Lacan and Critical Feminism

I0130391

This book takes a critical feminist approach to Lacan's fundamental concepts, merging discourse and sexuation theories in a novel way for both psychoanalysis and feminism, and exploring the possibility of a feminist subject within a non-masculine logic.

In *Lacan and Critical Feminism*, Carusi merges Lacan's theories of discourse and sexuation, not only from a gender/sexuality angle, but also from a literary, feminist, and women's studies framework. By drawing examples from literature, film, art, and socio-political movements to focus on discourse and sexuation, the text examines how tropes impact the subject's positionality within any discourse mode. The book also uses women's collective experience and action to illustrate ways that women have repositioned dominant narratives discursively.

This text represents essential reading for researchers interested in the relationship between Lacan and feminist theory.

Rahna McKey Carusi, educational developer in the College of Humanities and Social Sciences and Digital Innovation at Massey University, New Zealand.

The Lines of the Symbolic in Psychoanalysis Series

Series editor: Ian Parker, *Manchester Psychoanalytic Matrix*

Psychoanalytic clinical and theoretical work is always embedded in specific linguistic and cultural contexts and carries their traces, traces that this series attends to in its focus on multiple contradictory and antagonistic "lines of the symbolic." This series takes its cue from Lacan's psychoanalytic work on three registers of human experience, the Symbolic, the Imaginary, and the Real, and employs this distinctive understanding of cultural, communication, and embodiment to link with other traditions of cultural, clinical, and theoretical practice beyond the Lacanian symbolic universe. Lines of the Symbolic in Psychoanalysis provides a reflexive reworking of theoretical and practical issues, translating psychoanalytic writing from different contexts, grounding that work in the specific histories and politics which provide the conditions of possibility for its descriptions and interventions to function. The series makes connections between different the cultural and disciplinary sites in which psychoanalysis operates, questioning the idea that there could be one single correct reading and application of Lacan. Its authors trace their own path, their own line through the Symbolic, situating psychoanalysis in relation to debates which intersect with Lacanian work, explicating it, extending it, and challenging it.

Pink Herrings
Fantasy, Object Choice, and Sexuation
Damien W. Riggs

Sexual Difference, Abjection and Liminal Spaces
A Psychoanalytic Approach to the Abhorrence of the Feminine
Bethany Morris

Dolls, Photography and the Late Lacan
Doubles Beyond the Uncanny
Rosalinda Quintieri

Lacan and Critical Feminism
Subjectivity, Sexuation, and Discourse
Rahna McKey Carusi

Lacan and Critical Feminism

Subjectivity, Sexuation, and Discourse

Rahna McKey Carusi

Routledge
Taylor & Francis Group

LONDON AND NEW YORK

First published 2021
by Routledge
2 Park Square, Milton Park, Abingdon, Oxon OX14 4RN

and by Routledge
52 Vanderbilt Avenue, New York, NY 10017

Routledge is an imprint of the Taylor & Francis Group, an informa business

Library of Congress Cataloging-in-Publication Data
A catalog record for this title has been requested

ISBN: 978-0-367-19702-5 (hbk)
ISBN: 978-0-367-19709-4 (pbk)
ISBN: 978-0-429-24273-1 (ebk)

Typeset in Bembo
by Newgen Publishing UK

Contents

Preface

Lacan returned to Sigmund Freud through Ferdinand de Saussure's structural linguistics, opening the way to a radical rethinking of the relationship between the human subject and underlying enduring symbolic material that grounds our existence as speaking beings. In place of the reductive stories of biologically wired-in ages and stages of development in psychoanalysis, we then also had an opening to questions of discourse, the structuring of language as part of contradictory historical processes. Then it was possible to return to Freud again and again, making something new of psychoanalysis in such a way as to envisage change and, retroactively, to re-shape our possibilities for the future, to ground those possibilities anew in analyses of the past. Perhaps, some would claim, Lacan made a second return to Freud through Marx, but the political imperative driving the interest of many activists outside the clinic was feminist. This book pursues that re-reading of Freud, and, of course, of Lacan, returning to psychoanalysis through a critical feminist excavation and reconstruction of what we know of sexuality, and how we know it through what Lacan called "sexuation."

Woman figures at the heart of this re-reading, metaphorized and then erased by Lacan, as Rahna Carusi points out, but metaphorized and erased in such a way as to problematize the very masculine logic that essentializes, idealizes, and denigrates woman. To say that The Woman does not exist – and we should always remember that Lacan strikes through that positive definite article "The" – means that fantasies of what Woman is are placed in question. If, as Saussure argued, in language there are only differences, no positive terms, then Lacanian psychoanalysis, in feminist hands, is now able to shift emphasis to difference, historically culturally inscribed difference, and to what is productively negative about that; negativity as motor of resistance. Sexuality is now conceptualized as fixed in place through a discursive grid that determines what will be said about Woman – that her resistance is only to be understood as hysterical revolt, for example – and who will say it, what privilege and power will be accorded to men. What is said about sexuality is structured in the symbolic, what we sense we know about that symbolic grid is experienced in the imaginary, and something always resists, something of the real. This innovative book, *Lacan and Critical Feminism: Subjectivity, Sexuation, and Discourse*, makes it clear how and why we can grasp the shape of this grid through Lacanian discourse theory and through Lacan's account of sexuation.

Psychoanalytic clinical and theoretical work circulates through multiple intersecting antagonistic symbolic universes. This series opens connections between different cultural sites in which Lacanian work has developed in distinctive ways, in forms of work that question the idea that there could be single correct reading and application. The Lines of the Symbolic in Psychoanalysis series provides a reflexive reworking of psychoanalysis that transmits Lacanian writing from around the world, steering a course between the temptations of a metalanguage and imaginary reduction, between the claim to provide a god's eye view of psychoanalysis and the idea that psychoanalysis must be the same everywhere. And the elaboration of psychoanalysis in the symbolic here grounds its theory and practice in the history and politics of the work in a variety of interventions that touch the real.

Ian Parker
Manchester Psychoanalytic Matrix

Acknowledgments

I would first like to thank Tony and Umberto for your support while I was absent, and thank you for taking care of each other, too. Thank you to Ema and Richard for the use of your house and Ruby's company during the process. And thank you to Lara and Elsa for always being available when I needed a break. I would also like to thank the Routledge editors Kate Hawes, George Russell, and Elliott Morsia, Alec Selwyn and the peer reviewers for seeing promise in the proposal. Finally, I am grateful to Sally Hales for her keen eye to detail, as well as her patience and instruction during the copyediting stage.

1 Introduction

Why not make a book title out of it? [...] "beyond the phallus." That would be cute, huh? And it would give another consistency to the women's liberation movement. A jouissance beyond the phallus...

Lacan (being a dick), SXX, 74

On May 21, 2011, the internet *Star* article "Footloose and Gender-Free" covered a family who refused to reveal the sex of their baby, Storm, and the story went viral.[1] These parents are not the first to attempt to remove their child's "biological sex" from their social interactions: in June 2009, an article reported that a Swedish couple had not yet revealed the sex of their child, Pop, who was two and a half at the time.[2] Both sets of parents explained that they chose to withhold the sex of their child not only to offer "it" some agency in choosing and/or navigating its gender identification(s), but also to disrupt socio-cultural gender norms. Few people should find it surprising that in the second decade of the new millennium, in the wake of at least half a century of gender-based activism and scholarship, a trend to reconsider gender formation would arise. Of course, staunch traditionalists and neophobes struggle with change, and they tend to dominate mainstream platforms, most likely because their rhetoric provokes media drama. Ten years after the 2009 article, as we know, the gender conversation has evolved to one of mainstream visibility and rights activism where gender variant, non-binary, and trans folks are gaining more and more recognition and rights. The earlier (and still sometimes the later) media focus on dissenters to the reconsideration of gender formation, however, keeps mainstream media not only from asking critical questions about gender formation and representation, but also affects the masses who the media arguably tends to influence in terms of what holds present significance.

For example, the main complaint lodged by Storm's grandparents in 2011 is that they "resented explaining the gender-free baby to friends and co-workers" and that they have to use too many words to compensate for ambiguous pronouns or learn not to use pronouns at all and refer to the child as "the baby" or Storm all the time. They find this use of language difficult and think it sounds repetitive. It is significant that the grandparents' complaint is not that they do not know the sex of the child, but that it is difficult for them to speak about the child, to put "it" into words. Just like so many responders to the article who argue that the parents are forcing their ideological and political opinions on the child without realizing that all parents, even "normal" or "hegemonious" ones, are also always forcing ideology onto their children, the grandparents do not realize that the insistence on a gendered pronoun is also repetitive, in terms both of sound and the figuration of the child's subjectivity. Not only does the repetition of the articulation of gender manifest in the supposed one-to-one connection between a name and the body that it designates, but it also imposes discursive gender scripts on the subject through persistence and insistence. Gender(ed) pronouns are more than a mere signifying tool in our linguistic structure; they do much more than merely designate a person in the absence of their name. As queer theorists and activists have argued, gender(ed) pronouns are loaded with ideological and political implications marked on the psyche and the soma of the subject.

To be clear, this book is not a book about gender variance. Rather, this project explores the ways that discourse works upon the psyche and soma of the subject and, therefore, on social relations. I specifically want to explore the ways that discourse both shapes subjectivity and subjectivization (e.g., the discursive underpinnings at work in Storm's grandparents' complaints) and the ways that discourse can change and re-shape or even shape anew those identifications and social relations (e.g., the self-declaration of pronouns and use of they/their currently), particularly in regards to sexuation and gender formations. In a way, this exploration is aspirational in that it seeks to consider different ways of meaning as subjects, relating between subjects and within the subject, and breaking free from patriarchal and misogynistic constraints of understanding. My feminist scholar self and my psychoanalytic scholar self have never (or maybe on a rare occasion) been at odds with each other, though feminisms and psychoanalysis are rarely in conversation elsewhere. I find Lacan's work, particularly his mathematical logic, quite helpful in teasing out ways of understanding and thinking about multiple possibilities of socio-humanistic topics. So this project does just that: it explores various Lacanian mathemes and formulae to look closely at what is already happening, what occurrences are on the rise, and consider ways that we might create new possibilities, specifically in the narratives we rely upon and use to substantiate and manipulate in order to change our subjectivities and social relations.

Discourse, understood in Lacanian terms, designates the transsubjectivity of language as social link, as the social bond that occurs between subjects, as well as the transindividual occurrence at the level of the unconscious (*My Teaching* 79–86; SXI 207; SXVII 13, 100; SXX 21–22, 54). Discourse is transsubjective as it occurs between subjects, as well as transindividual as it occurs between and within parts of the individual as divided subject. Toward the end of his seminar career, Lacan says exasperatedly, "I can say until I'm blue in the face that the notion of discourse should be taken as the social link (*lien social*), founded on language, and thus seems not unrelated to what is specified in linguistics as grammar, and yet nothing seems to change" (SXX 17). Recalling Friedrich Nietzsche's *Twilight of the Idols* aphorism on the *I* and Being, "I am afraid we have not got rid of God because we still believe in grammar" (170), Lacan is focusing on the interrelatedness of discourse, the social link, language, and the subject. Lacan is theorizing that *the grammar of the subject is a physical* (rather than metaphysical) *effect* and the social link is a physical operation of discourse.

Lacan is discussing changes in discourse, the various possibilities of traversals – how they happen to us and how we can make them happen. I use the gender(ed) pronoun as an example because it discursively places, or situates, a subject for other subjects in terms of identity, which, for the purposes of this project and the field of theory in which I situate it, is a lie. The gendered pronoun signifies for others a figural and figurative identification – figural in the mathematical sense that designates a shape that consists of factors, as well as figurative in the sense of metaphor in speech that also connotes or engenders a visual representation – that subjects can then situate and interpret according to familiar significations. Lacan's insistence is that discourse is a "link," a metonymic structure of contiguous speech acts and meaning-making. Yet, gender(ed) pronouns function metaphorically; they stand in for a seemingly sedimented or "consistent" representation of similarity between two terms and of the difference that separates the two analogies – male is to masculine and female is to feminine – and most people try to perform within already socially scripted representations of them. But what happens when social and material conditions fail to provide sufficient support for these metaphors? Also, what happens when a subject, such as Storm or Pop, discursively forces the same social and material conditions to fail?

Much scholarship addresses the problematic in the metaphorical one-to-one (or word for word) relationship of sex and gender on subjectivity and subjectivization. This project contributes to this body of scholarship by revisiting Lacan's work on the connection between discourse and sexuation and considering the possibilities of traversing the figural representations with which identifications are formed, specifically in terms of sexual difference and sexuation, rather than through the more common focus on the identity politics of gender. As I will discuss in more detail later, sexual difference is a fundamental split that occurs both in subject formation and within the Symbolic as we know it, whereas sexuation is the logic of how that difference and split become articulated in language and on the body. Sexual difference and sexuation are both processes and failures of identification within the social field; gender, then, is the figural hegemony for an (always, sexed) "identity" demanded of all subjects within our cultural Imaginary.

Revisiting Lacan's treatment of metaphor and metonymy, I argue counter to much scholarship that focuses on what they read as Lacan's privileging of metaphor, not only that he does not privilege metaphor, but also that metonymy is more critically productive as the privileged trope. I make the argument for a privileging of metonymy in order to look more closely at Lacan's theories of discourse and sexuation, and the links which allow these two theories to be brought together. I use Lacan's method of turning, or "looking awry," at the master's discourse to read the sexuation graph in order to theorize possibilities of social change from the "feminine" side of the graph. I read Lacan's claim that "Woman does not exist, ~~Woman~~ (*La*)," (SXX 72, 78, 80–81) the term that appears in the bottom portion of the "feminine" side of the sexuation graph, metonymically in order finally to consider possibilities of a non-phallic consciousness available to anyone regardless of their sex and gender, which I argue is one way to pry discourse, and thereby subjectivization, loose from metaphorical gender structures as we know them. This project tries to contribute to contemporary feminisms, queer theory, and, tangentially, post-humanism and trans studies, all theories that are reconceptualizing not only subjectivity, but also the interfacings of the concepts of subject, object, and human by rethinking the figural as empty and, therefore simultaneously, full of potential within the social field.

Since the early 1980s, Foucault's work has dominated much of the academic trends in critical and literary theory, particularly for scholars concerned with social and political discourses. Joan Copjec's *Read My Desire: Lacan Against the Historicists* argues cogently, however, that Foucault's binary breakdown of discourse into conflicts of difference that produce and effect knowledge and power limits, rather than enables our comprehension of social possibility (18). For example, a Foucauldian perspective may make use of the argument about the gender-less child as a power struggle over identity politics and access to mobility, but both the argument and the power struggle function at the level of panoptic perpetuation. Copjec clarifies that the difference between Foucault's and Lacan's theorization of the connection between desire and the social is fundamental to the limitations and openings of these theories respectively: "Foucault conceives desire not only as an *effect*, but also […] as a *realization* of the law," whereas psychoanalysis argues that "it is the *repression* of this desire that founds society" (24, emphasis in original).[3] Tim Dean explains that this is a matter of Foucault's focus on positive terms – "forcing sex to speak" – brought on by a "critique of a naïve conception of repression," which he contrasts with Lacan's use of negation for his psychoanalytic understandings of repression, desire, and the unconscious ("Lacan and Queer Theory" 242). According to psychoanalysis, a primary repression must occur in order for desire to become; and the repression of drives, also known as the interplay between the reality and pleasure principles, propels desires that must occur for the establishment and continuation of social structures.[4]

Yet, many scholars, and many feminist and women's studies scholars, remain effusively resistant to Lacan's work. Most Foucauldian-based scholarship exists because his ideas privilege power; because they are useful for analyses concerned with subject marginalization, e.g., political issues of race, gender, and sexual practices. He is useful in these and other areas. There is a now decades-long dominant feminist backlash against Lacan because some of these scholars continue to claim that his work is misogynistic and patriarchal. In the introduction to *Sexuation*, Renata Salecl points out that postmodernist and deconstructionist thinking views sexual identity as "the result of complex discursive practices and of the interplay between power relations: what has been constructed in concrete historical constellations can also be deconstructed and radically changed" (1). Admittedly, I see this perspective as valid and real, but only up to a point. I do not dismiss the complexity of discursive practices and the interplay between power relations in the argument that follows, but rather I situate it in an interplay with the psychoanalytic notion of sexual difference, which is "first and above all the name for a certain fundamental *deadlock* inherent in the symbolic order" (2, emphasis in original). In order to think within the lenses of both feminisms and psychoanalysis, both issues of sexual identity or performance and of sexual difference need grappling with, a look at both the social link and at the subject.

Lacanian scholars, and particularly feminist Lacanian scholars, often have to explain and justify their methodology as if they are anti-Foucauldian, which often is not the case. Molly Anne Rothenberg, in her 2010 *The Excessive Subject: A New Theory of Social Change*, for example, reiterates Lacan's significance as she carefully, chapter by chapter, explicates the shortcomings and limitations of critical theory by Pierre Bourdieu, Michel de Certeau, Judith Butler, and Ernesto Laclau, four highly influential theorists (whom I respect), all of whom rely on Foucauldian theory and/or selective readings of Lacanian theory. Genevieve Morel's 2000-11 *Sexual Ambiguities* also provides a detailed argument that focuses on sexual difference and sexuation in order to steer away from the misguided emphasis of gender theory (xiv). In this way, the impetus of Morel's work is similar to this project; however, she focuses specifically on psychosis and transsexuality as her objects of analysis. Elizabeth Wright's *Lacan and Postfeminism* claims that postfeminism "has begun to consider the question of what the postmodern notion of the dispersed unstable subject might bring" (5), notes that the French feminists Hélène Cixous, Luce Irigaray, and Julia Kristeva never aligned themselves with the Anglophone feminisms (8), and that the descriptive – rather than prescriptive – approach to sexual difference in psychoanalysis has allowed for the possibility to "discuss a revolutionary interpretation" of the sexuation formulae within feminist discourses (13). I will argue here for a turn to Lacan through a feminist lens, particularly in regard to the way in which psychoanalysis can contribute to theories of discourse in order to continue rethinking subjectivity and subjectivization founded on the logic of sexuation. In other words, I think theories of psychoanalysis can provoke social change.

Lacan defines discourse simply as a transsubjective "social bond, founded in language" (44). The turn to Lacan, then, does not suggest, for example, that Foucault's discourse theory is not useful; again, Foucault's discourse theory connects directly and overtly to power relations, which are a real and valid consideration of socio-political issues, and, therefore, his work is compatible with this project and lurks in the background at times. One of Foucault's definitions of discourse explains that it is an "asset that consequently, from the moment of its existence (and not only in its 'practical applications'), poses the question of power; an asset that is, by nature, the object of a struggle, a political struggle" (*Archaeology* 120). A danger of relying exclusively on Foucault's power-infused conceptualization of discourse, however, is that further theorizations and arguments are often stifled by the sole focus on identity politics. Tim Dean also makes this point by situating it historically in the 1960s and 1970s movements for civil rights, the Equal Rights Amendment, when gay and lesbian rights benefited greatly from identity politics. But the criticism of identity politics' use value quickly arose in the 1980s and 1990s when AIDS spread and marginalized groups, specifically gay men, found that identity politics was easily turned on its head ("Lacan and Queer Theory" 239). In contrast to Foucauldian scholarship's consistent focus on power relations, Lacan's discourse theory centers on the function of language in the social link within which repression and desire are fundamental. Repression and desire can fit into the category of power dynamics, too, but they do so differently. Phallic desire, for example, may be about manifest power dynamics between subjects, but it is not the only kind of desire possible. I argue that we will find it productive to look more closely at structures of language as informed by desire; that is, at discourses in the Lacanian sense of the term.

From a psychoanalytic perspective, we are desiring subjects fundamentally, because we are subjects in and of language. The Symbolic, Lacan's psychic register of language and its acquisition, is the place where desire manifests through signifying systems within the social field.[5] Looking at the structures of language allows a closer examination of specific desires that inform traditional, perpetual narratives, and this examination of desires can provide insight into societal repressions. Insights into societal repressions that provoke hegemonic desires can incite a criticality that leads to social change in that the dynamic between subjectivity and subjectivization becomes evident as contingent rather than engineered or calculable. Through looking at how tropes function within our social myths to depoliticize discursive positionalities of subjectivity and subjectivization, we may begin to re-theorize the desires inherent, and operative, in the social field and bring to light and re-narrativize our own discursive positionalities.

A literary and critical approach to psychoanalysis

As that which holds one of the privileged positions of the social link, discourse is important. So many discourses are at play and at odds with one another that I think we often feel as if we are in a perpetual, energetic trapeze act – thrown or throwing constantly from one side to another with flips and grabs and holds and releases and falls between. Where we are positioned and/or position ourselves within the ideological play at work within these discourses and how we come to understand those positionalities often requires, not only birth, but narrative. Narrative, too, can determine who is in what (discursive) position on that trapeze – one of the two main handlers at the bars or a variety of artists who enter the routine.

As the main vehicle through which we communicate events, narratives are important. Narratives both shape our perspective on various issues and our worldview, as well as reflect, if not gauge, the way in which the world is already operating. We arguably only have narratives to grapple and play with, to argue about, to get excited about, and sometimes to fear. I find that the narratives in contemporary film or literature often reveal much more about the ideological holds gripping our subjectivities and subjectivizations than, say, the news, which moves and fades so quickly with our fleeting, distracted daily memory. Film and literature are often contemporary studies in an event or idea or subject dynamic that uncover the nuance that discourse impacts on our subjectivities. In narrative we can see discourse at work among and between characters, ideologies, and ruptures.

The discourses out of which the narratives in this project emerge all look critically at masculinity and patriarchy. I focus on these narratives and narrative discourses because the masculinist structures and ideologies need to be watched, need to be critiqued, need to be addressed, at least at this time. As much as I have wanted to do so, I cannot yet take my eye off of these structures because the dominant ideological powers at work continually manipulate, exploit, or even more violently harm folks who labor to liberate themselves and others from those oppressive narratives and discourses. These narratives and discourses are still generationally effecting the wellbeing of almost everyone. It wasn't until I heard Dr. Kim Tallbear explain what her DNA research was about – that, unrealized by a lot of people, she wasn't studying indigenous peoples but rather white people because, until genocidal and settler colonialism was truly not a threat anymore, we had to continue to keep a critical eye on them – that I felt resigned to follow through with this project on looking critically at the binary structures in discourse and sexuation, even though I want to move beyond it badly. As much as I want to move on to non-binary, less canonical, less structural, more creative and hopeful projects, this work has to be done first. The simple fact is that Western patriarchal and masculinist narratives and discourses are still very much at work on our subjectivities, subjectivizations, and sociopolitical realities, which I think I can safely say at this point in history are overwhelmingly harmful. So, if we do not continue to pay attention to masculinist narrative discourse, then those narratives will perpetuate even if we do not see them; they will continue to bubble up to the surface and push other narrative possibilities down.

The texts I work with in this project are often by men who are trying to look critically at masculinist narratives with some level of feminist influence lurking in the margins or informing the critique. Some of these men, not surprisingly in our #metoo era, have been scrutinized or fully rejected by cancel culture. Cancel culture is a fairly new phenomenon where something someone has said or done, no matter if it was years prior or in their current morning tweet, outrages enough people that they call for that person's cancellation of social belonging. In other words, a 20-year old-photo of someone in blackface at a high school party, a 10-year-old homophobic tweet, or last night's drunken sharing of a sexist meme can cause anyone to lose their job, be blacklisted from their profession, become ostracized from their family and friends, and openly attacked in public. In other words, cancel culture is the new method of exile punishment. I am not excusing bad behavior; however, I do fear that the power of exile currently being exercised is refusing to allow people to learn, and more importantly to learn publicly. Cancel culture ironically counters the supposed fundamental principles of inclusion and continual learning within left-leaning or progressive discourses, which started the cancelation phenomenon, and conjures the ancient oppressive religious practice of confession and persecution that harmed the subjects within those discourses for centuries. That said, some of the men who authored the texts in this book have been subjected to cancel culture. For example, Lars von Trier has long been criticized for being misogynist and racist; Quentin Tarantino has been accused of similar behavior; posthumously, David Foster Wallace was accused of abuse and stalking; and Slavoj Žižek, despite his complicated reputation, offers invaluable work on psychoanalytic sexuation. I do not condone any such behaviors, but I am not going to weigh in on a verdict for any of their offenses or the accusations against them, as this is not the purpose of the book. I will, however, do my best to show that a few of the texts are of value in being able to evidence the anti-masculinist narratives and discourses critical to our subjectivities and socio-political milieu.

Instead of critiquing the man, then, I want to turn to Kristeva's writing subject as a way to consider the internal, intersubjective discourse(s) at work in the creative process. Because this book focuses partly on the close reading and critique of masculinist narratives, I think it is important to look at texts created by men that critique and disrupt those narratives. Kristeva's writing subject is an insightful way to reconsider the ways in which masculine logics proliferate and can be subverted through the "purely symbolic channels" to which Bourdieu points in *Masculine Domination* that are the passive-aggressive violence or the micro-aggressions we often experience when positioned within someone else's patriarchal master's discourse. Leon S. Roudiez's introduction to Kristeva's *Revolution in Poetic Language* explains that Kristeva coins the idea of the "writing subject" over an "author" in order "to emphasize that consciousness is far from dominating the process and that the writing subject is a complex, heterogeneous force" (8). In considering the "writing subject" one "investigate[s] the forces that brought [the text] into being" (7). The "writing subject, then, includes not only the consciousness of the writer but also his or her unconscious" (8). Kristeva's writing subject helps explain the significance of the narratives about women written and delivered by cis-male subjects. It may or may not be apparent that the texts presented throughout this project only fall under this category, but all the major characters are women and they are depicted from the lens or pen of a man. And in these narrative depictions of women I see a discursive shift in the writing subject occurring, which I would hope is at least in part a long-term effect of feminisms.

The book's trajectory

This project progresses from a discussion on discourse to Woman to sexuation. Between the chapters are short interruptions, which I cheekily call quilting points, that try to illustrate textually in film, literature, or a socio-political event/ moment the broader theory discussed in the project. To lay the groundwork for an argument on sexuation as discourse, I first discuss briefly Lacan's four discourses as they are presented in SXVII: *The Other Side of Psychoanalysis.*[6] I focus this discussion on the hysteric's discourse and the feminine. In Chapter 3, I turn attention to tropes, specifically metaphor and metonymy, and trace the significance of these tropes in relation to discourse and the body in psycho-analysis, as well as how Woman, with a capital W, is a tropological fantasy. This tropological look at discourse and the body leads to a discussion of metonymy as the articulation of desire, the way in which language and desire work upon the body and the unconscious. In Chapter 4, I turn to the materiality of the letter and look at how affect – always an anxiety – works upon the body and the social with very real implications when defined by, or picked up on, by dis-course. In this study of the materiality of the letter, I revisit Lacan's "Seminar on 'The Purloined Letter'" to introduce the ensuing discussion of Woman.

Chapter 5 fleshes out this idea of Woman, specifically as metonymy rather than metaphor, in order to lead to Lacan's claim that Woman does not exist: ~~Woman~~. This chapter looks specifically at Irigaray-oriented literature on sexual difference and sexuation in relation to metonymy and develops an argu-ment that merges metonymy, the object, and figural identifications in order to foreground my concept of re-symbolizing identifications within logics of sexuation. To illustrate feminine discursive metonymy, I turn to specific examples of Latina activism, such as *Las mujeres negras*, that show the meto-nymic manipulation and disruption of metaphoric expectations of Woman. Chapter 6 argues for an ethical discourse of the body – an ethical jouissance – through the eradication of the (metaphor of the) phallus. Leading up to this chapter, I offer a close reading of Lars von Trier's *Antichrist* to illustrate what Rothenberg calls retroversive causality. Rothenberg's reading of the signifi-cance of extimacy for purposes of social change is salient to how *Antichrist's* She is monstrous both because of, and in spite of, this extimate causality.

In Chapter 7, I finally turn our attention to Lacan's sexuation graph. The argument builds upon the earlier metonymy discussion in order to look awry at the sexuation graph. I first turn the sexuation graph in the same way Lacan turns the discourse formulae in a counter-clockwise quarter turn in order to read the feminine side anew; that is, metonymically as a sentence. I turn briefly to three David Lynch films to show the ways in which narrative can not only expose the masculine problematic (like the other objects I use), but also create non-masculinist narrative. In Chapter 8, I replace the graph's phallus symbol, ϕ, with the general notation for the master signifier, S_1, to show how any signifier can function as the quilting point in this sexuation discourse. This replacement allows me to suggest a pushing beyond the temporary privileging of ~~Woman~~ as metonymy in order to move toward a privileging of the object over subject, where I build upon Copjec's claim that sex is empty and Rothenberg's development of the excessive, or Möbius subject, alongside Levi Bryant's democratic theory of objects to begin thinking of ways to open up non-phallic discursive spaces that put less or different emphasis on the figural. Woman, as symptom of man, is the privileged signifier of the master's discourse as we know it in masculinist form. Here, I work to argue that it is the metaphoric Woman, and secondarily the phallus, that we must move beyond. Leaning on Kristeva's notion of the writing subject, I argue that these narrative objects are already beginning to shift the way in which we can imagine sexuated positionalities. Finally, I hope to provoke through the starting point of ~~Woman~~ as metonymy possible manifestations of non-phallic discursive spaces conceived through identifications that occur via the collapsing of the figural as we know it.

Notes

1 Countless websites reproduced or poached from this one, so for brevity and efficiency I only provide one source: www.parentcentral.ca/parent/babiespregnancy/babies/article/995112. Tangentially related, but beyond the scope of this project, is the much more prevalent work on transsexuality. Rona Marech's article "Throw out your pronouns – 'he' and 'she' are meaningless terms in the Bay Area's flourishing transgender performance scene" in the *San Francisco Chronicle* does not so much discuss in detail, but it emphasizes the uselessness of pronouns. Monday, December 29, 2003: www.sfgate.com/entertainment/article/Throw-out-your-pronouns-he-and-she-are-2507407.php

2 www.thelocal.se/20232/20090623

3 Foucault argues, within the context of history, that the concept of authority is characterized by the *possible positions of desire in relation to discourse*:

> discourse may in fact be the place for a phantasmatic representation, and element of symbolization, a form of the forbidden, an instrument of derived satisfaction [...] In any case, the analysis of this authority must show that [...] the relation of discourse to desire [...] is extrinsic to its unity, its characterization, and the laws of its formation. They are [...] its formative elements.
>
> (68, emphasis in original)

As I will discuss later, Lacan's theory of discourse has everything to do with desire manifested as *objet a* and what type of *jouissance* a subject may access or be barred from. Also, Lacan's formulae provide four examples of how subject positions can function discursively, much like when Foucault says "discourse may in fact be." In this regard, I am not quite convinced that Foucault is saying anything incompatible with Lacan – and I must point out that they both presented their theory of discourse the same year, 1969-70 – except that Foucault emphasizes the idea of authority, and Lacan is specific not to place emphasis on any one "little letter" in his formulae. In fact, when it comes to authority, he specifically points out in a Hegelian vein that the imaginary perception of the absolute master is actually the absolute weakness of that subject position. Tim Dean, in his introduction to *Beyond Sexuality*, argues that "Foucault concurs with Lacan in the effort to move beyond psychology," but he wants to focus on categories of "bodies and pleasure" rather than the psychoanalytic focus on "sexuality and desire" (3). Again, Dean, in "Lacan and Queer Theory," states, "Although Foucault's conception of discourse differs significantly from Lacan's, his transindividual notion of power nevertheless is somewhat homologous with Lacan's theory of the symbolic order: both represent transindividual structures that produce subjective effects independently of any particular individual's agency or volition" (239).

4   Lacan's algorithm $\$\lozenge a$ – barred subject, lozenge, *objet a* – is the notation he places on the Graph of Desire between the signifier of the subject and the signifier of a lack in the other that bars, but could allow, jouissance. An interpretation of this algorithm may read as the barred subject *becomes* by entering into the Symbolic, the necessity of becoming a speaking being constituted by the loss of *being* in order that s/he must *mean*. What is lost through the process of castration is the original object of desire, *objet a*. The loss of *objet a* is what constitutes the lack in the subject – hence, its barring – as well as the subject's desire: *objet a*, then, is the object-cause of desire. The subject can never know what this lack is, can never define *objet a*, by the necessity of repression, but is propelled by desire to supplement (always temporarily) that lack. *Objet a* is lost once the subject exits the Real; therefore, desire becomes (*is*) the Desire of the Other, which is both the locus of this lack and of speech. $\$\lozenge a$, in this way, manifests in fantasy. Because the Law prohibits jouissance, the subject is propelled by desire rather than demand. The demand for the mother's breast, for example, is replaced by a desire for satisfaction and recognition, a kind of middle term between need and a desire for love. Once the subject must *mean*, which also occurs in conjunction with the recognition/identification of sexual difference, s/he is subject to an unconscious drive that is always articulated as symptom. It is an excess outside of articulation but constitutes the subject's very life in that it must be articulated, yet always fails in its articulation. One can never know the Other's desire – hence, *che vuoi?* – but this antagonizing/agonizing question speaks to how the focus shifts from demand to desire: the mother, who serves as the initial Other, eventually cannot meet the child's demand for unconditional love, and it is the father who steps in as the signifier for the Father/Law, that compels the child to speak; the child asks about the father, "what does he want from me?" Much like the Other as the locus of speech, the (F)father wants the child to speak.

5   The Symbolic, Imaginary, and Real are Lacan's terms for psychic registers which he explains are interconnected and cannot be separated from one another. He borrows the mathematical structure of the Borromean knot to diagram their interdependence. Like all Lacan's teaching, language is the basis for understanding how the three registers function: he places speaking/writing, the discourse of the Other (the unconscious) and the Law in the Symbolic, the signifying reservoir; whereas meaning, the signified and signification, are found in the Imaginary, the place from where a subject seeks (demands) meaning and to mean, where the ego is formed (in the mirror stage) and sustained in a desire for recognition; and historical discourse (for lack of a better phrase) is the Real to which subjects have no real access and that which escapes the other registers. The Real is impossible to signify; it is the place

of jouissance, which is impossible but has traumatic effects (Žižek, *Sublime Object*, 68–69). (However, my using Žižek as a reference for the psychic registers will inevitably provoke contention, especially concerning the Real. Yet, providing an adequate definition of the Real, the register discussed least and most abstractly by Lacan, is beyond the scope of this project, as it could be a whole chapter or book on its own.) Lacan cites Claude Lévi-Strauss' anthropological assertion that there is a universal Law that organizes social (kinship) relations and exchanges as the basis for his Symbolic register. The Law that governs these relations and exchanges is, for Lacan and Lévi-Strauss, a logical structure embedded in the linguistic signifying system. The unconscious, structured like a language, is the locus of desire and, therefore, discourse of the Other, which is strictly in the Symbolic. It is in this way that I understand the Symbolic as a reservoir, as its signifiers have no fixed relation to any absolute signified. This register is one of culture, hence the anthropological basis for it. The symbolic determines subjectivity, so a subject cannot occupy a place outside of it.

Initiated into the Imaginary through the mirror stage when the ego is formed, a child develops identity (subjectivity) through an identification with its specular image (its counterpart). The child develops a dual relationship of narcissism and aggressivity with this specular image, which is the foundation of the subject's alienation. This register is the realm of deception (illusion) of wholeness that provides the signifieds and significations of the signifiers in the Symbolic. Unlike his contemporaries, Lacan does not privilege the illusory, the Imaginary, in the subject as the place from where psychoanalysis should practice because the dual relationships in the Imaginary are "disabling fixations" (Evans 83). Rather, it is the triadic relationship in the Symbolic that will allow the subject to identify with her/his sinthome.

The Real first emerges in Lacan's teaching as the philosophical being-in-itself, but it quickly becomes more ambiguous and complicated. The Symbolic and Imaginary require differentiation, binary and tertiary relationships, and a loss, lack, or cut from being-in-itself. The Real is undifferentiated, lacks nothing, is the "*hic et nunc* of the all," and is the place in which a cut (castration) must occur (by the Symbolic) in order for a subject to come into being.

6 Throughout the book, I will often shorthand Lacan's seminars with the S, for seminar, followed by the seminar's Roman numeral.

2 A (re)turn to Lacan

In determining the scope of what discourse repeats, it prepares the question of what symptoms repeat.

Lacan, "Seminar on 'The Purloined Letter'," *Écrits* 13

This chapter's title refers to a few key points that inform or are aims of my thinking for this project. Firstly, just as Lacan declared that his oeuvre was a systematic return to Freud, I am referring to the resurgence in psychoanalytic scholarship, and particularly in a Lacanian vein, around sexuation and gendered identifications that has been occurring over recent decades. This is welcomed resurgence that adds to (and not necessarily opposes) the already prolific body of theory scholarship on gender and sexuality usually stemming from a Foucauldian perspective. Also, very little psychoanalytic scholarship has voice in the wider discipline of women's studies and feminisms, and, as I hope to show with this project, psychoanalysis can be relevant in these spaces, particularly from a literary and critical theory perspective. In this chapter, I introduce Lacan's four discourses, elaborate on psychoanalytic discourse through the "feminine" hysteric's discourse, which is a quarter turn from the master's discourse, and introduce the connections I see between the four discourses and the sexuation graph. Later in this project, I will also turn the sexuation graph similarly to how Lacan turns the discourse formulae in order to try to articulate how sexuation is also discursive. Just as discourse is a repetition, a return of sorts, so too, as this chapter concludes, is sexual difference, which is the symptom of sexuality as such.

Discourse, psychoanalytically speaking (or, discourse and the directionality of the subject)

As early as the 1953 Rome Discourse, "The Function and Field of Speech and Language in Psychoanalysis," Lacan explains that "speech confers a *meaning on the functions* of the individual; its domain is that of concrete discourse qua field of the subject's transindividual reality; and its operations are those of history insofar as history constitutes the emergence of truth in reality" (*Écrits* 214, emphasis added). Speech bestows meaning onto the individual through discourse within the social field – across, through, over, to or on the other side of, beyond, outside of, from one person to another as transsubjective – but also within the psychic and somatic functions as transindividual, or, rather, intersubjective. The way in which Lacan describes this transitivity of the subject's reality within discourse provokes the image of vectors of discourse that make or direct meaning.

Here, I want to emphasize the conceptual difference between the two terms intersubjective and transsubjective, as not only is Lacan's use of them confusing, they may also become confusing throughout this project. The idea of *the* individual implies an extradiscursive being. But the subject, especially in psychoanalysis, is a subject of, and in, language who gets meaning and recognition transsubjectively through discursive practices/performances with other subjects. In this instance within the Rome Discourse, Lacan does not seem to make a clear distinction between intersubjectivity and transsubjectivity. Considering that this project takes on both discourse and sexuation, and understanding sex/sexuation as a complex spectrum, I would like to make a clear distinction between the two terms. For Lacan, intersubjectivity is not the simple idea of communication or the message that subjects convey to one another. Rather, for Lacan, intersubjectivity refers to the act of transmission and the articulation of language because it calls into question primarily the subject of enunciation itself (*My Teaching* 84–85). Because I find some ambivalence in the use of the term "intersubjectivity," viz. that it is not clear if the term refers to the way language acts on the subject's relation to itself or the way language defines relations between subjects, I feel the need to make a distinction between these two ways language acts discursively and impacts the two different subject relations. For this project, I reorient this term to transsubjectivity. Intersubjectivity is the discursive relation between the body and the psyche, and transsubjectivity is the discursive relation across subjects.

The reality of the subject within discourse is an historical fact only in terms of the structural ahistoricity of speaking beings and the social link, and the social link is the conscious truth of reality as such. The social field always – universally and transhistorically – presupposes the social link, which Lacan defines as discourse. The subject is always only a function within it, an apparatus of sorts as a signifier to another signifier (SXI 207; SXVII 13, 100; SXX 54; *My Teaching* 79–86). The signifier is a function of the representation of the subject to another signifier once the subject has been established. All signifiers at the start, according to Lacan, are equal in the sense that none – or *not one* – is privileged.[1] Lacan asserts that *all signifiers are equal at the start.*

In his 1958 "The Signification of the Phallus," Lacan does indeed place the phallus on the utmost signifier pedestal. But he places the phallus on the pedestal within the context of a descriptive reading of what already exists. As I hope to make clear in the following chapter, his emphasis on metaphor and metonymy in this text, just as in much of his early work, implies that the functions of language within discourse also determine the ways in which subjects perceive reality. A few years prior, in "The Function and Field of Speech and Language in Psychoanalysis," Lacan eloquently explains:

> Psychoanalytic experience has rediscovered in man the imperative of the Word as the law that has shaped him in its image. It exploits the poetic function of language to give his desire its symbolic mediation. May this experience finally enable you to understand that the whole of reality of its effects lies in the gift of speech; for it is through this gift that all reality has come to man and through its ongoing action that he sustains reality.
>
> If the domain defined by this gift of speech must be sufficient for both your action and your knowledge, it will also be sufficient for your devotion. For it offers the latter a privileged field.
>
> (264–65)

He is not claiming to create this structure or its effects; rather, he is showing how it manifests and persists. Later in his work he makes it a point to devalue this propping up of the phallus as privileged signifier and, in fact, even goes so far as to devalue the Father as well (SXVII 122–24). As I will discuss in more detail later, he comes to the understanding that the Oedipus complex is a "myth," that Freud's appropriation of the story in the Oedipal complex functions as the mythical ground of a mere cog-like "structural operator" (123) and that "the Oedipus complex is Freud's dream" (137).

Lacan's theorization of discourse as the fundamental principle of the subject and the social link provides the framework through which I conceive, within this project, sexuated articulations as the primary enunciation for the possibilities of discursive positions. Specifically, sexual difference is the primary difference marked onto the body and psyche through sexuated subjectivization as the primary way in which the subject identifies within and is situated by discourse. Sexual difference is the initial signifier that forms the subject. The multiple discursive formations that produce subjectivity and identity that are "a result of the subject's entry into language [are] always already shot through and informed by figurations and encryptions of power, politics, historical, cultural and ideological remainders organized through particular relationships and networks" (Wolfreys 66). Psychoanalysis purports that it is through this already established linguistic structure that the subject comes into meaning by other subjects' anticipation of her/him. Discourse necessitates and makes possible the subject and their identification(s): "Man thus speaks, but it is because the symbol has made him man" (*Écrits* 229).

In "Cutting Up," Copjec explains language's duplicity: "the fact that whatever it says can be denied [...] ensures that the subject will *not* come into being as language's determinate meaning" (*Read My Desire* 56, emphasis added). Rather, she argues, the subject has a "desire for nonbeing, for an *in*determinate something that is perceived as extradiscursive" (56). This seemingly "*extra*discursive" thing is *objet a*, which "causes the subject" but "has historical specificity (it is the product of a specific discursive order), but no historical content" (56, emphasis in original). Here, Copjec explains the important difference between Lacanian and Foucaultian notions of discourse and its function for the subject: *objet a* is the manifestation of desire within discourse. Desire may be perceived as "*extra*discursive," as that which "causes the subject," but desire is both discourse's latent and manifest ground. The subject's use of discourses, as well as the subject's insertion into various discursive spaces, come into being only through the production and reproduction, i.e., *repetitions*, of meaning, and *discourse is the vehicle of lack*, i.e., of desire. Lacan reads the stirring up of discursive activity as the very thing that makes the subject a subject and not something else: the subject can only engage within the social link, which requires the subject to enter into the discourse(s) present to it, but the impetus for this engagement is only ever a primordial lack that propels desire. As Copjec explains: "Instead of an external opposition between the subject and society, we must learn to think their necessary interrelation: the very existence of the subject is simultaneous with society's failure to integrate, to represent it" (124). Society's and the subject's reciprocal misrepresentation and misrecognition are each other's essential vehicle. For example, P.D. James' *Children of Men* portrays the impending destruction of society due to the lack of children being born, and exhaustion which cancels the making of the subject in (at least) two senses: there are no more subjects coming into existence, in the simple sense, but, more importantly, there are no more infants at the breast, no more mirror stages, no more splittings, no more Oedipal complexes, no more vehicle and ground for/of desire – in short, no more repetition of the social link.

To return to Lacan's theorization of how "speech confers meaning on the individual," what he at the time terms the transindividual discursive "truth in reality" determines culture and cultural practices of identification and difference. The fundamental social determination is arguably sexual difference, the primary meaning written on the body and psyche that determines its functions within cultural narratives and practices. It is not coincidental that Lacan, in his psychoanalytic appropriation of Saussurean linguistics in the 1957 "The Instance of the Letter in the Unconscious," complicates the basic linguistic structure, or really reduces and imbues the formulation with the fact of sexed articulation through the example of the two siblings on a train who arrive at a station and argue over where they are according to their view of the bathroom stalls (*Écrits* 416–17).[2] It is important that the two subjects in the example are brother and sister; that is, that one is a boy and the other a girl and that they are produced from the same biological make-up. "To these children," Lacan explains:

> Gentlemen and Ladies will henceforth be two homelands toward which each of their souls will take flight on divergent wings, and regarding which it will be all the more impossible for them to reach an agreement since, being in fact the same homeland, neither can give ground regarding the one's unsurpassed excellence without detracting from the other's glory.
>
> (417)

Lacan's sarcastic tone indicates the irony of the divergent paths these two children, serving as paradigms, must take. The "two homelands," the two paths of desire that inform the identifications at which they arrive, re-write upon their already marked bodies the psychic difference that the Symbolic requires of them. Symbolic Law requires them to disagree even though their arrival is "in fact [at] the same homeland," that is, as subjects within the Symbolic required to identify according to the laws of discursive signification by engaging in power relations between and against identifications marked on the sexed body. Lacan's point, to which I will return later, is that "this structure of the signifying chain discloses the possibility [a subject has] – precisely insofar as [a subject] share[s] its language with other subjects" in order "to use it to signify *something altogether different* from what it says […] namely, the function of indicating the place of this subject in the search for truth" (420–21, emphasis in original). In other words, the discursive functions of language are such that they don't mean what is said, but are rather the way in which what is said is said, which both situates the subject's desire and the way in which other subjects interpret (or interrupt) it. Rather than an identity, the subject gets only a directionality, which manifests on the signifying chain of desire.

The four discourses

Because a number of texts have painstakingly described the discourse formulae symbols and positions, I will keep this explanation brief and succinct. Lacan diagrams four formulae of discourse in Seminar XVII: *The Other Side of Psychoanalysis* to designate the directionalities upon which the subject embarks and within which the subject partakes in the social field. The subject can occupy a plurality of directions: it can and may occupy, as well as be forced into, any of these discourses at any given time. The four formulae – master, university, hysteric, and analyst – address both the performance and transmission, but not the message or mere communication, that take place within the subject and between subjects.

Each formula arises from a quarter turn, and the same four letters comprise the four positions of each formula. The master's discourse is the paradigm from which the university discourse is a counter-clockwise quarter turn, the hysteric's is a clockwise quarter turn from the master's, and the analyst's is another quarter turn from the hysteric's, thereby making it the inverse of the master's discourse. The four letters are S_1, the master signifier; S_2, knowledge (*savoir*); $, the split subject; and *a*, surplus enjoyment (jouissance).[3] The side-by-side mini-formulae represent the "essential functions of discourse," which Lacan designates *in terms of function* as agent/truth on the left of the formula and Other/production on the right of the formula, and *in terms of meaning* as desire/truth and Other/loss, respectively (93). The agent is the position of that which speaks from the place of desire, underlain by the truth of its desiring position; the Other is that which the subject desires to know or manifest as knowledge, and production is the desired content from the Other, or the knowledge

Master

University

$$\frac{S_1}{\$} \rightarrow \frac{S_2}{a} \qquad \frac{S_2}{S_1} \rightarrow \frac{a}{\$}$$

$$\frac{\$}{a} \rightarrow \frac{S_1}{S_2} \qquad \frac{a}{S_2} \rightarrow \frac{\$}{S_1}$$

Hysteric

Analyst

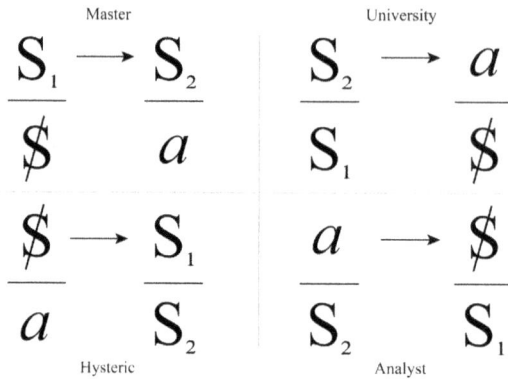

Figure 2.1 The four discourse formulae

the agent presumes the Other has and the subject desires. The left-hand side designates the speaking subject and the right-hand side the receiving subject. The formula's top portions designate manifest content and the bottom portions designate latent content.

The hysteric's discourse

Because the hysteric's discourse plays a formative role for the analysis that follows, I will focus on its positions and symbols for my analysis of the discourse formulae. The agent in the hysteric's discourse is symbolized by $, the barred/split subject. From the subject-who-speaks' perspective, $, then, the agent is fully aware of her division/alienation both within the social link in terms of satisfaction or identification with other discursive scripts, so she acts transsubjectively as antagonist and disruptor. She refuses to accept "master-ized" discourse, exposes its falsity, yet still wants and is reliant upon a master for her to dominate (94, 129). It is significant that Lacan considers the hysteric, no matter its sex, a feminine subject. As Lacan explains more than once, he is not theorizing anything new, but merely reading what already is. He uses the term feminine, I will defend, because the master's discourse as we know it (patri- archal, paternalistic) is a master's discourse only because it excludes her, and, more specifically, her jouissance (97). The hysteric is the feminine subject who recognizes that she is the Other *for* this discourse.[4] She is aware of her extimacy but does not know what to do with the awareness that what is most interior is also what is most Other, so she performs the discursive act of making present this truth. Recalling again the hysteric's discourse formula, with the master signifier in the position of Other (A) and *objet a* in the position of truth, a par- ticular extimate relationship occurs: we find, or locate, the embodiment of the alterity of the Other (Miller 79). This grounding of the alterity of the Other, to follow Jacques-Alain Miller's summation of extimacy, is jouissance, specifically a jouissance, unlike the phallic jouissance of the master, that has no signifier.

Objet a, the object-cause of desire, is positioned in both function and meaning as the latent truth for the hysteric subject. This little *a(utre)* must be a part of all subjects, but subjects of the master's and university's discourses position it as something discursively outside of themselves, even though the speaker in the master's discourse knows nothing of this, because of primary repression. Rather than displacing desire into another category, such as the Other or production or loss, the hysteric knows that the truth of her subjectivity is that her desire is displaced and she is split as a desiring subject because of that displacement. This knowledge is of primary importance in distinguishing the hysteric's discourse from the master's and university's discourses, as well as for the proceeding argument, because the awareness that her desire is displaced and its concomitant split bring to the fore the forceful oppression inherent within the master's discourse through subjectivization.

To reiterate, the master's discourse as we know it is patriarchal, paternalistic, but *the content of the master's discourse can shift*. In Lacan's view, the analyst's discourse, as the master's inversion, which also provokes purposefully the hysteric's discourse in patients/subjects, cannot prevent the burgeoning of another master's discourse. What other subjects forget is that they (we) all started out as *objet a*s: "This is what is important to grasp if we wish to understand something that has to do with – what? – with the forgetting of this very effect […] each one of us is initially determined as object small *a*" (SXVII 160). The hysteric does not necessarily forget this; rather, she speaks from the place of *objet a*, which brings out the fact that the master's discourse is a lie, that it is merely a "'master-ized' discourse" (103).[5] The repression of this fundamental desire is, to reiterate Copjec's argument discussed earlier, the foundation of subjectivity and society. The hysteric somehow does not repress it or displace it as well as dominant discourses desire her to do. Even though *objet a* is the latent position, it is nevertheless on the side of the speaker in the position of truth and motivates the discursive act.

The hysteric and the feminine

Lacan characterizes the subject of the hysteric's discourse as the *feminine* subject, but not as *female*. Early in the seminar, Lacan begins to clarify that the characterization of the hysteric as "she" is not supposed to limit this position to women. Yet, he says that men may "pass through the hysteric's discourse" only during analysis (33). I argue that he makes this claim because our society is structured by a discourse that privileges men, and men consciously and unconsciously assume this privilege. Men undergoing analysis must interrogate their unconscious, which pushes them into the hysteric's position. As I will explain later when I discuss the sexuation graph, the feminine position is liminal in that it is situated intersubjectively between the phallus and the unconscious. Lacan seemingly equates the hysteric and women by saying, "What hysterics ultimately want one to know is that language runs off the rails concerning the magnitude of what she as woman is capable of revealing concerning jouissance" (34). But Lacan repeatedly reminds his audience, mostly psychoanalysts, that he proceeds slowly with his explanations because of the novelty of the subject matter (23, 112, 137, 147, 175, 178). In reading Lacan to the letter, we read "she as woman" as a simile, not as a denotation.[6] At this point, Lacan has not built up his argument against Freud's short-fallings – namely, Freud's continual falling back into heteronormative gender paradigms and his inability to read his development of the Oedipus complex as his own dream – and so he likens the hysteric with woman as Freud did in order not to have to move too quickly, as well as to develop his theory of discourse and show how sexuation is interconnected with it.[7]

Later, in addressing the infamous woman question – worded specifically as "What does *a* woman want?" – Lacan emphasizes the indefinite article because the question is one of desire rather than of the subject so as to highlight that the subject is only ever situated as a particular manifestation of desire (129). In doing so, he specifies precisely that "'She' is the hysteric, but this is not necessarily specific to one sex" because, in articulating the question of want, the speaker "enter[s] the function of desire [and produces] the master signifier" (130). What the hysteric manifests in her relation to the master is the fact that there is jouissance beyond the privileged signifier of the phallus within existing Symbolic Law.[8] The Law is the Symbolic structure that acts as prohibition to jouissance, and discourse is the vehicle within the Symbolic that organizes social relations according to the Law. The Law's function (as we know it) is to prohibit incest and promote exogamy *a la* Freud's heteronormative, patriarchal primal horde myth and Oedipus complex. However, by redirecting emphasis from the subject to desire and access to a non-phallic jouissance, Lacan begins to consider the subject differently, as a subject of possibility, a subject that changes, even due to its subordination to desire within the functions of discourse.

In referring to the hysteric's discourse formula pictured above, we can recall that the hysteric directs her discourse toward S_1, the master signifier, in the position of Other, where S_2, the function of knowledge that takes on the meaning of loss, is in the place of production as the latent content. The hysteric's discourse, reliant upon the master signifier as receiver of her speech, acts through resistance rather than opposition. In thinking opposition phonologically as the functional or potentially functional contrast between two linguistic elements, we see that the hysteric's discourse does not function as full contrast: it functions as a pushing back and against the privileged linguistic element, the phallic signifier and, psychoanalytically, as resistance to what the phallic signifier represses. The analyst's discourse fits into the oppositional category more neatly. The hysteric's discourse, again, exposes the master's discourse as not wholly master, much like the master's discourse renders the feminine subject as having excess outside of phallic jouissance. But the master is only master through the myth of wholeness, the myth of the One. In this decentering of the master's discourse, the hysteric plays a role similar to the mythologist (Barthes 156–58), as she is only partially revolutionary: she, perhaps, is more the impetus for revolution, but what she does is not a revolutionary act in itself.

Recalling the connections between the Law, the Symbolic, and jouissance, however, we can understand that the hysteric, speaking from a place of the bubbling up of the cause of desire, acts from a place of jouissance. Although the hysteric subject is still subject to the Law, the Law fails to prohibit her jouissance, at least fully, and there is a potential for a non-phallic jouissance. Sexual difference is a structure of the Law, of a particular function and meaning within language, within discourse, as Lacan illustrates with the siblings on the train. All people are sexual, have sexuality as such, but sexuality is more akin to *savoir* as unconscious knowledge. Sexual difference is not necessarily prediscursive or akin to Freud's oceanic feeling in *Civilization and Its Discontents* (65) or Lacan's amorphous blob (the lamella) because it does designate something differentiated as sexuality; however, sexuality is different from the discursive designations of sexual difference. The content within the master's discourse inscribes sexual difference on the psyche and the body, or, rather, *makes sexuality figural*.[9] Sexuality as such is reined in, symbolized mythically through discursive narratives of sexual difference. The sexual difference myth is segregating both inter- and transsubjectively in that it segregates men from women, but also segregates the subject in that the subject always fails to be one or the other sexually scripted category.

Lacan's sexuation graph explains sexual difference as discursive, specifically within the master's discourse. The way in which *objet a* is positioned in relation to the $'s directionality toward it is an Imaginary and Symbolic directionality that narrativizes and mythologizes subject and object within discourse. However, Lacan's claim that the sexual relationship does not exist, as Ed Pluth argues in "On Sexual Difference and Sexuality 'as such': Lacan and the Case of Little Hans," is an "anti-imaginary claim" (73). Pluth parses well the difference between "sexuality as such" and sexual difference: sexuality as such is traumatic in that it is Real, unsymbolizable; sexual difference is the attempt to symbolize the unsymbolizable – a catachresis – to inscribe a logic of sexuation to sexuality as such. However, sexuality is only Real, unsymbolizable, retroactively in the sense that we cannot recognize sexuality as such until we are situated within sexual difference. Sexual difference is not an "answer or solution" to sexuality as such; rather it is a "repetition and inscribing of that real impasse in a symbolic impasse, without its having any claim to being right or accurate" (76). Even more salient to this project is Pluth's insight into the connection between the way Lacan defines the symptom and the way Lévi-Strauss defines myth: the symptom "forg[es] a relationship between two enigmas," and in this case the two enigmas are the presence of signifiers and sexuality as such (SXVII 76). Lévi-Strauss "suggests that myths formalize and organize impasses without really dissolving them" (76–77). For example, the myth of the masculine and feminine attempts to formalize and organize the tension within sexuality as such through sexual difference, and the myth fails at covering over the indissolvable tension between the two enigmas. If this is the case, then giving the sexuation graph a counter-clockwise quarter turn allows us to conceptualize sexuation not only within discourse, but also as discursive, which opens up possibilities of the transformation of subjectivity.

Discourse and sexuation

> *There is nothing vaguer than the question of belonging to one side or the other [...]*
> *Still, I have to find a point of departure, which is a [...] mere supposition, the supposition that there is a male and female subject. It is a supposition which experience*
> *shows us to be quite obviously untenable.*
> Lacan, *Les non-dupes errant* (unpublished), January 15, 1974

In *Encore*, Lacan highlights explicitly the truth in reality as fundamentally discursive: the "dream" of prediscursive reality "must be considered mythical," because "[e]very reality is founded and defined by discourse" (SXX 32). He connects this discursive reality directly with the social relationships between masculine and feminine subjects, particularly in the fact that subjects are defined and identify as such through discourse both in terms of subjectivization and objectivization, which sexual difference, as defined above, serves to do. "What constitutes the basis of life," he claims, "is that for everything having to do with the relations between men and women, what is called collectivity, it's not working out (*ça ne va pas*)" and "a large part of our activity is taken up with saying so" (32). The relations between masculine and feminine subjects – not really men and women – are impossible in terms of their inability not to substitute something in the place of the other for the masculine subject, and the split directionality of desire for the feminine subject. Lacan points to how socio-political discourses deal with this "large part of our activity" in his example of the two siblings who arrive at the train station as "the immeasurable power of ideological warfare" (*Écrits* 417). Society, social relationships, and the cultural reproductions therein have everything to do with the discursivity of sexuation and the impossibility of the sexual relationship through division and exclusion. Lacan's claim that there is no sexual relationship (SXVII and SXX) means that there is always something between the masculine and feminine positions because sexual drives are directed toward part-objects rather than people (Evans 181). The socio-cultural "conventions, prohibitions, and inhibitions that are the effect of language and can only be taken from that fabric and register" are such because "Men, women, and children are but signifiers" (SXX 32–33). Society perpetuates the myth of the sexual relationship, which does not exist, both through cultural conventions and the primary societal prohibition of incest that are only products of the language (*langue*) function in the Symbolic order.[10] The presupposition here is that of discourse in which signification embodies everything else. The siblings on the train will have to (mis)identify, will fail at identity, and will never be in agreement because of the bar that prevents them from avoiding the metonymic train of signifieriness, the great chain of signification.

As mentioned above in the context of the subject, the structure of the signifier is such that it can only signify through its relation to other signifiers.
A signifier may "slip" into the position of the signified and be "replaced" on the
signifying chain, but that replaced signifier is always metonymically connected
to it. Therefore, the bar between the signifier and signified can never be crossed
because the signifier inevitably arouses other signifiers.[11] Language is always
prior to the subject and determines one's sexuation, i.e., causes one to mean
discursively as feminine or masculine.[12] This bar is what makes possible the production of writing (34), and "[e]verything that is written stems from the fact
that it will forever be impossible to write, as such, the sexual relationship" (35).
The "immeasurable power of ideological warfare" (re)produced through the
writing of the cultural, which makes identification significantly political, stems
from the fact of the bar that prevents "what is written [...] to be understood"
(34). Copjec reiterates that "sex is produced by the internal limit, the failure
of signification" to encompass all understanding because there is a *"radical
antagonism between sex and sense"* (*Read My Desire* 204, emphasis in original).
It is only in this failure, she explains, "where discursive practices falter – and
not at all where they succeed in producing meaning – that sex comes to be"
(204). Pluth's careful musings on sexuality as such and sexual difference support
Copjec's claim. The "radical antagonism between sex and sense" in that sense,
in the sense she uses it here, is a fully Symbolic construction, whereas sex is
Symbolically constructed as an attempt to signify the unsymbolizable trauma
of sexuality as such.

At this point, I should probably address the contrast between what I am
arguing as the fundamental ideas of sexual difference and sexuation for this
project and the currently dominant discourse on sex and gender. Judith Butler's
now canonical, politically and rhetorically useful undoings of sex and gender
are similar to those within psychoanalytic scholarship, but she privileges
conclusions rooted in Foucault's queering of traditional understandings of
power. Similar to Lacan's prediscursive reality as dream, Butler theorizes that
language is structured by the Law, so cultural narratives are always limited by
what is inside the Law. Anyone who makes a narrative claim based upon what
is "before" the Law temporally is only able to do so retroactively, but we cannot
know what is really "before" and the Law always affects any account provided
of it. Butler argues that if gender, traditionally binarized into male and female,
is a social construct, then this construct is a performative articulation dictated
by dominant culture. Performativity is a set of linguistic codes embedded in
language by the Law, and the Law mobilizes these discourses so that they act
upon the subject, who is forced to internalize the codes and act out regulated
performativities: her appropriation of the term "performativity" provides an
historically rooted deconstruction of the relationship between language, the law,
and the psychic and bodily marks on the human. Since the effects of complex
signifying chains within discourse(s) are "vectors of power" (Butler, *Bodies* 187),
the circulation of dominant discourse (read: regimes of compulsory heterosexu-
ality/ heteronormativity) imposes the impossible and unintelligible gender and

sex constructs on subjects and masks them as normal and intelligible. Moreover, the referent to which these discursive significations refer is not a designation, but rather an act; therefore, gender and sex do not and cannot designate a natural or centered being. Foucault's theory that power does not exist in the traditionally understood hierarchical structure, but rather as a decentered structure that has multiple nodal points of origin arising and disappearing at any given moment, as well as his insight into the multiplicity of discourses occurring in the same fashion that overlap and function in opposition to one another simultaneously (Foucault, *History* 99–102), allow Butler to argue that it is not only within discourse that subjects experience oppression, but discourse is also the place from where subjects can and will access the power to move away from oppression. However, Butler occasionally mistakes *characteristics of language, which can change, and the condition of possibility of language as such, which cannot be altered*. Even though Butler offers up some libratory wiggle room – e.g., a subject, through acts of parody, irony, and pastiche (i.e., characteristics of language), can denaturalize dominant performativity that potentially bring about new conceptions of sex and gender articulation – she fails to acknowledge that new constraints of identificatory articulation must, perforce, arise. In "Restaging the Universal," Butler explains the unpredictability in the ways that the universal becomes contaminated – much like Rothenberg's unpredictable retroversive causality[13] – but her frustration gets the better of her as she concludes that "the purification of the universal into a new formalism will only reinitiate the dialectic that produces its split and spectral condition" (41). Butler seems to be searching for a final negation of the fundamental negation of subjectivity – the very constitution of the human condition – which would mean, psychoanalytically speaking, a return to the Real, a radical loss of subjectivity, an exile from the social link. Butler also contradicts her own desire for multiplicities and disruptions by desiring a utopic wholeness, or oneness, of the individual, almost, it seems, a desire to eradicate the subject.

Copjec demonstrates that psychoanalysis, against trends in sex and gender studies *a la* Butler, provides a politically useful argument *via* Lacan's declaration that the sexual relationship does not exist: "sex," as empty, "in opposing itself to sense, is also, by definition, opposed to relation, to communication" (*Read My Desire* 207).[14] Sex fails in signification; therefore, discourse, reliant on the subjects' transsubjective sense-making, cannot account for it. In her philosophical explication of the emptiness of sex and picking up on Freud's claim that to understand sex one must look to the drives, not culture, Copjec offers up a bit more liberating wiggle room than Butler. She argues that the subject "who is an effect, but not a realization of social discourses is […] free of absolute social constraint," but "he or she is nevertheless not free to be a subject any which way" because "within any discourse the subject can only assume either a male or female position" (210). The subject is not the origin of the social; rather, the subject is the first excess of language – through alienation from the Real – and it is in and through enunciation that the subject must occupy this space as, on Copjec's reading, one of two options. Later I will add to Copjec's idea of the subject's having to occupy one of the two positions in discourse by arguing that the occupation as one of the two positions is not an absolute or static positionality; rather, the subject can and does position herself within discourse as either/or and, at times, both/and, and neither/nor masculine or feminine. Additionally, I will take issue with Copjec's political fatalism in regard to this either/or in trying to highlight the incongruity between sexuation understood as discursive and the binary in which we struggle with the body as already ascribed masculine or feminine by focusing on the object rather than the subject. In privileging the object, similar to, if not in direct correlation with, the way in which I hope to foreground this focus on the object by privileging metonymy, we must re-figure the ways in which we understand identifications.

The tension I find between Lacan's work as productive for the transformation of subject positionality and Copjec's assertion that we must mean (only and forever) as men or women is one that I could have never made without more current psychoanalytic work influenced by posthumanism and object-oriented ontology. For example, Rothenberg traces not only Butler's use of the psychoanalytic subject's untotalizability within the social field but also her misreading of the Real so that she can find a way to get at excess for socio-political change that leads to a disavowal of psychoanalysis and ultimate return to Foucault to find possibilities of political agency: "When it comes to certain performances, [Butler] forgets about the slippage, the opening for re-interpretation, that iterability confers on *every* person. [...] Butler reserves the power of such insurrectionary speech for those who have been the objects of injurious speech, the marginalized or abjected" (98, emphasis in original). Butler does not want to accept the transsubjectivity of all subjects in the social field, as well as the social field's contingency due to the transsubjective, inevitable unpredictability of retroversive interpretation. Copjec explains, "Instead of an external opposition between the subject and society, we must learn to think their necessary interrelation: the very existence of the subject is simultaneously with society's failure to integrate, to represent it" (*Read My Desire* 124). Copjec, though, restricts subject possibility by sticking to the narrative Lacan uses to introduce his theory of sexuation, which, as my language here suggests, is only an illustrative narrative, a way to impart substance to a difficult, abstract structure of subject formation and manifestation. Butler claims that psychoanalytic theory is not and never can be political because it is ahistorical. As Fredric Jameson summarizes succinctly, Butler thinks "that in Lacan the Symbolic is radically separated from the social: this means that [...] Lacan's structural psychoanalysis will always be implicitly or explicitly ahistorical and thus anti-political – something that has frequently been affirmed in the context of a 'tragic vision' in Lacan" (385–86). In her refusal to see that the Symbolic and the social are overly determined by each other, she takes up an anti-psychoanalytic, pro-Foucaultian/historical position in order to forward an identity politics argument. Rather than queering the problematic of identity politics itself by recognizing the libratory emptiness afforded by the social and Symbolic relationship, she inserts her argument into traditional heteronormative discourse.

Political momentum (along feminist and queer party lines) occurs through opposition; that is, the positioning of discursive strategy outside of dominant discourse through the recognition of absence therein, as well as a refusal to engage with it. And it is this possibility of opposition that Lacan tries to set up, both in SXVII and SXX, for further discursive practices. Butler misses the mark because she does not fold into her theory that the sexual relationship qua discourse and the social always fails. Dean suggests a non-gender focused revision of Lacan's grappling with this failure as "sexual relationality's failure as such, independent of gender" (*Beyond* 17). To attempt to suture this failing through identity politics is to misrecognize identifications as identity, and this borders on utopist essentialism articulated through the Foucaultian denial of discourse as inherent in and of the subject, and thus as a species of voluntarism. If sexuation is fluid, are non-absolute positionalities within discourse indices of the always failing sexual relationship? And does the social field from which sexuation comes and continues to (mis)represent identity for the subject always fail too? If we can answer these questions affirmatively, then society, in the sense of its inability to become a place devoid of this "ideological warfare," is not utopic or dystopic, but nevertheless always fails. Cultural reproductions proliferate in order to cover over what fails. Society – following Yannis Stavrakakis in *Lacan and the Political* and in light of the idealist suturing desire inherent within political conflict – does not exist because identity does not exist.[15] Stavrakakis makes this claim in the wake of Laclau, who does so a bit differently than Stavrakakis in that he appropriates partial psychoanalytic terms to complicate socio-political relations. Laclau often uses the terms *suture* and especially *identity* more broadly in order to focus on the relationship between identification and the political. Stavrakakis, though, points out that the "radicality and importance of the Lacanian critique depends on its ability to keep its distance from fantasmatic politics [...] which is not the same as saying that psychoanalysis is apolitical" (119). A subject only has politically situating identifications that always miss the mark, always open up fissures within meaning, and discourse qua the emptiness of the Symbolic allows choices, particularly from the so-called feminine subject position. This so-called feminine subject position, due to its evident excess apart from the phallic function and its dual trajectory, particularly the non-phallic one, functions, at least, as proof that phallic discourse is *not all* (encompassing), and it is an opening to something Other and to new possibilities.

The hysteric's discourse is important for this project not only in terms of its interrogation of the master's discourse, but also its specificity as a (read: *the*) "feminine" discursive mode. Also, the analyst's discourse has a transdiscursive relation to the hysteric's discourse in that it provokes the hysteric's discourse, but the hysteric's discourse also functions as the subject's movement away from the master's discourse and toward the analyst's: if the subject functions within and from the analyst's discourse, then societal revision becomes more possible in that a different master discourse may arise. Lacan muses, "it is fairly curious that what [the analyst] produces is nothing other than the master's discourse, since it's S_1 which comes to occupy the place of production [...] perhaps it's from the analyst's discourse that *there can emerge another style of master signifier*" (176, emphasis added). What we find in his turnings of the discourse formula is not only an explanation of the ways subjects occupy the social field and/or ways the social field defines subject positions, but also, as we see in this rare moment of incitement, a desire for, almost (should I dare write) a belief in, something other than the phallus as master signifier. These discursive revisions come out of disruptions of sexual difference as we know it, i.e., the *symptom* of sexuality as such. Disruptions of the symptom put the myth of identity in crisis, expose the discursive reality of subject relations, and break down the myths that hold up these relations. We are speaking beings who live by, through, and in discourse, so we will make new myths from new symptoms of the crisis.

Notes

1 If we can take on Lacan's equalizing of all signifiers, then Foucault's discourse theory, with its emphasis on power rather than possibilities of discursive positions, just as Copjec insinuates, perpetuates itself through insistence upon an assumption of the very power dynamic he intends to redefine and open up.

2 I want to note briefly that the bathroom stalls diagram reads as a rudimentary or preliminary sketch of Seminar XX's sexuation table and/or a discursive materiality of (or symbol of) sexuation. I will revisit this in later chapters.

3 *Savoir* is different from *connaissance*: the former is an order of knowledge that, for psychoanalysis, is not known that it is known. It is thus situated as unconscious knowledge and/or knowledge of the unconscious, and the latter is a knowledge of representation or acquaintance (SXVII 30). *Savoir*, then is a latent knowledge that affects the subject's interaction with discourse, i.e., within the social field. Lacan's distinction between these two terms differs from Foucault's, who also makes an important distinction between the two terms. For Foucault, *savoir* refers to a general knowledge, and the conditions of knowledge necessary for particular knowledges to arise; *connaissance* refers to particular types of knowledge, such as literary studies, psychoanalysis, biology, etc. (*Archaeology* 15 fn 2).

4 However, as I will try to show throughout this project, the master's discourse does not have to mean within patriarchal and/or paternalistic discourse. Rather, the feminine subject as Lacan has written it in the sexuation graph takes on this gendered signifier only because it is the content that grounds the current master's discourse.

5 Lacan writes:

> The object *a* is what makes it possible to introduce a little bit of air into the function of surplus *jouissance*. You are all an object *a*, insofar as you are lined up there – so many miscarriages of what has been, for those who engendered you, the cause of desire. And this where you have to get your bearings from – psychoanalysis teaches you this. [...]
>
> Nothing can function without [segregation] – what is happening here, as the *a*, and the *a* in living form, miscarriage that it is, displays the fact that it is an effect of language. Be that as it may, there is in every case a level at which things do not work out. It's the level of those who have produced the effects of language, since no child is born without having to deal with this traffic by the

intermediary of his beloved so-called progenitors, who were themselves caught up in the entire problem of discourse, with the previous generation behind them also. And this is the level at which it would really be necessary to have made enquiries. (SXVII 178–79)

6   Referring back to the opening discussion on the difficulty of pronoun use within the psychoanalytic language of sexuation, even the master cannot escape the trap.

7   Freud's Oedipal complex narrates the moment of recognition of sexual difference in children. This occurs differently for boys and girls. When the little boy recognizes the girl's lack of a penis, castration anxiety sets in; when the little girl recognizes that she lacks a penis, is castrated, then she turns aggressive toward the mother and identifies father as love-object. Lacan, however, revises Freud's ideas in order to theorize that castration occurs the same in all children: it is the Symbolic loss of an Imaginary object. With this view, Lacan removes the anatomical focus of the phallus as penis and develops the concept of Imaginary phallus. (Trans subjects repeatedly and *un*uniformly make this clear in their individual foci on what will and does make them a man or a woman. For example, a female-to-male may focus on having an excessively large scrotum while another may focus on sideburns. A male-to-female may focus on having large breasts while another may focus on hairlines. Of course, these are outward significations and are in no way meant to insinuate that it is such that will and does make a trans person who they want to be.) Therefore, the Oedipal complex occurs first and the castration complex follows once the child recognizes a lack both in the Other (mother) and the self that the child desires to fill. This leads the child to take up a position as man or woman, a position that imposes sexual difference on the subject and within the social field.

8   Lacan, in his revision of Freud's Oedipal stage, replaces Freud's literal penis with the Imaginary phallus. His revision reads a movement from an initial triangulation of the mother-child-phallus relationship (the child wants to be the phallus for the mother once it recognizes that the mother lacks a penis) to a fantasy of an interruptive fourth term. This fourth term is the father who possesses the phallus. (This revision stems from Freud's primordial horde myth where the horde's father, who is killed and devoured, returns mystically/mythically as an internalized "No"!) This interruption begins the castration complex for both boys and girls. The subject comes to mean (rather than be) in and through language, which is displaced desire (the phallus as signifier). The phallus as signifier is the residue of the Imaginary that manifests as a double play of desire in the Other and in relation of the Other to the subject. And this residue is, for Lacan, what makes the phallus the primary signifier. Language, as the colonizer of man, is invisible, incomprehensive, and the phallus first as signifier (interruptive fourth term) then slides into the position of the bar in the Symbolic to "unveil" the meaning of the phallus as that which signifies the *Spaltung* of man. Many theorists take issue with Lacan's construction of the Imaginary phallus as privileged signifier. For example, Jacques Derrida argues that Lacan reintroduces the transcendent/ metaphysical signifier with which poststructuralist theories disagree, because Lacan asserts that the phallus has no signified as the privileged signifier. Feminists (e.g., Irigaray and Butler) take issue with the phallus as privileged signifier because Lacan seems, to them, to reify and/or perpetuate phallogocentrism and patriarchal dominance over women. In addition, Lacan says that in the Symbolic and Imaginary men *have* the phallus and women *are* the phallus (for men). Of course, this theory is problematic for most feminist thinkers because it suggests that men are in

possession of the privileged signifier and women must represent themselves as that privileged signifier for or be recognized as it (as an object) for men. I will continue to address this issue of feminist tensions with the phallus throughout this project.

9 I develop this point further in chapter four by arguing that sexual difference metaphorizes sexuality, as sexual difference comes about by a spark that arises from metonymically situated signifiers within the Law that results in an occulted signifier. Metaphorizing sexuality into sexual difference, that is, replacing sexuality with sexual difference, is the mythologizing of sexuality.

10 For Lacan, *langue* designates a specific language, as opposed to *langage*, which is the structural paradigm. Lacan later coins the neologism *lalangue* "to refer to […] non-communicative aspects of language which, playing on ambiguity and homophony, give rise to a kind of *jouissance*" (Evans 97).

11 Cf. Ferdinand de Saussure, *Course in General Linguistics*. Open Court Classics, 1972; Jacques Lacan, "The Instance of the Letter in the Unconscious." *Écrits*, translated by Bruce Fink. W. W. Norton & Company, 2006, pp. 412–41. I will return to this issue of the crossing of the bar later in order to detail the nuances of it by way of metaphor and metonymy.

12 I recognize the heteronormative implications of this statement. I do not think this is an all-inclusive claim; rather, it is a dominant claim. Just as Lacan continually reminds his audience that he is only reading what is already out there, in making this claim I am doing the same. The queering of this binary has become part of dominant conversation and takes on a variety of discursive positionalities.

13 I will discuss Rothenberg's concept more fully later. Briefly, though, unpredictable retroversive causality is exactly what it sounds like. Rothenberg uses the example of Julius Caesar's murderers' inability to foresee, that is, predict, the way in which their murderous act would be interpreted and judged by themselves, their peers, and especially future historical moments (1–3). The linearity of social change, and particularly singular events such as the murdering of Caesar, are myth.

14 Foucault and Lacan both read the subject as empty, but not quite in the same way. In theorizing the statement, the enunciative function and the subject, Foucault says the subject is an "empty function" in that anyone can put together the statement and anyone can enunciate or occupy the position of a variety of statements and positions to them (*Archaeology* 93–95). Differently than Foucault's empty function and its "vacant place" (95) in the statement, Lacan's four discourses formulate how the subject can occupy a variety of positions within discourse and how discourse and the subject *inter-function*. Bruce Fink, following J.A. Miller, in *The Lacanian Subject: Between Language and Jouissance*, uses mathematical logic to describe the subject as empty set, Ø, to further explain alienation – the coming into the Symbolic and differentiation – and how the subject is eclipsed by the signifier and, therefore, becomes a signifier for another signifier (52–53). In Copjec's "sex is empty" statement, she explains that this is a signifying position, not an ontology, and the Symbolic's support of this position is unstable.

15 Cf. Bellamy, J.E. "Discourse of Impossibility: Can Psychoanalysis Be Political?" *Diacritics*, vol. 23, no. 1, 1993, pp. 24–38.

Quilting point

A literary discussion on metaphor and metonymy

This first quilting point provides a canonical background for my upcoming workings of tropology that derive from literary theory and which also informed some of Lacan's thinking. So as not to take the reader's knowledge for granted, I outline briefly here Ferdinand de Saussure's origins of the signifier and signified, Victor Shklovsky's literary techniques of metaphor and metonymy, and Nietzsche's thinking around tropes, the subject, and the subject's perception of objects and truth. (I will incorporate Roman Jakobson's discussion on tropes into Chapter 3's discussion.) This quilting point foregrounds the workings of metaphor and metonymy on the subject and within discourse and sexuation that follow throughout the project.

Psychoanalysis is the talking cure. We use language because we have to mean; we cannot only be (Thomas xv). The only way we know the unconscious exists is because it peeks out through language, as slips of the tongue or dream states, for example. Tropes are a socio-discursive, linguistic moving force. Our society and social structure/connection are built on metaphors. Yet, language is inherently metonymic. Sentences are a chain of signifiers. In literary theory, we have a clear lineage of tropological philosophy, which I briefly outline here.

In *Course in General Linguistics* (1906–11, first published in 1916), Saussure's focus on *langue*, the structure of language in general, rather than *parole*, the individual speech act, provides a platform for structuralism.[1] Saussure suggests that semiology, a science of language focused on the study of the system of signs, could, and should, become an intellectual imperative.[2] In order to provide the groundwork for semiotics, Saussure maps a dyadic sign comprised of a signified (Sd) placed over a signifier (Sr) separated by a bar (Sd/Sr), written like a mathematical fraction. The signified is the concept referred to by a signifier as acoustic image. He distinguishes the sound pattern from the speech act by using the example of the way we read silently and still have a voice in our head that functions by way of sound patterns. The signified and signifier are intimately linked, but the link between them is arbitrary. However, because language is a structural system, the arbitrariness of the sign is not absolute – i.e., we cannot willy-nilly replace one sign for another or mix up signs, e.g., call a cat a banana and expect others to understand – because of the social relations within language systems that create values between similar and dissimilar things.

According to Saussure, relations and their values are contingent upon comparison and substitution. We must compare signifiers with other signifiers to produce meaning. Saussure explains that "instead of pre-existing ideas … we find *values* emanating from the system. When they are said to correspond to concepts, it is understood that the concepts are purely differential and defined not by their positive content but negatively by their relations with other terms of the same system" (117). Language has no positive terms, only differences. Saussure explains that syntagmatic relations, the linearity of words (signifiers) strung together in a structured sequence like a phrase or sentence, for example, are necessary because a word's value depends upon what frames that word. All words in a sentence gain their value through the comparison, or opposition, of other words within the syntagm. Just as significant, but quite different from the syntagmatic relation, is the associative relation of words; that is, substitution. Unlike the necessary discursive position of syntagmatic relations – a sentence needs a subject and a verb – the associative (or substitutive) part of language relies upon the interchangeability of words, dog for cat, for instance.[3] The substitutive relation, then, occurs on another scene by sustaining itself in a mental reservoir of exchangeable words, which allows variety and possibility within language as a living system; that is, as an actively differential system.

To bridge Saussurean linguistics with literary theory in order to show how signifieds and signifiers and syntagmatic and associative relations matter to the operations of metaphor and metonymy, I turn to Shklovsky's 1917 "Art as Technique," which distinguishes the poetic from the prosaic in order to show what Literature does and how it does it. Here, I first lay out Shklovsky's explanation, and then in the following paragraph I situate the significance of his treatment of metaphor and metonymy for this project. Shklovsky's interests lie in the Formalist distinction between Literature as art and other writing, as well as the way artistry works by way of the perception of the art. He focuses on the manipulation of language as that which, when artistic, is poetic regardless of the genre (i.e., formal poetry or prose). Metaphor, briefly, is a substitution of one word with another. Metonymy is often reduced to, or aligned with, synecdoche, which is the linguistic use of part of a thing to refer to the whole thing, e.g., a thousand sails to refer to a fleet of ships. Metonymy, however, emphasizes the function of linkage, a word to word connection, rather than a mere part to whole association. To begin to distinguish between metaphor and metonymy, Shklovsky uses the infamous "Butterfingers" examples to explain the difference between the two tropes.[4] If a child eating buttered bread has the butter all over her fingers and someone calls out, "Hey, Butterfingers!," then that person uses the child's buttered fingers, a part of her person, to refer to her "whole" person, which is synecdochal (i.e., metonymic). If a child is playing with a toy and drops it and someone calls out, "Hey, Butterfingers!," then that person substitutes the child with a metaphoric idea (776), i.e., the child doesn't have butter on her fingers in this case but, instead, is metaphorically substitutable for the slippery, butter-adorned fingers.

Shklovsky's distinction between the two tropes serves as an example of the difference between the prosaic and poetic. The metonymical butterfingers is prosaic because it is realistic: the child really has butter on her fingers. More salient to my argument for the (transitional) privileging of metonymy is that this example shows the linking of metonymy with physical contiguity: not only is there a synecdochic part-to-whole contiguity of the child with her own fingers, but also the contiguity, the link, of the butter and the body, again specifically, through the fingers. Metaphor is poetic because it is said to be more imaginative: it is "as if" the child has butter on her flesh. Metaphor, then, negates metonymy's "realism." Shklovsky, privileging metaphor, uses these basic literary tropes to discuss the way in which poetry as Literature, both as artistic technique and as perceived by the reader, is poetic. With quotidian discursive spaces, metonymies and metaphors can become habitual, automatic. In fact, our quotidian, as Shklovsky describes it, is largely habitual and automatic (778–79).[5] What Literature does, then, and perhaps especially with the aid of metaphor, is defamiliarize what has become familiar. The function of defamiliarization is not necessarily, if at all, to provide a specific meaning for an object, idea, or event; instead, it is to create perceptions that provoke readers to re-evaluate these things and events.

Artistic techniques must work to defamiliarize again what has become familiar when once innovative poetic techniques eventually become habitualized. Language works upon the subject, but artistic and perceptive subjects must also work with and through language in order to resist mental and internalized cultural fascism.[6]

Nietzsche, in his 1873 "On Truth and Lies in an Extra-Moral Sense," addresses this problematic relation between the subject's consciousness and language. Years before Saussure's claim that the sign is arbitrary, Nietzsche, a defected philologist, also proclaims this very idea and he does so by discussing explicitly metaphor and metonymy.[7] The subject of language, whom we all are, is at least three times removed from the thing-in-itself: a nerve stimulus provokes an image (Saussure's signified), which then provokes a sound (Saussure's signifier) (116).[8] Additionally for Nietzsche, the concept is also removed from an "essence" in that concepts only come about through difference. So, he shatters the philosophical legacy of searching for and/or professing Being and Truth in an absolute sense. Our very anthropomorphism removes us from essences (116–18).[9] So what are truths for Nietzsche? They are illusions, metaphors, and metonymies. In alignment with the above notes on Shklovsky, truths are human relations poetically worked upon.[10] Nietzsche also emphasizes that this poetic language becomes "forgotten," and he signifies this by the metaphor of a coin that has lost its distinctive marks; the coin, worn through the passage between hands, no longer has monetary or fetishistic value as a coin, but is only metal (117).

For Nietzsche, the subject to object relation is nothing but metaphor from the start. There is no original essence upon which our perceptions build metaphors. He explains that:

> "the correct perception" – which would mean "the adequate expression of an object in the subject" – is a contradictory impossibility. For between two absolutely different spheres, as between subject and object, there is no causality, no correctness, and no expression; there is, at most, an *aesthetic* relation: I mean, a suggestive transference, a stammering translation into a completely foreign tongue.
>
> (119, emphasis in original)

If I understand Nietzsche correctly here, he is talking about how "man" perceives the world metaphorically, or in terms of metaphor, in order to make himself stable and secure; man makes the world seem consistent to himself in order to feel less inconsistent in himself. There is no "correct" or "true" way to perceive an object; truth is merely a matter of what works to stabilize the perceiving subject, which is to say, perhaps, that there is only one "correct" way to perceive an object, i.e., whatever way that offers stability. Nietzsche's brief but dense musing on man and perceptions can be read as a precursor to Freud's pleasure principle. The pleasure principle is Freud's concept of the way the subject reduces excitement, a destabilizer associated with unpleasure, in order to feel stable and comfortable, i.e., rather than trying to achieve pleasure, which is an affective manifestation of anxiety, the subject seeks to reduce the level of anxiety to which it is subjected.[11] What I find most interesting about Nietzsche's construction here is the way in which "the adequate expression of an object *in* a subject" can mean both how the subject internally perceives external objects and how the subject perceives the corporeal self as object.[12] That "suggestive transference" that is "a stammering translation into a completely foreign tongue" could just as well be understood as the processes that occur between the unconscious and conscious, or even the conscious and discursive articulation, according to psychoanalysis. In this regard, Nietzsche posits that the human drive is nothing but the drive (from and) toward metaphor, and it is in the revision of metaphors that desire manifests (121). As I have already hinted, this enlightenment is crucial to understanding why metaphor and metonymy are major keys within psychoanalysis, and, as I will explain when I revisit this passage later, it is also crucial to understanding Lacan's claim that there is no such thing as a sexual relationship (SXX 33–35).

The upcoming chapter fleshes out the significance of tropes on the body and how they play out often as symptoms. I will first look at Freud's use of tropes for dream analysis and how that leads, seemingly always, to the body, in order to discuss how Lacan adapts Freud's work in conjunction with the influences outlined here to begin developing a theory of the subject as a signifier to another signifier. This discussion of metaphor and metonymy will ultimately lead to the articulation of desire and the function of the gaze.

Notes

1 Note that Saussure's *langue* and *parole* are different from Lacan's *langue, langage,* and *lalangue*. Cf. endnote 10 in Chapter 1.

2 The term *semiology* later turns into *semiotics*. Both indicate the study of signs and sign systems. I will use the term semiotics.

3 As I will show below, the associative is now more commonly referred to as paradigmatic *a la* Jakobson.

4 Metonymy also has a close association, for my thinking, with Derrida's *différance*.

5 He specifically homes in on Leo Tolstoy's use of "unconsciously" to make his point. This is significant particularly as these ideas come in the wake of Freud's *The Interpretation of Dreams* where Freud discusses the properties of condensation and displacement of unconscious communication in dreams, as well as in the analysis of them, and Jakobson's and Lacan's later adaptation of condensation and displacement as metaphor and metonymy, respectively, as well as Lacan's mapping of metaphor and metonymy onto the symptom and desire, respectively. I will talk more about condensation and displacement in the following chapter.

6 I am referring not to fascism in the strictly political sense; rather, I am referring to how Foucault uses it at the end of his preface to Gilles Deleuze and Félix Guattari's *Anti-Oedipus*: "the fascism in us all, in our heads and in our everyday behaviour, the fascism that causes us to love power, to desire the very thing that dominates and exploits us" (xiii).

7 The basics of semiotics are not new even to Nietzsche; as is well known, we find these philological ideas in Plato (4th century BCE) and Augustine (354-430 CE) among others.

8 For Saussure, the concept or image is the primary process; for Lacan, however, this is not necessarily the case.

9 Nietzsche is aware that this is a truth claim, which he states explicitly to underline the paradoxical "nature" of language.

10 Human relations as we know them can only be relations dependent upon and provoked by language.

11 Nietzsche's link between perception and metaphor is also similar to Lacan's semiological building upon Freud's pleasure principle in his concept of fantasy as one of the primary functions that interlocks the Imaginary and Symbolic.

12 A subject's perceiving itself as object is later picked up by Irigaray, both in *Speculum of the Other Woman* and *This Sex which Is Not One*. I will expand upon this connection later.

3 The troped body

The unconscious is neither the primordial nor the instinctual, and what it knows of the elemental is no more than the elements of the signifier.
Lacan, "The Instance of the Letter in the Unconscious," *Écrits* 434

I want to turn now to tropes as a function of language, a function that repeats inter- and transdiscursively with very real consequences for the body and for the subject as a signifier to another signifier. I will follow on from the previous chapter's discussion to develop the hysterical symptom and its inscription on the body, then turn to metaphor and metonymy. I examine the development of tropology in psychoanalysis in relation to sexual difference; I ask how discourse, through the functions of tropes, affects the body; and I establish why these concepts matter for feminisms. I begin with the notion of the hysterical symptom as a focus of understanding language and the body in "The Function and Field of Speech and Language in Psychoanalysis," which lays out Lacan's merger of linguistics with Freud's psychoanalysis that leads us to consider the body as a complex and divided system. As the opening epigraph suggests, the elements of discourse and the ways in which they mean determine the logic of one's sexuation, which is arguably unconscious. The hysteric, taking the speaking being's position in discourse, interrogates what seems primordial and/or instinctual and reveals that meaning to be a symptom of a particular discourse or discursive position. For example, Ruth Padawer's August 8, 2012, multi-page cover story in *The New York Times Magazine* "What's So Bad about a Boy Who Wants to Wear a Dress?" asks her readers goadingly about the apparent rise in gender-variant identifications among children under the age of ten. These children simply explain that they are in the "middle" in terms of "being" a boy or a girl, and that they act out one or both genders as a performance and engage in the discursive interrogation of normative demands. I then turn to "The Instance of the Letter in the Unconscious" in order to describe how Lacan, influenced by structural linguistics, maps metaphor and metonymy in the relationship of the body to discourse. "The Instance of the Letter in the Unconscious" also provides an understanding of the materiality of the letter, which I use to reconceptualize the connection between discourse and sexuation. I look to the "post face" of the "Seminar on 'The Purloined Letter'" in order to explain the L schema as a prototype for Lacan's later discourse formulae. Because the L schema focuses on the gaze, I argue that the gaze is the link between the L schema and the discourse formulae in order to foreground an argument I make later that the discourse formulae embody a gaze function.

The hysterical symptom and its inscription on the body

> For this ego, distinguished first for the imaginary inertias it concentrates against the message of the unconscious, operates only by covering over the displacement the subject is with a resistance that is essential to discourse as such.
>
> Lacan, "The Instance of the Letter in the Unconscious," *Écrits* 433

As I note in the previous chapter, Lacan asserts in the Rome Discourse that "speech confers a meaning on the functions of the individual; its domain is that of concrete discourse qua field of the subject's transindividual reality; and its operations are those of history insofar as history constitutes the emergence of truth in reality" (*Écrits* 214). In addition to the commentary regarding discourse that I provided in the previous chapter's discussion of this passage, I also want to show that this conferral of "meaning on the functions of the individual" is a way in which the body comes to be defined, delimited, and shaped. The unconscious, Lacan explains, is the "censored chapter" of one's history that can be "refound" because it is "written elsewhere," in other locations, such as on the body. This censored history manifests corporeally through "the hysterical core of neurosis in which *the hysterical symptom manifests the structure of language*, and is deciphered *like an inscription* which, once recovered, can be destroyed without serious loss" (215, emphasis added). I want to emphasize here Lacan's declaration of the way in which the structure of language arises, and the way in which we can transform (apparently without much ado) the realization of its symptom. The body, understood in psychoanalysis, is not the biological body, but *a body complexly constructed of a relationship between psychic perception and physicality, as well as often infringed upon by unconscious* (and specifically hysterical) *inscriptions*, such as the inexplicable paralysis suffered by analysands in Freud's accounts documented in "A Comparative Study of Traumatic and Hysterical Paralyses." Lacan, following Freud, asserts that everyone who falls into the category of the neurotic is, at root/core, a hysteric. The subject's hysteric core is what makes analysis possible. As I tried to show in the previous chapter, the hysteric's discourse is not only a necessary stage of analysis, but it is the discursive stage upon which the analysand pushes the boundaries of their understanding of their own meaning as a subject.

The hysterical symptom manifests in the neurotic subject the "structure of language [...] deciphered like an inscription" (216). Similar to Foucault's popular insight that homosexuality as an identity category did not exist until heterosexuality became a category and needed a different category to serve as its other, the hysterical symptom manifests the structure of language because it is that which serves as the difference for or disruptor to the seemingly invisible "normal" neurosis. Additionally, "Normal hysteria has no symptoms and is an essential characteristic of the speaking subject. Rather than a particular speech relation, the discourse of the hysteric exhibits the most elementary mode of speech. Drastically put, the speaking subject is hysterical as such" (Wacjman, n.p.). The hysterical speaking subject, rendered as $ in Lacan's algebra, functions as both subject and object within the hysteric's discourse as the subject who demands knowledge of "her" identity from the master, thereby serving as the object-cause of the master's desire and as the object of his desire. The demand to know who "she" is, to be affirmed as a subject, is the fundamental impetus for speech.

Once we are able to decipher the structure of language, we can analyze its inscription on the body. In defining the body as one of the sites of the hysterical symptom's inscription, Lacan explains that the body is itself a metaphor; the body is "but a symptom for the symbolic displacement brought into play in the symptom" (*Écrits* 216).[1] The body is one of the many metaphors used to describe the locations where the censored chapter of the subject's history can be refound. To carry over my introductory question – can we not consider the sexuated body an object of discourse within the logic of sexuation (or possibly *the fundamental logic and object of Discourse*)? – I argue that sexual difference is the overriding metaphor that situates the subject within discourse, specifically in response to the subject's hysterical demand "who/what am I?" Lacan elaborates on this connection between the hysterical symptom and the body:

> if [Freud] teaches us to follow the ascending ramification of the symbolic lineage in the text of the patient's free associations, in order to detect the nodal points [*noeuds*] of its structure at the places where its verbal forms intersect, then it is already quite clear that symptoms can be entirely resolved in an analysis of language, because a symptom is itself structured like a language: a symptom is language from which speech must be delivered.
>
> (223)

To clarify, "the ascending ramification of the symbolic lineage in the text of the patient's free associations" is Lacan's definition of the symptom for this particular point he is making. The analyst can detect the nodal points of the symptom's structure at the places where the symptom's multiple verbal forms intersect, which are the points from which analysis works upon the subject.

We can begin to understand what Lacan means by his often-repeated claim "the unconscious is structured like a language" (SIII 167; SXI 20) in this claim that "a symptom is itself structured like a language." In consideration of the link between the speech of the hysteric and the lack that the other three discourses mask with un- or less-than-truthful speech, if the neurotic is at core a hysteric, and the hysteric speaks consciously from the place of the split subject, then the speech of the hysteric directly symptomatizes the lack that other discourses mask with un- or less-than-truthful speech.[2] *The symptom marks the arrival of the letter, the Real materiality of the signifier.*[3] This Real materiality of the signifier designates the core indivisibility of the signifier *prior to* its insertion or usage in the Imaginary and Symbolic registers.[4] In other words, the materiality of the letter implies that signifiers are "embodied, materialized, they are words that wander about and as such they play their role of fastening together" (SIII 289). We can read this materiality of the letter as a metaphor for the sexually differentiated body "signifying about" in order to fasten itself to another signifier. The ascription and use of signifiers fill a lack inherent in the subject that wells up symptomatically on and in the body.

Freud's theory of hysterical paralysis illustrates the materiality of these nodal points, translated elsewhere as "bonds" (*Écrits* 225), in similar fashion to Lacan's idea of quilting points. In *Vital Signs: Nature, Culture, Psychoanalysis*, Charles Shepherdson connects this discovery of hysterical paralysis with the drive, specifically the sexual drive, as understood in psychoanalysis. Freud's "A Comparative Study of Traumatic and Hysterical Paralyses" (1893c) concludes that hysterical paralysis emerges not because of some organic or physical cause but rather because of *the idea of the body*, for example, the nodal point, if I may use this term, of the intersection where the leg meets the hip, or the arm meets the shoulder (Shepherdson 96–97). In other words, the anatomical reality and even at times the visible understanding of the body and its parts differ from the idea of the body in the ways in which hysterical paralysis manifests. Shepherdson asks:

> When Freud says that the arm is paralyzed *up to the point where one sees* it join up with the shoulder, or that the paralysis follows *the common idea of* the arm, *what we commonly designate by the word* "arm," are we dealing with a symptom governed by *the image or the word*? Is the "hysterical body" the visible body, or the body divided by the signifier?
>
> (97, emphasis in original)

Hysterical paralysis is a paralysis of the psychical idea of the body by the signifier, which stays intact but separated from the larger idea of the body. The arm, in this example, becomes the guiding signifier as symptom and, hence, as metaphor. "Freud," Shepherdson writes, "recognize[s] that, in the course of analysis, a discursive chain (a consciously spoken discourse) will intersect, at a particular point, with a bodily effect" (98). As we see later in *Three Essays on the Theory of Sexuality*, Freud theorizes erotogenic zones similarly: he understands the entire body as a site of pleasure that gives way to the oral and anal stages that (may or may not always) give way to an idea of genital pleasure and excitement, and this transference of pleasure from the entire "polymorphously perverse" body to localized (and Symbolically scripted or libidinally normalized) areas can be understood as an intersection of the body and the idea within discourse.[5] As another example, the Oedipus complex serves to institute law in terms of corporeal regulation, teaching us how to direct desire psychically and physically.

In a kind of shorthand, we can understand the symptom transmitted from interaction with the unconscious and inscribed onto the subject's understanding of its body, according to Lacan, as a metaphor of censored history. However, to complicate matters, the way in which we talk about the symptom is also *through* metaphor, i.e., within the domain of metaphor. As sexual difference, articulated as masculine or feminine, is the founding difference within the master's discourse, and it is sexual difference that subjectivizes each and every one of us symptomatically, not only for ourselves, but also for others. To be sexed and subsequently gendered – that is, to be subjected to an identificatory objectivization and then to internalize that subjectivization and, ultimately, a gendered form of subjectivity – is also to become an object to oneself. Working from Lacan's claim that "speech confers a meaning on the functions of the individual" (*Écrits* 214), I turn now to the question of the ways in which the individual's functions mean tropologically, specifically metaphorically and metonymically, and of how these functions determine the subject's positionality within discourse.

Metaphor, always behind the throne of metonymy

To bring us back to somewhat more current usages of metaphor and metonymy in literary theory, Jakobson's 1960 "Linguistics and Poetics" merges Saussurean linguistics with literary studies in order to delineate its structuralist practice, considered as objective, from prior literary criticism, considered as subjective evaluation. He notes both the sequential and spatial movements of syntagmatic relations, which he designates as the horizontal vector of an axis. In addition, he renames the substitutive relations as paradigmatic relations, a more narrowed and specific way of theorizing this concept, which he designates as the vertical vector of an axis. The paradigmatic relations provoke meaning through analysis of absent signifiers that could be substituted by what is present in a linguistic sequence; therefore, it would seem that significance depends upon the selections made. The structure of the poetics of selection (paradigmatic axis, metaphoric) and combination (syntagmatic axis, metonymic) produces effects of signification. Yet, Jakobson privileges the axis of combination, i.e., the functions of metonymy – a much debated assertion – as that which determines meaning, that is, the way in which words function next to each other, not in the selection of how or why a writer places them (Jakobson 858).

Overlapping with structuralist trends in linguistics and literary studies in the mid-20th century, Lacan marries Freud's psychoanalysis with semiotics. In "The Instance of the Letter in the Unconscious, or Reason since Freud," Lacan inverts Saussure's "signified over signifier," Sd/Sr, to "signifier over signified," Sr/Sd, and removes the enclosure and the arrows that suggest movement. Lacan is able to theorize that "the unconscious is structured like a language" because of his version of metaphor and metonymy. This major thematic claim means that the unconscious, just like language, is a structure of signifiers (Evans 97, 218). However, Lacan is very specific upon the first utterance of this claim that the unconscious is not a discourse, nor is it expressed as such (SIII 166–67). We can recall from the previous chapter that desire is a key component of discourse. Referring to Freud, Lacan reiterates that the unconscious is a site of drives that allows the subject to shape himself in language, and the elementary structures of language are the laws of combination and substitution (*a la* Shklovsky and Jakobson) and kinship relations (*a la* Lévi-Strauss and Freud), that is, of a relation between signifiers and signifieds (167). And he turns to Freud's *The Interpretation of Dreams* to explain his point.

In *The Interpretation of Dreams*, Freud uses the terms condensation and displacement to try to prove the unconscious' existence, as well as to explain the relation between the unconscious and conscious. Condensation, on the one hand, occurs metaphorically because it always depends on a negation, on an *as if*.[6] Aristotle's explanation of metaphor in *Poetics* is an often-used example for metaphor as condensation: "As old age is to life, so is evening to day," a four-term analogy, may be condensed to the two-term "old age as the 'evening' or 'sunset' of life" (2333). Freud presents the content and provides analysis of one of his own dreams, commonly titled "Irma's injection." He inspects the interior of Irma's mouth and observes that Irma "showed signs of recalcitrance, like women with artificial dentures" to which he thought "that there was really no need for her to do that" (Freud 131). In his analysis, he realizes that the word *recalcitrance*, first associated with an organic symptom associated with false teeth, is also associated with her attitude toward psychoanalytic treatment. Initially, she has a recalcitrance (possibly a stubborn stain, irritated skin or gums, an infection) *in* her mouth that he then, within almost the same breath, thinks of as a behavior (a reserved refusal or shying away). Freud thinks she is stubbornly resistant to his supposedly successful diagnosis and treatment, and he compares her to her friend whom he "perhaps" holds in higher regard because of her recalcitrance and ability to treat herself so far (134). On the one hand, through transference (which is the root meaning of the word metaphor, which means "to carry over") he condenses his irritation toward Irma's resistance to her treatment and his anxieties regarding medical culpability into Irma herself, who, as an image of recalcitrance, appears in the dream as if she were the word (134–35).

Displacement, on the other hand, is metonymic because it occurs syntactically and syntagmatically; just as the reader's attention moves from one word to the next when reading a sentence, so the dreamer's affect or libidinal energy is displaced from one idea or object or image to another in the dream-work. For example, as Freud furthers his analysis of "Irma's injection," he recalls that his wife opens a liqueur that has "the word 'Ananas'" on it, which he notes "bears a remarkable resemblance to that of my patient Irma's family name" (138). Within this same moment, Freud begins to link the chemical names together: the liqueur smelled of fusel oil, amyl, connected to propyl, part of the injection ingredients, which then led him to the trimethylamine associated with sexuality, specifically his association with one of his colleagues who made this medical claim alongside one of "the female organs of sex" (139). Here, we not only see displacement occurring within the dream, but also within Freud's analysis of it in that he not only dreams by way of the syntagmatic structure between one word that sparks a chain of words, but his analysis also progresses along the same lines, e.g., by way of a chain of free association. The "chain of free association" itself shows the convolution of metonymy and metaphor.

In "The Instance of the Letter in the Unconscious, or Reason Since Freud," Lacan builds upon Freud's dream-work, specifically on condensation and displacement, and inverts Saussure's diagram of the sign. He places metaphor and metonymy's functions in the signifier's "impact" on the signified in order to develop a topography of the unconscious. In terms of the basic semiotic diagram (now "signifier over signified," Sr/Sd), metonymy never crosses the bar of signification, but in order for metaphor to work, it has to cross the bar to an extent. However, this crossing is never complete and never satisfactory.[7] To demonstrate why, Lacan offers up the narrative mentioned in the previous chapter of the siblings riding the train and their opposing perspectives on the bathrooms at which they arrive.

The image of the bathrooms with the names placed appropriately above the identical doors, separated by a wall (a bar), as well as the children on the train, barred from the bathrooms by the railroad tracks, complicates (what is now) the simplicity of the Saussurean diagram. According to Lacan, then, "no signification can be sustained except by reference to another signification" (*Écrits* 415). The structure of the signifier is such that it can only signify through its relation to other signifiers. A signifier may "slip" into the position of the signified and be "replaced" in the signifying chain, but that patent signifier is always metonymically connected to the replaced signifier. Therefore, the bar can never really be crossed because the signifier only perpetuates other signifiers. Lacan does say that one crosses the bar in metaphor, but he is talking about metaphor, the trope of *as if*-ness. In light of the above discussion of the symptom and metaphor, we can understand that a signifier does not actually cross the bar; rather, in metaphor, it is *as if* one crosses the bar.

Recalling Lacan's definition of the subject as only a signifier to another signifier, we can transition to an understanding of why metaphor, the *as if* of

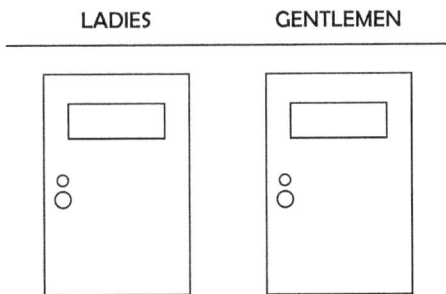

Figure 3.1 The bathrooms in "The Instance of the Letter in the Unconscious"

the signified dependent on negation, is the symptom of the anthropomorphic moment. The chains of metaphor and metonymy can be linked:

> Paradigmatic → substitution → metaphor → similarity → condensation
>
> Syntagmatic → combination → metonymy → contiguity → displacement[8]

Metaphor evokes an idea of identity as similarity – even though the evocation is really only a similarity that is metaphorized as identity – by condensing multiple terms or concepts into one. For example, a queer man who performs in the style of the effeminate diva, but also within the rules of queer culture, is commonly referred to as a queen; the Queen of the United Kingdom is required to perform according to the rules of royal pageantry. This metaphorically evoked "one," a highly problematic idea for Lacan and most contemporary thought, appears on the surface of the subject as symptom. As I tried to show at this chapter's outset, the symptom is the surface condensation of that which is repressed, or censored, to use Lacan's language. Lacan's formula for metaphor, $f(S'/S)S \cong S(+)s$, articulates that the signifying function, written as f S, occurs because of the substitution of one signifier for another (what Lacan refers to as one signifier's need of another signifier's slippage below the bar) in order to mean, (S'/S), which is structurally similar to, but also produces, $\cong$, the play of the signifier, S, and, +, the signified, s (429). In order to gain a fuller understanding of the metaphor function, it is useful to note the difference between geometry's use of $\cong$ as congruence and abstract algebra's use of $\cong$ as isomorphic. I think Lacan's intent is to signify isomorphism here. Congruence basically denotes equivalences of measurement. Isomorphism is a bit more complex in that it does not denote basic equivalence, but rather connotes structural relationships of identity even if differences are present. The S′ is the "signifieriness," the signifying effect that is explicit, overt, or "patent" in metaphor (441 fn 20). The substitution of a signifier for another (or others) is made on the surface and is apparent. "Metaphor's creative spark," Lacan elaborates, "does not spring forth from the juxtaposition of two images, that is, of two equally actualized signifiers. It flashes between two signifiers, one of which has replaced the other by taking the other's place in the signifying chain" (422). If two signifiers were "equally actualized," then a metaphoric substitution, or condensation, could not occur. There would be no slippage, no *as if*-ness of the one thing for the other, as in the girl who is a butterfingers. One (at least) of the signifiers must take a backseat for the other to evoke meaning. The "spark flies that fixes in a symptom" (431).

Metonymy, the articulation of desire

Because language is always already in operation before the subject's entrance into it, Lacan argues that language, not biology, determines one's sex. Biological genitals alone are not enough to determine sexual difference (416–20). The bathroom problem, discussed above, complicates the sign structure. The separation of the word from the thing designates (ultimate, primordial) separation in determining sexual difference. Language is not giving one an identity; it is giving one a directionality in that the person, to qualify as "a person," must go through one linguistically marked door or another. One starts on the path of signification toward death, and the Symbolic Law requires the subject to mean through sexual difference in that process. Language acquisition is anthropogenic in that it marks "the moment at which desire is humanized" (262). In the signifier's taking of its place along the signifying chain in metaphor, "the occulted signifier [remains] present by virtue of its [metonymic] connection to the rest of the chain" (422).[9] Metaphor cannot occur without metonymy; however, as I will argue and illustrate below, this does not mean that metonymy should be relegated to a place of mere function, a tool, for other tropes to arise and make more satisfactory meaning; such satisfactions would perforce be those of the ego in the Imaginary.

Desire functions along a signifying chain metonymically. Metonymy – different from metaphor in the way in which it means – approximates; it puts the subject in the proximity of that which s/he desires, and displaces/disrupts the subject from metaphoric identification. The subject, through the function of metonymy, becomes other to itself, an object to itself, as in a self-othering. Metonymy's matheme, $f(S'...S)S \cong S(-)s$, articulates the signifying function, f S, that occurs in metonymy by the chain of signifiers, $S'...S$, which is structurally equivalent to, $\cong$, the signifying chain, S, that does not cross the bar, $-$, but that nonetheless still attempts to "get at" a signified, s (428). The matheme of metonymy makes clear the impossibility of language to encompass ontologically or epistemologically a whole, full, or absolute Truth because the signifying chain cannot cross the bar and be equivalent to that which it functions to signify. Signification always presents a resistance toward the signified, hence the contiguity of displacement. In other words, metonymy's function is to approximate the signifieriness of the subject to another signifier, whether that signification is inter- or transsubjective. We can think of this contiguity of displacement in connection with the "censored chapter of one's history." Metaphor's signifieriness is "patent" and metonymy's is "latent" (441 fn 20). Lacan asks, "what does man find in [metonymy], if it must be more than the power to skirt the obstacles of social censure? Doesn't this form, which gives oppressed truth its field, manifest a certain servitude that is inherent in its presentation?" (423). He likens metaphor to "the signifier *esprit*" and metonymy to the letter (423), and he reminds us of the adage "the letter kills while the spirit gives life," in order to argue that the spirit cannot live without the letter (423). Displacement, or the "display" of metonymy, as we see in "Irma's injection," is "the unconscious' best means by which to foil censorship" (425). Metaphor, then, functions to cover over, and metonymy functions to convey, even bring forth, the truths of desire. The letter, again associated with metonymy, is the letter of discourse (424) – and I will return to this claim shortly in the following chapter – which is why, in this project, I turn to the hysteric's discourse, the discourse that interrogates the master's, connecting that discourse with metonymy to "skirt the obstacles of social censure" and begin to read the field of "oppressed truth."

The issue at stake here is the continued maintenance of the desire for "identity" through the demand of sexual difference, which I equate here to the demand for (and of) subjectivity. The way our society has sustained the dominance of metaphor, has held it in the privileged position of meaning and creativity, speaks to the persistence of (what I consider archaic) modern intellectual paradigms, namely the Enlightenment and Cartesian *cogito*. I do not think this dominant focus on metaphor is actually what Lacan intends for psychoanalytic practice and theory, except for a pointing up of metaphor for the purposes of criticizing these (archaic) paradigms. Indeed, Lacan spends much more time discussing metaphor in "The Instance of the Letter in the Unconscious" than metonymy, but he does so in order to show topographically metaphor's dominant role within Descartes' problematic *cogito*. After all, Lacan declares at the outset of "The Mirror Stage as Formative of the *I* Function" that "this experience [of the *I* function] sets us [analysts] at odds with any philosophy directly stemming from the *cogito*" (*Écrits* 75). *Cogito ergo sum*, "I think therefore I am," is a statement that claims absolute subjectivity through the firm grasp of oneself as a cognitive object. The *cogito* relies on a circular argument that assumes being, even though it does not deliver it. The fundamental difference, the incompatibility, between being (*ontos*) and meaning (*logos*) – *l'être* and *la lettre* – is that one cannot be without meaning, or, rather, that one cannot be because of meaning. Metonymy is crucial in this difference because it "allows for the elision by which the signifier instates lack of being [*le manqué de l'être*] in the object-relation" (428).[10]

We can think of this lack *of* being as the lack *in* meaning, a persistent and insistent failure to mean fully by means of subjective identifications. Descartes' *cogito* provides the illusion that one can mean fully. Psychoanalysis, though, systematically provides evidence that meaning can never be full (of itself). Meaning means lack, emptiness, in that to mean is to empty the word, the self, of "real" content.[11] In working through the metaphoric and metonymic topography of the unconscious, Lacan refers to Freud's *Wo Es war, soll Ich werden*, "Where it was, I must come into being," in order to revise and complicate Descartes' *cogito* (435).[12] In Lacan's revision, or demolition, we have to continue to position more and more *I am*s into the question of being when talking about signification and the unconscious: "What we must say," Lacan insists, "is: *I am* not, where *I am* the plaything of my thought; I think about what *I am* where I do not think *I am* thinking" (430, emphasis added). In this insistence, Lacan revokes the ability of either of these tropes to deliver Cartesianism's desired Truth of self-certainty and self-identity. Instead, he shows how both tropes lack in truthfulness as past philosophy has defined Truth; they both fail to mean in any way other than as signifying functions that do different things, neither inherently better than the other. To think that a signifier can cross the bar to the *space* of the signified – and here we must recall that a subject is only a signifier to another signifier – is to misunderstand the relationship between the subject and language: "the S and *s* of the Saussurian algorithm are not in the same plane, and man was deluding himself in believing he was situated in their common axis, which is nowhere" (430–431).

Lacan's quip (*a la* Rimbaud) in "Aggressiveness in Psychoanalysis," "I is an other" (96), works to articulate the relationship between different planes. "'I'm a man,'" Lacan explains, "at most can mean no more than, 'I'm like the person who, in recognizing him to be a man, I constitute as someone who can recognize me as a man'" (96). Here we have another way to articulate that the subject is only a signifier for another signifier, which is a transsubjective and intersubjective metonymic relationship in that the Symbolic is always lingering within this relationship as a third term, and, as we fail, or never stop failing, to metaphorize our identity, we must proceed with our failure via metonymy's linkages. In light of the insistence that makes the subject ex-centric – that ensures "the self's radical eccentricity with respect to itself" (435) – identification originates from and is sustained by self-alienation. The act of meaning – of speaking, of identifying – is a fundamental dehiscence from being because one has to occupy one's "place" in the signifying chain that constantly unfolds but never *arrives*. If one says *I*, then one is splitting itself; if one thinks *I*, then one is thinking of either/or that one is not in that one must negate one *I* in temporal favor of another *I*: "I am not where I am the plaything of my thought; I think about what I am where I do not think I am thinking" (430).

Because language is always prior to the subject, it determines sexual difference. The doctor has a linguistic concept of what makes this or that little thing a boy or girl and ascribes said marker accordingly. The logic of sexuation, though, does not necessitate the ascribed sexual difference to match the masculine or feminine position. Sexuation does not require a more active role, defined by and inherent in the demand of castration, from the subject as it navigates the obstacle course of discursive positionality. Rather than an identity, the subject gets only directionality, which manifests on the signifying chain of desire (*a la* Nietzsche). To complicate the directionality even more, the siblings on the train are not only barred by the tracks and the symbols on the bathroom doors: a bar also sits between them that cannot be crossed. Referring to Kaja Silverman's linking the enunciated and enunciating *I* as that which Lacan distinguishes as the difference between "being" and "meaning," (45–47) I look to the syntagm *I am a man*.[13] To *proclaim* oneself as a man or a woman or trans or gender-variant is to *displace* one's being into meaning and to position oneself discursively. A subject can never fully or finally *be* a man, or woman, or trans being; a subject can only (fail to) mean discursively as such, i.e., attempt to represent or disrupt the characteristics expected socio-culturally of these signifiers. And, most importantly, these signifiers' meanings do not have stable, absolute definitive characteristics as is exemplified by the increasing public expressions of gender-variance, as well as the examples in Padawer's article and the efforts of Storm's and Pop's parents who resist genderizing their child.

The ways in which the subject occupies a position within discourse connect directly with the subject's desire and its attainment of jouissance. The hysteric, for example, speaks from the place of demand and attains enjoyment from the master's desire for her as object. In "The Subversion of the Subject and the Dialectic of Desire," Lacan explains that discourse is what allows for the inverse attainment of phallic jouissance through submission to castration and the Symbolic Law of desire.[14] As subjects, we imagine retrospectively that the undifferentiated, precastrated little being is in a state of pure jouissance, and the little *infans* must refuse this jouissance, undergo castration, for subjectivization, first through the Imaginary "negativized" (696) representation of the phallus in the specular image and the prohibition that ensues, and then through fantasy structures ($\$<>a$) that positivize the signifier through desire, "which is a defense [...] against going beyond the limit in jouissance" (699).[15] In this sense, jouissance is phallic: all subjects submit to this inverted trajectory toward jouissance through castration and submission to the Law of the Father, which unites desire and Law (698): "*I* am in the place from which 'the universe is a flaw in the purity of Non-Being' is vociferated. And not without reason for, by protecting itself, this place makes Being itself languish. This place is called Jouissance, and it is Jouissance whose absence would render the universe vain" (694).

The gaze and the L schema

Lacan formulates the gaze as the observational knowledge between the subject and the object, the object being *objet a* both/and the Other: "the eye which looks is that of the subject, while the gaze is on the side of the object, and there is no coincidence between the two, since 'You never look at me from the place at which I see you' (SXI 103)" (Evans 72).[16] Lacan's phrasing of the subject and object gaze dynamic echoes the rewriting of the *cogito* discussed above. (Not) thinking and (not) seeing where the subject is/may be are key components of understanding Lacan's poststructural contributions.[17] Not only is the subject decentered in this formulation – the subject does not have control over, or even awareness of, the perspective of the gaze – but the object is also not the central perspective because it also desires, and it desires from a non-centralized place. The topography implied within these statements of (not) thinking and (not) seeing is more like a flat expanse than a layering of depth (as in the popular idea of the unconscious as located in the mind's depths).

In "The Orthopsychic Subject," Copjec appropriates psychoanalytically Gaston Bachelard's term "orthopsychism" so that "in Lacan 'orthopsychism' [...] grounds the subject. The desire that it precipitates *transfixes* the subject, albeit in a conflictual space, so that all the subject's visions and revisions, all its fantasies, merely circumnavigate the absence that anchors the subject and impedes its progress" (38, emphasis in original).[18] As Žižek explains in "The Seven Veils of Fantasy," the subject's inscription in the fantasmatic narrative is difficult to pin down: the subject's appearance does not always correspond with or recognize its identification; rather, the subject identifies with how the desire of the gaze depicts the subject so that the Other desires it (193).[19] The gaze, then, is not something through which a subject views external symbolic representations. The gaze comes from *that other part* of the split subject and maps onto how the subject's ego desires. The Other, whose desire the subject desires, is the Symbolic's ideological content. Žižek explains that the subject's (mis)recognition of him/herself within this content is the way in which the letter arrives at its destination:

> when I recognize myself as the addressee of the call of the ideological big Other (Nation, Democracy, Party, God, and so forth), when this call "arrives at its destination" in me, I automatically misrecognize that it is this very act of recognition which *makes* me what I have recognized myself as – I don't recognize myself in it because I'm its addressee, I become its addressee the moment I recognize myself in it. *This* is the reason why a letter always reaches its addressee: because one becomes its addressee when one is reached.
>
> (*Enjoy!* 14, emphasis in original)

Understanding the gaze in this way – that is, as something with which we choose to please the Other, which the subject experiences as something external to itself – allows for a theorization of how the split subject's identifications occur through an intersubjective relationship to the Other that is largely dependent upon already narrativized, discursive scripts, such as gendered norms of sexual difference. If we can follow Lacan's claim that the social link is discourse and there are only subjects (i.e., not individuals) in this context, then the gaze from which subjects operate and make choices of their social insertion depends upon how the subject, through the Other, internalizes the external power(s) of language. The internalization of the power of language, as we see in the continual insistence of the letter and the subject's servitude to it, provides the material for the social link, and social scripts are the way in which that materiality manifests Symbolically. The Other is the space of the contentless Symbolic where we locate language, the reservoir of signifiers, as well as a way to make the radically impersonal appear coherent by making a kind of anthropomorphism of the Symbolic.

In order to better describe the gaze and begin to relate it to a topography of flat-ness in an effort to rethink the idea of the object, I turn now to the L schema. The L schema, included in the "post face" of "Seminar on 'The Purloined Letter'," is the first in a series of schemata Lacan develops that maps the way in which the "discourse of the Other reaches the subject in an interrupted and inverted form" (Evans 169). The interruption and inversion occur because the Imaginary relation always blocks the Symbolic relation between the Other and the subject. Let us look at the L schema:

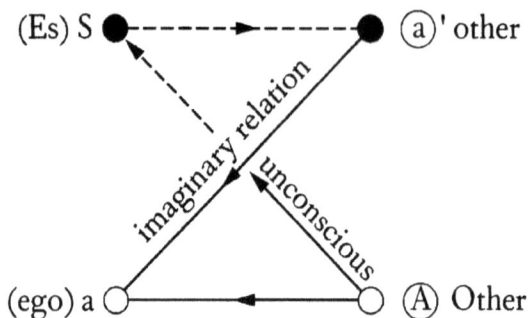

Figure 3.2 L schema

The S in the top-left corner represents the Subject of the unconscious, the other *I* in the *I* articulation discussed above, not the "self." (Es) is a translinguistic pun: in German, Freud uses "*das es*" to mean "the it." The Strachey translation of Freud's writings transforms this into the *Id*, the term most familiar today in the Anglophone world. Therefore, (Es)S is a rough equivalent of the inter-subjective relationship between the other of the split Subject's, S, and the Id's, (Es), interrelation. The ego(a) in the bottom-left corner represents the conscious subject and the little other, the relationship between the conscious subject and the object of desire, *objet a*. The (ego)a cross-connected to the (a´) other is an imaginary relation, keeping in mind the imagistic orientation of the Imaginary, and designates the relation between the subject and its own specular image, which blocks and distorts the relation between the unconscious and the Other (A), of the Symbolic order and the other Subject (Es)S. The Subject (S) addresses the Other, but it thinks it is addressing the other; the subject (ego) thinks it *is* because it sees its image in the other (a´). The imaginary wall of language, represented by the solid diagonal line, inverts, as a mirror does, the message and its representation.[20]

Lacan's discussion of the gaze in Seminar XI: *The Four Fundamental Concepts of Psychoanalysis* helps to illustrate and contextualize the L schema and its connection to the gaze. He makes a distinction between seeing and showing in waking and dream states and focuses on the dream state in order to best describe the gaze:

> our position in the dream is profoundly that of someone who does not see. The subject does not see where it is leading, he follows. He may even on occasion detach himself, tell himself that it is a dream, but in no case will he be able to apprehend himself in the dream in the way in which, in the Cartesian *cogito*, he apprehends himself as thought.
>
> (SXI 75)

The subject leads and follows simultaneously here, but, in leading, the subject is "it" and, in following, the subject is "he." For example, David Lynch, in *Inland*

Empire (2006), saturates the scenes and plot with the subject who does not see. Laura Dern plays multiple characters in the film, all of whom are interrelated, if not the same person at different stages of waking and dreaming. In one of the earliest moments of the Dern character split, she has shifted from actor-Susie to character-Susie by following an ancient riddle recited in the film's second scene. Actor-Susie finds herself in an alleyway, enters a door, and is then thrust into character-Susie, who is presumably performing a sex scene but may actually be engaged in sex outside of the film within the film's script, when she becomes confused and conflates herself with character-Susie and cannot "apprehend" herself. She sees herself (not) seeing herself (and the Other's gaze is also present in the form of her husband in the doorway). She is incapable of deciphering this gaze. She gets caught up in the identificatory desiring chain provoked by this gaze, as the majority of the film consists of a variety of Susies playing out similar scenarios, but *always with a remainder*. The subject's ego and conscious "part" play only a partial role in the subject's function, and that part is always interrupted and inverted by its very servitude both to discourse and that from which discourse borrows, the letter. Each of Dern's characters do not, cannot, know they *are* as the *cogito* would have them think they can constitute themselves. In their very thinking, these characters become more confused, more displaced, but at the same time more aware of their confusion and displacement. The Imaginary relation that provides the barrier between the subject and the Other begins to perforate for Dern's characters, and they are no longer protected from the anxiety for which the Imaginary provides a cushion.

In understanding the dynamic relations of the L schema, I suggest we shift our thinking from that of multi-dimensionality (i.e., the depths of the mind) and consider these relations along a flat plane, similar to the way in which we can consider metonymical tropes as always functioning along the same axis, *above* the bar. The way in which I imagine the tropes along the same axis above the bar is as a pulsation of spreading and condensing meaning rather than pushing meaning into a depth below or pulling it closer to the subject. The topographic reorientation provides a more cohesive correlate to the vectors of discourse that make or direct meaning within the transitivity of the subject's discursive reality. As well, I would like to point out the similarity between the L schema and the discourse formulae, except that the L schema focuses specifically on analytic discourse and that which occurs within the subject. The L schema resembles the basic structure of the discourse formulae in terms of the complicated interrelation between the four points of each diagram. In terms of the agent/truth, Other/production structure of the discourse formulae's four positions, I think that reading the L schema with these points and adding the dimension of the gaze to the trajectories that the L schema maps could make sense for furthering the conceptions of subject and object relations.[21]

The internalization of the gaze influenced by the external linguistic structure in the Symbolic appears in the L schema as that which both enjoys and regulates enjoyment on the surface of the post mirror stage physico-discursive body. Both the compulsion to speak and the ways in which the significations of speech so often exceed the intentions of the ego are an effect of the Other

upon the *I*. Desire, or the object cause of it, a′, also works upon the ego subject, and Lacan makes close equivalence between the gaze and *objet a*: "In so
far as the gaze, *qua objet a*, may come to symbolize this central lack expressed
in the phenomenon of castration, and in so far as it is an *objet a* reduced, of its
nature, to a punctiform, evanescent function, it leaves the subject in ignorance
as to what there is beyond the appearance" (SXI 77). In "The Mirror Stage
and Formative of the *I* Function" and "Aggressiveness in Psychoanalysis" Lacan
clarifies what he introduces in the "post face" and, again, in the claim "I is
an Other." In the fundamental split between the ego and the Subject, the *I* is
an object in that it is other than itself. The Subject is necessary for action to
occur, just like it is necessary to the grammatical construction of a sentence.
When Nietzsche laments – as I pointed out earlier in the context of Lacan's
exasperation at having to repeat until he is "blue in the face" that discourse is
the social link – "I am afraid we have not got rid of God because we still believe
in grammar" (170) we can hear him talking about our linguistic and, therefore,
identificatory emphasis on this (part of the) subject, this ego, that appears to
stand at the forefront of our thought.

The linguistic subject is determinative of the action, yet the subject as identity has been lost along the signifying chain. Moreover, and I will return to this
later, Lacan argues that there is a "routine of the signified" as always having the
same meaning no matter what signifiers are used because subjects, dominated
by the ego consciousness, always signify a center, but that center is contingent.
For example, for the collective human psyche, the sun once revolved around the
earth and now the earth revolves around the sun, but the sun is not the center
of the universe anymore, as well as the idea that the spheres do not necessarily
"turn" *a la* Copernicus so much as they "fall" *a la* Kepler. Lacan's point here is
that no matter how we define, formulate, and understand objects and concepts,
the signified takes on a center for our stability (SXX 42–43). The (ego)a subject negates or rejects a part of itself because it has entered the Symbolic order,
but, perhaps more significantly, the negation is a product of the Symbolic order
structured in such a way as to demand the persistence of the negation that
culminates in the regulation of the body's enjoyment via discourse positionality.

Yet, what is at stake in the grammar of the linguistic subject is still more
dire than what I present above. In "Love and the Signifier," Lacan explores
this connection between language, grammar, the letter, writing, and the non-
existent sexual relationship. He explains that the "letter reveals in discourse [...]
grammar," which "is that aspect of language that is revealed only in writing"
(SXX 44). Prior to this moment, Lacan is discussing speech, specifically his
speech at that moment as well as the importance of speech in analytic discourse. One of the differences, for Lacan, between speech and the grammar
that only writing reveals is that speech, when produced as the analytic discourse,
takes "the function of the signifier" as its "starting point" – not its center –
and the "meaning effect[s]" of the function of the signifier are unpredictable
(43). The difficulty is in understanding what Lacan designates as writing: writing
produces an effect "beyond language" (44), which happens no matter what, but
the "beyond" also has a polar opposite of "shy of" (44). Language, he says, both

"imposes being upon us" and forces us to "admit that we never have anything by way of being" (44), and that we instead get a "para-being" that is beside, alongside being, or shy of being. The relation between language and this para-being is where "we must articulate what makes up for the sexual relationship *qua* nonexistent. It is clear that, in everything that approaches it, language merely manifests [itself in] its inadequacy" (45).

The quotient that comes of this relation between language and para-being is love, which makes up for this inadequacy, but is also that which we cannot speak, that which is beyond language. "The Other," Lacan explains, "is the only place, albeit an irreducible place, that we can give to the term 'divine being'" (45). However, the significant point to understand is that we produce this God in and of language: Lacan, in what seems a direct and conscious allusion to Nietzsche, proclaims, "As long as things are said, the God hypothesis will persist" (45). Here, we notice an interesting and difficult conflation between "writing" at the beginning of this exposition and things being "said" at the end. The Other – that which becomes the subject's desire, the locus of both lack (*objet a*) and speech; i.e., we speak because we desire (love) – is that with which the subject can never become one. Love is beyond language and attempts to get at a subject unconnected with, or shy of, jouissance. Love and desire are not the same. Like love, desire is not linguistic but, unlike love, desire is in language. Tim Dean explains "that although desire is 'in' language, *desire is not itself linguistic*" (*Beyond* 178, emphasis in original). I understand this similar to the way in which I outline above Lacan's function of the signifier and its meaning effects. Of course, the signifier and its meaning effects are both linguistic; however, desire is a meaning effect of the drive, which is not linguistic but in language, and, moreover, desire has its own meaning effects. Indeed, the sentence, for example, functions as a trajectory of desire, or, simply put, desirously, in that we desire to get to the end of the sentence, for the sentence to be over so that we can grasp its meaning. Yet, the desire itself is not made up of or defined by the words that make up that sentence – nor is it, say, the elements of discourse – but we only know the meaning effects of that desire in language.

Notes

1 The body and parts of the body as metaphor have a history in contemporary theory. For example, later I will address Luce Irigaray's "two lips" and the contentious critical reception of her concept in terms of metaphor and metonymy. Additionally, Tim Dean, in *Beyond Sexuality*, emphasizes this moment in Lacan's essay within a similar context to my own. Dean says, "By emphasizing that the censored chapter of my history 'has already been written down elsewhere,' Lacan reinterprets that 'other scene' […] in terms not of more or less private mental space, but of public discourse, the symbolic domain of language and culture, which is necessarily transindividual yet also historical" (7).

2 As I discussed in Chapter 2, the subject speaking in the master's discourse takes up the "identity" of S_1, the master signifier, which takes the form of the desiring subject to master-ize a lie, or, at the very least, to veil unknowingly the truth of the split/barred subject.

3 I flesh out the materiality of the letter in the section below with that title, but I use this opportunity here to foreground that section and the connections I make throughout this chapter.

4 Indeed, a signifier is a signifier because it is different from a signified; however, the signifier *in itself* cannot be divided from itself. This indivisibility from itself is the Real materiality of the signifier. The signifier obtains meaning(s) once subjects differentiate it from other signifiers, but the signifier *in itself* can glom onto the subject, define the subject, manipulate the subject without the subject's control or awareness of it. If we can follow Pluth's differentiation of sexual difference and sexuality *as such* discussed in Chapter 2, then we can perhaps begin to understand the ways in which sexual difference means as a signifier *in itself* apart from a signified and prior to Symbolic establishment.

5 Lacan says, "language is not immaterial. It is a subtle body, but body it is. Words are caught up in all the body images that captivate the subject; they may 'knock up' the hysteric, be identified with the object of *Penisneid*, represent the urinary flow of urethral ambition, or represent the faeces retained in avaricious jouissance" (*Écrits* 248).

6 Freud does not use the terms metaphor and metonymy. I am using them here in order to explain his concepts of condensation and displacement, as well as to situate the terms within the larger study of metaphor and metonymy. I pull from "Irma's injection" in order to illustrate the way in which condensation and displacement function within the dream and within the interpretation of a dream.

7 The bar, for Lacan, is the bar of prohibition, specifically (in following Freud's Oedipal complex) the prohibition of incest with the mother, and metaphor is a way of doing what one cannot do, that is, crossing the bar of prohibition against incest and merging with the "mother."

8 Dean adds "figure" to the end of the metaphor trajectory and "syntax" to the end of the metonymy trajectory.

9 Earlier, in "The Function and Field of Speech and Language in Psychoanalysis," at this moment in the text I am quoting here, Lacan *repeats* the same language, the same terms, without naming metaphor, that he uses to talk about metaphor. In the middle of a discussion on the death drive and the *Fort! Da!* game, he explains that "These are the occultation games which Freud, in a flash of genius, presented to us so that we might see in them that the moment at which desire is humanized is also that at which the child is born into language" (262). (Arguably, I would say that it is the moment we are born into death.) Lacan is saying here that Freud, through metaphor, realizes metaphor's function in our humanity.

10 This statement has no relation to object-relations theory. Object-relations theory, although partly influenced by psychoanalysis, leans more toward developmental psychology and the over emphasis of mapping one's relations with the mother and father to one's psychological ticks in adulthood, particularly how he gets along with other people. Lacan's use of the term object-relation here refers to the production of desire and its manifestation along the signifying chain.

11 Here we can recall Saussure's concept of negation and differential relations between words within the linguistic system.

12 Freud presents this sentence in his 1933 *The New Introductory Lectures on Psycho-Analysis*.

13 I discuss this enunciation in more detail later.

14 Lacan does not use the term "discourse" in the essay. I am inserting it as a retroversive understanding given his later ideas in Seminars XVII and XX.

15 Lacan says that the move from the Imaginary to the Symbolic is a move from negative to positive, respectively, "even if it fills in a lack" because it is "the signifier of jouissance" (697). Also, significantly, he explains the retroversive interpretation of the movement from *infans* to subject:

> When we say 'primary' and 'secondary' for the processes, that may well be a manner of speaking that fosters an illusion. Let's say, in any case, that it is not because a process is said to be primary – we can call them whatever we want, after all – that is the first to appear. Personally, I have never looked at a baby and had the sense that there was no outside world for him. It is plain to see that a baby looks at nothing but that, that it excites him, and that that is the case precisely to the extent that he does not yet speak. From the moment he begins to speak, from that exact moment onward and not before, I can understand that there is [such a thing] as repression. The process of the Lust-Ich may be primary – why not? It's obviously primary once we begin to think – but it's not the first.
>
> (SXX 56)

16 Lacan's concept of the gaze is different from Sartre's reciprocal gaze, which is conflated with the act of looking.

17 Elizabeth Wright points out that not only is Lacan's gaze different from Sartre's, but it also has been misunderstood by earlier feminist film criticism due to a widespread misreading of Laura Mulvey's 1975 infamous essay "Visual Pleasure and Narrative Cinema," as well as due to an incorrect conflation of it with Foucault's panoptic gaze, which, like Sartre's gaze, is a gaze between subjects, even if one side of the gaze is the other as a system such as patriarchy (Wright 46–47).

18 The absence Copjec refers to here is the gaze. For Bachelard, orthopscyhism, "in providing an opportunity for the correction of thought's imperfections – allows the subject to wander from its moorings, constantly to drift from one position to another" (Copjec 38). Cf. Gaston Bachelard, *The New Scientific Spirit*. Beacon Press, 1984.

19 Žižek refers to Seminar XI, here, where Lacan explains that

> the identification in question is not specular, immediate identification. It is its support. It supports the perspective chosen by the subject in the field of the Other, from which specular identification may be seen in a satisfactory light. The point of the ego ideal is that from which the subject will see himself, as the one says, as others see him – which will enable him to support himself in a dual situation that is satisfactory for him from the point of view of love.
>
> (SXI 268)

20 If the logic of the L schema makes sense, which I think it does, then we can better understand how Descartes' *cogito* is further illusory in terms of its promise of fullness and being.

21 I will return to this point and develop it later.

4 The materiality of the letter

Isn't that precisely what psychoanalytic experience presupposes? — the substance of the body, on the condition that it is defined only as that which enjoys itself (se jouit).

Lacan, SXX, 23

I tried to argue in the last chapter that the gaze, as a materiality of the Imaginary relation between the Other and the subject, provokes manifestations of affect. In order to better explain how the body is a function of discourse and the consequences that function has on the subject in the social field, I look at the way guilt, as affect, is a masculine logic within patriarchal narratives. I consider the letter and symbolization as bodily, in the psychoanalytic sense, which ultimately brings me to questions of Woman and the feminine. I then look at shame, again as affect, as a feminine position within the masculine logic of those narratives and try to illustrate how Woman is a problem (or problematic) therein. At the chapter's end, I turn to Lacan's 1956 "Seminar on 'The Purloined Letter,'" where he maps in Poe's narrative the connection between the signifier, the subject, the Symbolic, the feminine, and, ultimately, the Real. He plays both on the title of Poe's story and the structure of the narrative by way of the events therein to illustrate what he means by *la lettre*, particularly in terms of how the analyst finds the letter literally in the gaps of the analysand's speech. Rather than the patency of the symptom in the nodal point, though, the letter is the materiality of the Real, the latent truth that what is lacking is nothing, at least in Symbolic terms.

The materiality of the letter

The letter, Lacan declares, is "that material medium [*support*] that concrete discourse borrows from language," which is not the same as the ways in which the subject's functions "serve" the letter (*Écrits* 413). As I introduced the letter earlier, Lacan defines it as the insistent and indivisible property of the signifier, and this property that is also meaningless, i.e., not Symbolic, is the materiality of the signifier in the Real. Put differently, the letter exists (within the Real), but it does not mean as a signifier. Rather, the letter's materiality wanders around, always permeates, but only means as a signifier once it is differentiated as a signifier to another signifier, once it has glommed onto a subject, for example.

Both Freud and Lacan use the Egyptian hieroglyphs to exemplify what Lacan coins as the letter: prior to the discovery of the Rosetta Stone, the inscriptions, the writing, meant nothing except that we assumed that they meant something as a signifying system (Evans 100; Lacan *Écrits* 243, 424). The letter, like Derrida's arche-writing, is the presence of inscription, a materiality, prior to meaning, which, once in the Symbolic, always ends up meaning something. In SIII: *The Psychoses*, Lacan touches on the letter through a discussion on the signifier and meaning in regards to neologisms as "meaning *as such*" and empty meaning. The neologism has "a meaning that essentially refers to nothing but itself, that remains irreducible," and empty meaning occupies the "opposite pole" as "the form that meaning takes when it no longer refers to anything at all. This is the formula that is repeated, reiterated" (SIII 33). Regardless, the letter always insists in "inscribing itself into the subject's life" (Evans 100). The indecipherable hieroglyphs, for example, meant at the very least the presence of writing, the desire for meaning; they served as a metaphor for the letter's inscription. Lacan sees the metaphoric function as the way in which "man defies his very destiny" (*Écrits* 423), but "*a letter always arrives at its destination*" (30, emphasis added).[1] The subject can veil the Real "until s/he is blue in the face," but s/he will have to do it as the servant of the letter. The defying of destiny that the metaphoric function enables does not necessarily mean that "man" is successful in the endeavor.

In Poe's "The Purloined Letter," Lacan reads the repetition of the psychoanalytic letter's insistence in the story's letter that passes from one person to another "as a metaphor for the signifier which circulates between various subjects, assigning a peculiar [discursive] position to whoever is possessed by it" (Evans 100).[2] Lacan's purpose for the Seminar is "to illustrate […] a truth," which is "the major determination the subject receives from the *itinerary* of the signifier" (7, emphasis added). He introduces as his purpose, then, the trajectory of the signifier that determines the directionality of the subject; that is, a subject as a signifier in the signifying chain and in discourse. And the letter, the signifier without meaning that comes to mean by its itinerary and inscription on the body – *the physico-discursive transindividual reality of the subject* – materializes as sexual difference upon each subject who comes in contact with it, particularly as placing them within the logic of sexuation, for a time, in the "feminine" space.

The letter in Poe's story, which Lacan uses as a narrative representation of any letter, changes hands throughout the story, and each time the possessor of the letter, as Lacan reads the details, becomes "feminized" discursively. In *Enjoy Your Symptom!*'s "Why Does the Letter Always Arrive at Its Destination?" Žižek explains that "In the network of [transsubjective] relations, every one of us is identified with, pinned down to, a certain fantasy place in the other's symbolic structure" (6).[3] The other may take on the "fantasy figure of a Woman" or the "real father," (7) and the characters in Poe's short story take on the fantasy of

Woman intersubjectively so as to occupy the feminine place transsubjectively in the master's discourse. In understanding how the letter in Poe's story situates and then repeats the transindividual reality of the subjects involved in its possession, the search for it, and the desire to have it, we can begin to understand a topography of sexual difference and sexuation, the affect and logic of discourse and the body. Lacan claims that "There is only one affect" (SXVII 150), and it is in analytic discourse – the place from where Lacan reads "The Purloined Letter" – that one "determines [the speaking being's] status as object" (151). Before I add to Lacan's reading of "The Purloined Letter," though, I want to turn our attention to affect and its potentially sexuated manifestations in discourse. I hope this detour will help substantiate the way in which I outline the determination of the speaking being's status as object in the "feminine" discursive position brought to light in Poe's story and Lacan's reading of it.

Affect: shame and guilt

In this and the following section, I try to work out and develop the distinctions I want to make between shame and guilt as feminine and masculine safeguards against differing experiences of jouissance. Earlier I defined extimacy, particularly in the hysteric's case, as the grounding of the alterity of the Other (Miller 79). In making a connection between Lacan's concept of *extimité* and his claim that man's desire is the Other's desire – that is, man desires what he perceives to be the Other's jouissance, or, at the very least, the way in which the Other desires that provides a pathway to another jouissance – I begin to understand that non-phallic jouissance is the jouissance of the Other. The subject as ego (as discussed earlier with the L schema and the gaze), in its extimacy, understands the Other as outside itself, even though it is not. The subject internalizes the Symbolic in her coming into meaning; the Other, as the Symbolic writ large, is the psychic manifestation of the subject's internalization of the Symbolic: the Symbolic may seem as if it is "out there" when it is both external and internal. By way of this (mis)understanding, or (mis)recognition, of the Other as outside rather than as one's own alterity, the manifestations of anxiety as affects – e.g., shame and guilt – can be understood as socially implicated. The distinction is productive, I think, in that it can add to our already established understandings of the sexuation graph's representation of differing ways to negotiate jouissance by building upon the subject's experience of anxiety within the self and with others due to social scripts. As well, understanding the affective manifestations on one side or other of what we at present understand as jouissance delineated according to sexual difference can provide us with a way to reconsider the categories of sexual difference through the subject's discursive position according to the relation or tension between affect and jouissance rather than as feminine and masculine.

The affect resulting from a persistent demand on the part of the Symbolic upon the subject to engage a part of the self is the inscription of sexual difference, a physico-discursive materiality that fails because it always arrives at its destination – that is, that the signifier always becomes a stabilizing center from which the subject will identify and/or ground itself. Lacan discusses affect – which is always an anxiety in that all affects such as love, shame, guilt are manifestations of anxiety – through shame as that which provides the subject with an ethical relationship to being, what Lacan terms *hontology* (XVII 180). (Lacan merges the French *honte*, shame, with ontology here.) Shame is "that which protects us from [anxiety's] borderless enigma" and plays on the surface with the always veiled "true jouissance" (Copjec "May '68" 111). If I understand Copjec's explanation correctly here, she is saying that anxiety is that which can potentially destabilize the subject, as that which lacks a solid place in the Symbolic, as that which can propel the subject toward a (sometimes dangerous) encounter with the Real. Guilt, as Copjec distinguishes it from shame, is a manifestation of affect that "treats every surface as an exterior to be penetrated, a barrier to be transgressed, a veil to be removed" (111). This penetrative characteristic of guilt (which ironically Copjec sees active in the university discourse) always fails in its desire because once it has successfully penetrated the surface "the Real has fled behind another barrier" (111). Nevertheless, anxiety, as we learn from Freud's pleasure principle, is also that which stabilizes the subject by its always fluctuating within the Symbolic-Imaginary relation. Different from guilt, shame

> does not seek to penetrate surfaces or tear away veils; it seeks comfort in them, hides itself in them [...] Our relationships to the surface change in shame, as compared to guilt; we become fascinated with its maze-like intricacies, its richness and profundity.
> [...] Shame is not a failed flight from being, but *a flight into being* – the being of surfaces, of social existence [...] Unlike the flight or transformation of guilt, however, shame does not sacrifice jouissance's opacity, which is finally what 'keeps it real.' [...] this opacity now gives us that distance from ourselves and our world that allows us creatively to alter both; it gives us, in other words, a privacy, an interiority unbreachable even by ourselves.
>
> (111)

Guilt as a manifestation of affect/anxiety seems aggressive, violent. As well, guilt's penetrative and colonial mode of operation is characteristic of the masculine traditionally defined in patriarchal narratives. Shame, though, functions at a planar, rather than a depth, level. Rather than approaching anxiety as something to hierarchize or demolish, shame allows the subject to spread and turn, to approach the self and the world as a möbius with variant possibilities of interpretation.

The way in which the subject approaches and copes with experiences of anxiety determines an ethics of affect and transsubjectivity. The "true jouissance" that Copjec claims is "always veiled" is that encounter with the Real, that mystic encounter that removes the subject from the social link. In light of the above discussion on jouissance, desire, and the Other, this mystic encounter could also be a realization of the Other's desire. The difference between what Copjec calls "true jouissance" and some other jouissance is the way the subject enjoys: the "sham" jouissance is one affected by guilt, a guilty enjoyment, that coincides with phallic jouissance. Shame, as opposed to guilt, consumes the subject's conscious experience and forces the subject into a reflective/reflexive abjectness. Shame, similar to abjection, is a manifestation of anxiety about excess jouissance and the fear of either not resituating oneself back into the phallic or solitude in one's excess. With guilt, the subject does not feel excluded from the dominant order and their identification with it; rather, the subject's position is complicit and identification with that order is reiterated, even affirmed. There is some correlation between the subject's Imaginary from which he enjoys, and Symbolic Law. With shame, though, the subject feels a threat of not being anchored within the Symbolic, both in terms of external exclusion and internal identification, but shame guards the subject from crossing that boundary into the Real. As such, shame is that which society marks as anxiety's furthest margin in that the subject is denied a correlation between her Imaginary and the Law, while guilt is that which marks successful subjectivization.

The distinguishing features of guilt and shame provide another pathway into examining the masculine and feminine positions, respectively. I think that the L schema does not represent the feminine discursive position within the transsubjective relation; rather, the schema represents only the masculine discursive position prior to any possible experience in the hysteric position. Applying this differentiation between shame and guilt to Lacanian sexuation, we see that a subject in the masculine position, always wholly subject to the Law, experiences guilt instead of shame in that his identification as masculine subject is always at play transsubjectively only within the boundaries of the Symbolic. He is always blocked by the Imaginary wall of language represented by a solid bar on the L schema.[4] A subject in the feminine position, not wholly subjected to the Law, can experience shame, which we can visualize as a perforated, rather than solid, Imaginary wall of language. In the forthcoming discussion of Lacan's reading of Poe's "The Purloined Letter," I show the interconnections between the gaze, the L schema, and shame, as well as the way these interconnections function to situate a subject, particularly a male subject, in the feminine discursive position, thus supporting my claim that sexual difference is the affective effect of a physico-discursive translinguistic troping of the body.

The repetition of two scenes in the story, the first of which Lacan dubs the primal scene, is a narrative structure representative of desire's function, of the ways in which the subject accesses jouissance, the ways in which the subject desires the Other's jouissance, and also the ways jouissance eludes the subject. By beginning *Écrits* with this essay, Lacan sets a precedent for the rest of the tome; that is, to emphasize that it is not merely the subject who is in question for psychoanalysis (even though this is the title of one of his essays), but it is more so the subject's jouissance, or lack thereof; that is of interest instead. Lacan and those who have written on this seminar emphasize the positions of looking by the characters in the story because the directions of their looking denote directions of desire and organizations of jouissance. Lacan illustrates the transsubjectivity of this desire within the context of looking by playing with the ostrich's poor survival tactic of burying its head in the sand. The ostrich thinks that another ostrich or a predator cannot see it because it buries its head in the sand, which allows for that other ostrich/predator to get at it from behind. His neologism *l'autruiche* (*Écrits* 10), which blends the French *autre* (other) with German *Ich* (I) to play on the French *autruche* (ostrich), refers to the other *I* of the split subject, the *I* who laments, "You never look at me from the place at which I see you." Lacan sees in Poe's "The Purloined Letter" a similar performance of the ostriches by the possessors of the letter in that each of the letter-holders hides their self and the letter in plain sight. Their performances, I argue, are manifestations of the affect internalized by the subject and the externalization of that affect both/and the Imaginary blockages, described by the L schema, within this discursive transitivity: "What interests me today," Lacan says, "is the way in which the subjects, owing to their displacement, relay each other in the course of the intersubjective repetition. [...] their displacement is determined by the place that a pure signifier — the purloined letter — comes to occupy in their trio" (10). The letter serves as a fourth term in the intersubjective discursive structure, but the intersubjective actions that position the subject in discourse cannot occur without the letter's inscription on the possessor's body, i.e., without a signifier to determine its identification within a discourse dynamic.[5]

Guilt, as an affective response to anxiety, arises out of content that culture provides for the subject to experience, viz. experiential content that simultaneously and paradoxically puts the subject's social stability at risk and affirms its status as a subject. For example, when a man, taught to "be a man" through our culture's systemic denigration of women, rapes a woman (because he feels entitled to her as object and "knows" that she is the "appropriate" receptacle for his aggression), he knows that the law criminalizes this act (sometimes), but he also experiences guilt-enjoyment in that patriarchal society simultaneously affirms (and enables/encourages and protects) the act of using women as objects. However, in our subjectivization to a masculinist/patriarchal structure, we are all to a degree phallic, masculine subjects in that we (mis)recognize ourselves in that particular ideological Other, and even predominantly feminine subjects are marked with a masculinist consciousness. In this regard, we are all subjects of guilt, what, perhaps, Žižek, after Lacan, eludes to as "the stain":

> When the letter arrives at its destination, the stain spoiling the picture is not abolished, effaced: what we are forced to grasp is, on the contrary, the fact that the real "message," the real letter awaiting us is the stain itself. We should perhaps reread Lacan's "Seminar on 'The Purloined Letter'" from this aspect: is not the letter itself ultimately such a stain — not a signifier but rather an object resisting symbolization, a surplus, a material leftover circulating among the subjects and staining its momentary possessor?

[…] the subject is strictly correlative to this stain on the picture. The only proof we have that the picture we are looking at is subjectified is not meaningless signs in it but rather the presence of some meaningless stain disturbing its harmony.

(*Enjoy!* 10)

The law, as in the legal system, has nothing to do with the guilt the man feels; rather, the masculinist Law provides him with a *guilt-enjoyment*, a "right" that demands the penetration and colonization of his enigma, of the object of his anxiety. As non-masculine subjects become more vocal about their own rights to non-violence with movements like #metoo, we in turn see a more public and communal rise (rather than just the business-as-usual individual offences against women) in the vocalization of and demand for traditionally pro-masculine (read: pro-violence and oppression) entitlements with movements like "incels" and various alt-right factions. The guilt-enjoyment is that which covers over the meaninglessness of the subject's surplus, his unsymbolizable stain that "spoils the picture" of ideality.

Guilt-enjoyment, different from guilt, does not carry with it remorse or bad feelings; rather, guilt-enjoyment provides the "masculine" subject with an affective manifestation of anxiety that safeguards him against a non-phallic jouissance. In this enjoyment, the masculine subject finds Symbolic-Imaginary scripts to ground his experience. In fact, his masculinity is precisely that which is affirmed through guilt-enjoyment as such: guilt-enjoyment is written into the Symbolic as a phallic apparatus.[6] The campaigns fighting violence against women since the 1970s, when addressing a male audience, most often try to reverse this inherited understanding of masculinity by using the language of man as protector, which, with unfortunate irony, still invokes violence and props up the phallic apparatus. Moreover, this language of man as protector is a myth taken as a truth for some people, as if violence against women did not exist in some not-so-far-off-bygone era of chivalry. To exemplify my point, I turn to a short editorial written by Margaret Miller Curtis, a women's rights political activist in Georgia. After reading Carol Ashkinaze's disturbing report of the abuse victim, Elaine Mullis, who was given a life sentence for killing her husband in self-defense, Curtis sends a short editorial to the *Atlanta Journal Constitution*. She quotes the outrage by a prominent Southern gentleman upon hearing the news of a man's trial on wife abuse.

"Men have changed," he said. "In my youth, Southern men were raised to believe it was their duty to protect women, and that included the protection of the law."

My mother agreed, reporting an identical case in her county when she was a girl. That jury not only let the woman go, but the judge told her she deserved to collect a bounty for ridding the county of a no-good varmint.

Margaret Curtis, *AJC*, Friday, December 5, 1980

The lack of socio-political resources and platforms for the prevention of and recovery from such violence up until 40 years ago – and even then the law deliberately allowed this physical, sexual, emotional, and financial violence against women, e.g., considered property, no access to personal financial accounts, and rape within legal marriage under the terms "contractual consent" – and the focus on the violated rather than both the violated and violator, speak to this culture of guilt (for men) and shame (for women) that divides subjects along the lines of sexual difference. Within this master's discourse, guilt is an acceptable affective response; we have a juridical system wrought with language that holds up guilt as a functioning part of the transsubjective reality, in that the system affirms our humanness as such. Lacan, in discussing Aristotle on religion, declares:

> Nobody dwells on this [punitive fantasm] – it's because at the heart of religious thought that has formed us there is the idea of making us live in fear and trembling, that the coloration of guilt is so fundamental in our psychological experience of the neuroses, without its being possible for all that to prejudge what they are in another cultural sphere.
>
> (SIII 288)[7]

Culture provides the content and the opportunity for this guilt-enjoyment as a persistent, fictive taboo that subjects repeat – are expected to repeat – in order both to build identifications and to police (and capitalize on) their levels of enjoyment. In one of many explorations on the question of whether life has anything to do with death, Lacan, toward the end of his seventh seminar on ethics, returns to this idea of fantasm, not in the guilt-specific punitive sense, but in terms of the "fantasm of the phallus" (SVII 299). This guilt-enjoyment, defined as that which is situated within the Symbolic and has signification therein, is a masculine enjoyment because it is inscribed within Symbolic law. Said differently, culture provides for and expects guilt: culture creates *the hegemony of guilt.*[8]

As a "parallel function of the beautiful," shame functions as a barrier that prevents "the direct experience of that which is to be found at the center of sexual union" (298), namely, jouissance. The beautiful here is perhaps the Kantian beautiful that provides an aesthetic grounding of, safeguard from, Symbolic expression for, the sublime. The sublime, for Kant, is similar enough (but not at all the same) as Leo Bersani's self-shattering or Lacan's encounter with the Real.[9] Shame, rather than guilt, provides an ethical affect for the subject's experience with itself and with others in the "sexual union" in that it brings the subject to the precipice of jouissance, but in relation to the other from another gaze at the same time. Guilt fails as an ethical affect because it is a manifestation of affect wholly within the Symbolic-Imaginary structure; it is a manifestation from this structure rather than reflective about it. Guilt and debt, *a la Nietzsche*, force unethical relations. In recalling Žižek's commentary on the stain earlier, we can begin to see the way in which the subject's (mis)recognition of himself and the ensuing discursive production within that hegemony is the paying of the anthropomorphic debt, "our very symbolic existence" (*Enjoy!* 26). "The symbolic debt," Žižek writes, "has to be repaid. The letter which 'arrives at its destination' is also a letter of request for outstanding debts; what propels a letter on its symbolic circuit is always some outstanding debt" (*Enjoy!* 19). The experience of shame is without debt; rather, the subject is removed from debt; the Law wants nothing from the subject in/of shame.

But, more importantly, shame seems "to be at the origin of all kinds of questions that cannot be answered, including notably the matter of feminine sexuality" (SVII 298). I fear that Lacan's use of the term "sexuality" here may be misunderstood to mean the choices and practices of a feminine subject or in the earlier, Freudian sense rather than the way in which the feminine subject enjoys. Yet, this enjoyment, here at least, is tied directly to the notion of the body. Significantly, these questions that cannot be answered lead him to Heraclites' ambiguous denouncement of religious ceremonies, specifically of Hades (god of death and the dead) and Dionysus (god of wine and fertility) that induced Bacchic trance states because they provide a space for people to experience ecstasy (299). The ambiguity Lacan finds in a clever deconstructive moment is in the use of Heraclitus' word that means both shameful and venerable (299). The ecstasy that Hades and Dionysus represent is desired – even venerated as we see in Bernini's representation of the mystic Saint Teresa (SXX 76) – repressed as that desire is, as well as shameful in that it provides reprieve or temporary escape from the structured demands within the Symbolic. The affective experience of guilt is not a function of any reprieve or escape from the Symbolic, but is the experience of the Symbolic itself. Shame, though, participates in the ambiguous ecstasy/trauma of the subject's contact, however temporary, with the Real. Through this ambiguous encounter with the Real, the subject is able to hold the Symbolic-Imaginary reality through another gaze, which allows for a differential, or, perhaps, ethical, perspective and understanding.

Shame, the "feminine" position, and the letter

The Symbolic, as we know it, disavows shame and society signifies it through exclusion. Society has systems written into it to deal with guilt, but shame is an affective response that has no language, no system *per se.* In the introduction to *Feeling Backward: Loss and the Politics of Queer History*, Heather Love discusses shame as a form of containment forced onto queer subjects through abjection from heteronormative, hegemonic desires. She shows how *The Celluloid Closet*, a documentary of queer Hollywood, represents via the careful editing of Martha's coming out scene and subsequent suicide from *The Children's Hour* the shame of what I would call a non-masculine experiential representation and the way in which the participants in the original film neglected, if not ignored, the problematic of shame in queer subjectivization (Love 15–17).[10] Love extends the issue of shame out to current queer experience, as well as queer criticism: "Although there are crucial differences between life before gay liberation and life after, feelings of shame, secrecy, and self-hatred are still with us" (20). Love's issue here is that there is a lack of attempt to address or speak of this shame carried within the queer subject and queer communities. In other words, shame lurks in the shadows of every moment of progression in the liberation movement and the images of words of pride. Shame is, as of now, written into queer history and queer life, but its inscription is both repressed and disavowed.

Women are written into shame and exclusion in complex ways, too. So much so that I have too many narratives to choose from. Nevertheless, the 2003 film *Code 46*, even if in a heavy-handed way (which is why I chose this film) exemplifies this shame and feminine position. We learn that Maria Gonzales (Samantha Morton), the film's narrator and co-main character, literally has written in her genetic code the Law's taboo, which William Geld (Tim Robbins) is supposed to uphold but ultimately breaks. Through cloning technologies, Maria is genetically William's mother, a *repetition*. The Law's Code 46 explicitly makes sex illegal with a genetic match as such in order to prevent incestuous offspring. Not only is Maria illegitimated by her status as woman within patriarchy and as outlaw to such a regime, but she has the added script literally written into her body when she becomes (unknowingly) the illegal lover of a government employee (who does know) and whose job is to expel people like her. At the end of the film we see Maria banished to the outside of the Symbolic order, a kind of representation of the desert of the real. She is shame in that she is the rem(a)inder of the prohibition disavowed by the society that made her possible, and whose exclusion reaffirms its fantasmatic consistency as society. Moreover, she is a passport forger and smuggler, which one could read as her "playing on the surface" of reality in that she is not so much penetrating borders, but rather creatively being productive with them. Differently, William Geld is literally trying to penetrate suspects' minds while upholding the colonized boundaries and protecting the inside from the outside. Geld is guilty in that he and his fellow men made such a breach of prohibition possible in the achievement of cloning humans successfully to the extent, moreover, that they had to rewrite the Law, a repetition but different. He is trying to uphold the Law while finding guilt-enjoyment in his breaching that Law hegemonically.

Love's understanding of shame is pejorative, but potentially productive if embraced. Similarly, our dominant culture has scripted femininity as shameful, both for boys and girls. Obviously, if a boy shows signs of femininity – liking pink, playing with dolls, wearing dresses, etc. – he has been made to feel shameful historically in the way Love explains shame. A bit more complicatedly, girls are also made to feel shameful for the femininity culture expects of them. Girls are taught to feel shame for providing boys with guilt-enjoyment, to feel shame for lacking physical and intellectual superiority (even though none of this is true), to feel shame when outnumbered by masculine subjects, even paradoxically to feel shame for accomplishments outside of the maternal/domestic script. Essentially, feminine subjects are expected to function by way of shame, to be at the margin of phallic Law because, within this phallic Law, feminine subjects are the Other for masculine subjects, while they are also occupying that marginal position to define a masculinist center. We see this embedded shame in the Queen's position in Poe's "The Purloined Letter."

The paradigmatic queen

In Poe's short story, the letter is first in the Queen's possession, and the Queen is who if not the very icon of Woman *par excellence*, the phallic Woman, in that the purpose of Woman is to validate and make apparent man's discursive position of power to himself. Not only does she, through representation of loyal wife, legitimate the king's power, but she is, by traditional demand, expected to further produce with her body a legitimate heir. Let me be clearer here, though, and I will revisit this point as Chapter 5 is dedicated to explicating it: the Queen, as Woman, does not exist except as the fantasy object within the narrative of masculine power. As such, the Queen is only a manifestation of *objet a*, the object cause and the object effect of masculine desire. She also occupies discursively the "feminine" position in this first scene. According to Lacan's reading of the story, the Queen sets the paradigm for all future possessors of the letter, particularly the Minister. The only woman in the story, the woman "of certain personage," however, does not speak, has no letter attributed to her, but only *the* letter. Also, the Prefect who tells Dupin and the narrator of the Queen's situation attributes no guilt to her either. She has not done anything wrong *per se*, but the letter compromises her position as Woman in that she is bound in her role as Queen to be the exceptional "guardian of the power that royalty by law incarnates, which is called legitimacy" (*Écrits* 19). She has been interpellated into this royal scene of loyal subject and occupies her position therein metonymically, but from the place of her metaphoric position as Woman: "the existence of the letter situates her in a symbolic chain foreign to the one which constitutes her loyalty" (19). She occupies her position metonymically in that the desires placed upon the Queen are contiguous with her displacement as subject. Arguably, she is not a loyal subject at all, but a royal object instead. In this way, she occupies her metonymic position with the metaphoric veil of Woman.

This possible compromise marks her as occupying the place of shame, not guilt. The letter's existence, which is prior to its signification, and subsequent presence as signifier makes patent the contingency of her "identity" as Woman. The woman does not speak for two reasons: as Woman, she cannot be written (SXX 81), and language has no place for shame, only guilt. The Queen, as for any woman, embodies partly and always-already shame by her very status as Woman; that is, by virtue of being "not all," she is always partly excluded from the socio-symbolic. In terms of the narrative of "The Purloined Letter," though, the onset of that first scene, which propels the structural repetition into motion, is where we find an explicit representation of shame. G., the initial reporter of the letter's purloining, describes the scene:

The document in question – a letter, to be frank – had been received by the personage robbed while alone in the royal boudoir. During its perusal she was suddenly interrupted by the entrance of the other exalted personage from whom especially it was her wish to conceal it. After a hurried and vain endeavor to thrust it in a drawer, she was forced to place it, open as it was, upon a table. The address, however, was uppermost, and, the contents thus unexposed, the letter escaped notice.

(Mabbott 8)

Alone in the second most private room the letter comes to the Queen. Neither can we know nor help but speculate how she had received the letter – from a messenger? From the person who addressed it to her? The Queen is silent in her perusal and in the interaction between the King and the Minister. The Queen's hurrying "to thrust" the letter out of sight indicates her shame prior to the entrance of the men and the robbery. Her inability to hide the object that causes her shame – that she was "forced to place it, open as it was" in plain sight – is the predicament of the body occupying the "feminine" position and sounds all too close to that which occurs at the onset of rape, if interpreted from the master's discourse perspective. As the victim's body is forced open and exposed for the rapist – who only cares for the victim's surface, for to consider the contents therein would most likely stop the rape[11] – the message of the rape returns to the victim in an inverted form. The victim of rape most often is *covered* in shame, and just as the Queen takes her time to go to the police to report the theft that is haunting her, so does a rape victim often take time to report the crime, if s/he reports it at all. The surface exposed and the contents unexposed to a guilt-subject explain the violence women experience as object in the presence of men represented by the master's discourse as we know it. The subject of guilt-enjoyment only cares to penetrate (and in this case purloin), not creatively alter. The Queen is thrust into the position of truth and product, according to Lacan's discourse formulae, within this master's discourse as patriarchy within the hegemony of guilt.

The letter conflated with Woman

As I tried to lay out earlier by making a connection between the L schema and the discourse formulae, discourse always involves a gaze. From the gaze of the master's discourse, the Queen doubles in the discursive position of truth in her possession of the letter and her position as the primary gaze in the primal scene, and she is the product in that knowledge of her truth is repressed. Yet, the master's gaze also causes her subversion. The Queen must lay the letter open, but inverted, upon the table in plain sight in the same way the letter, also inverted, must hang in plain sight in the middle of the Minister's fire-place mantle. The inversion of the letter in both instances, and the difficulty in acknowledging its purloining and seeing its presence later speak to the repression of the gaze, but these positions do not occur from only one place. Her demand for the letter's return shows her subject position straddling that of the hysteric's and the master's discourses. From the position of the hysteric's discourse, the Queen demands and needs the master, but refuses to be complicit within the master's script of her as Woman. Yet, in the demand to regain the letter and, extra-textually assuming the Prefect delivers it *tout de suite*, her successful re-possession of it places her back within the master's discourse in her original position, but with a remainder, a lack. Those who know the letter's content do not, perhaps cannot, speak it, because it is contentless, cannot be spoken, and they find themselves in the "feminine" position that straddles the hysteric's and master's discourses. The letter, as Lacan argues, holds a specific power "either by prolonging its detour" or by its destruction, which signifies "the canceling out [*annulation*] of what it signifies" (*Écrits* 23). More pointedly, the subject who loses possession of the letter has the power to bestow upon or refuse a position of power in discourse from the new possessor. Lacan asserts that the Queen "confers upon [the Minister] a position that no one can really assume because it is imaginary, that of absolute master" (24). Even though Lacan follows this immediately with acknowledging, in the vein of Alexandre Kojève's reading of Hegel's master/slave dialectic, that the Minister's position as master is really one of absolute weakness, it is not clear that Lacan's discursive positioning of the characters here is in sync with the later discourse formulae laid out in Seminar XVII, or perhaps his layout is just more focused on the L schema and the impatient aggressiveness developed in the mirror stage toward the specular image (24). However, perhaps straddling the master's and hysteric's discourses, so to speak, is indicative of this very impatient aggressiveness.

Barbara Johnson's well-known essay "The Frame of Reference: Poe, Lacan, Derrida" argues a similar tack as my own here, except she focuses specifically on the rhetorical situation of the letter:

> The way in which the letter dictates a series of circumlocutions, then, resembles the way in which the path of the letter dictates the characters' circumvolutions [...] The character and actions of each of the letter's holders are determined by the rhetorical spot it puts them in whether or not that spot can be read by the subjects it displaces.
>
> (242)

Johnson explains that the letter is a substanceless signifier and its function is a division along a signifying chain. Building upon her, and Lacan's, notion of the letter, this project looks at what the letter does to the subject in the act of displacement in order to bring to the fore the significance of Lacan's work on sexuation and discourse and push back, perhaps repress, the current emphasis on gender within the phallic apparatus. Gender, a mere performance, does not get at the concept that "the signifier's displacement determines the subject's acts, destiny, refusals, blindnesses [...] irregardless of their character or sex; and that everything [...] follows willy-nilly the signifier's train" (*Écrits* 21). The subjects, as we see in Lacan's reading of the story, "by passing beneath [the signifier's] shadow, […] become its reflection. By coming into the letter's possession […] its meaning possesses them" (21). The letter, as the signifier that reflects, as we see written in the L schema and explained through the gaze, reverses the intention and forces the subject into a discursive position s/he did not necessarily choose. I want to extend Johnson's argument that whether the letter's content is hidden or revealed is immaterial (Johnson 242) to say that the letter's content is immaterial in that the letter is, in Lacanian terms, a pure signifier, but the letter materializes the subject within discourse by displacing the subject in its intersubjectivity. As Derrida and then Johnson point out, the *a* as letter designates a lack (242–43).

The Queen, as I said earlier, is a representation of Woman, i.e., *objet a*, and then the feminine position *par excellence*, but the Minister, as Lacan points out, becomes feminized when, in possession of the letter, he interacts with Dupin, who succeeds ultimately in retrieving the letter. The Minister and his apartment, as Lacan dwells upon them, are a representation of a "feminine" topography, as the Minister functions as the "feminine" discursive articulation situated within the "feminine" physical space as body. The Minister, due to his possession of the letter, is in a sort of exile from his usual social appearances; he must take on a different appearance in relation to the phallic apparatus in that the letter's inscription now affects his body. In *The Ethics of Psychoanalysis*, Lacan makes a connection between the shadow of death and the beauty of the image – particularly in his use of the still life and the curves of a vase – that is a representation by the human body. These representations are Imaginary factors, shadows and reflections, parodies of representation representatives (SVII 297–98). The Minister as actor in the discourse becomes an imaginary reflection of the Queen in his possession of the letter and its displacement of him within the dynamic of hiding and seeking. Lacan maps his position as "in the trap of the typically imaginary situation of seeing that he is not seen," and, in invoking the *autruicherie* he embodies "the attributes of woman and shadow" (*Écrits* 22). The Minister now occupies what Lacan reads as the metaphor of Woman: "what is blinding in a flash of light, no less than the shimmering that shadows exploit in order to release their prey" (22). He occupies the space of the occulted signifier in terms of an imaginary representation of meaning as subject to another signifier. The Minister is able to occupy the feminine position just as the Queen does in that what he hides is contiguous with his own displacement, if not sets his displacement in a particular trajectory. Also, he tries to veil this displacement with what Dupin is able to detect as a "feint" attempt at effeminacy. The Minister's attempt to be the metaphor of Woman fails. Apparently, he does not make a good queen.

The signifier is dominant over the subject. According to Lacan's argument here, Woman functions as the first sign:

> For this sign is clearly that of woman, because she brings out her very being therein by founding it outside the law, which ever contains her – due to the effect of origins – in a position as signifier, nay, as fetish. In order

to be worthy of the power of this sign she need but remain immobile
in its shadow, managing there by, like the Queen, to simulate mastery of
nonaction.

(22)

Woman functions in the Symbolic order as the first sign, the signifier of male
authority by way of one's division from the mother, but she learns how to exercise power. Passivity does not equate with helplessness.[12] Woman, as we see in
the Queen's actions and the Minister's predicament in his inability to use the
letter for powerful political gain, lends herself to the Symbolic order, but she
is only there metonymically as Imaginary metaphor, as substitutive object for
others. The Minister tries on this affect successfully with the imbeciles who
occupy the police force, but fails as Dupin, who functions as analyst, sees the
farce. Dupin reads the Minister as affecting femininity in his "aura of noncha-
lance [...] listlessness" and "ennui" (25), and also notices that the script the
Minister writes upon the inverse of the letter is "feminine." The Minister essentially affects the metaphor of Woman, and Lacan reads this artifice as a "beautiful image of the fact that this is the very effect of the unconscious [...] in the
precise sense that man is inhabited by the signifier" (25).

Woman does not exist, but neither, perhaps, does the phallus

The first line of Lacan's "Seminar on 'The Purloined Letter'" has its basis
in metonymy – "the instance of the signifying chain" (6) – and its correlate
ex-sistence "in which we must necessarily locate the subject of the unconscious" (6). Dupin, though, only sees the remainder of the Minister's affective
performance written not only on his body through his feminine appearance,
but also on the letter. The letter, in a sense, has become the eccentric place of
his unconscious. *Woman, thought of as metaphor within the masculine, master's discourse, becomes, rather, the truth that veils masculinity as the actual metaphor of sexual
difference.*

M.A. Franks explains that "Metonymy [...] is horizontal, a relation of word
to word. It is characterized by lack, and is associated with realism and servitude, that is, the servitude to the burden of the bar, which in its mathematical
formulation [gives] the appearance, not merely coincidentally, of a minus sign."
Woman does not exist: it is an affect of the anxiety of the masculine subject's
truth as metaphor.[13] Franks continues, "while it would appear that Lacan casts
metaphor in strong, positive terms and metonymy in weak, negative ones [...]
He refers often to the 'insufficiency' of the metaphor, and criticizes the ten-
dency of linguists to privilege metaphor over metonymy." If Franks is correct in
following Lacan's "letter *en souffrance*" (*Écrits* 30), then the letter, like Woman, is
an object of violent pursuit in that it holds the Imaginary promise of a release
from anxiety. But this metaphor, which reveals the truth of the Imaginary barrier between the split subject and its Other, will always escape the pursuer and
return to the object transformed. I end here with Franks' quiet boldness:

And do we dare suggest, as we read Lacan reading literature, that haunting the straight line of his intention, with its proliferation of discourses on the phallus and metaphor, there might be a shadow, a fear, an unconscious letter that insists, contrary to all intended purposes, *that the phallus does not and has never existed*, and that we have long been playing with the most apparent and childish of fantasies. (emphasis in original)

The following chapter will delve into this daring pronouncement in hopes of bringing to light the discursive and affective aggression with which feminist and queer scholarship has approached Lacanian thought. I begin with Irigaray's discussion of the body and her critique of Lacan in order to review the way in which critics have tried to use her theory to discuss woman as metonymy. I then engage with the concept of woman as metonymy in order to develop more clearly the metonymic function of the feminine in discourse. However, I ask that you indulge me in another quilting point that illustrates the issue of essentialist metaphor function in language, as well as Woman as metaphor, this time through two events from two different, but significant, historical American moments, an early civil rights protest and two women polarized on the Equal Rights Amendment (ERA).

Notes

1   I italicize the indefinite article in this statement in order to link it to Lacan's emphasis in SXVII and SXX on Freud's asking "What does *a* woman want," which has often been revised to ask "What does *the* woman want?" and "What does Woman want?" in his formulation of *La*. The distinction between *the* letter and *a* letter is important because Lacan is not emphasizing one letter that will always arrive at its destination over all other letters that may or may not arrive at a/ the destination. Just as many critics misunderstand Lacan's use of the phallus as the privileged signifier as not an arbitrary choice – let's consider his admiration for Saussure's work and the importance that the arbitrary plays therein – I do not want my readers to misunderstand the importance of the indefinite article in Lacan's work, and in my intentions throughout this project. However, Lacan does suggest that

> The very terms we use to talk about [the signifier and signified non-relation] are still slippery. A linguist as discerning as Ferdinand de Saussure speaks of arbitrariness. That is tantamount to slipping, slipping into another discourse, the master's discourse, to call a spade a spade. Arbitrariness is not a suitable term here. [...] To say that the signifier is arbitrary does not have the same import as to simply say that it bears no relation to its meaning effect, for the former involves slipping into another reference. (SXX 29–30)

And in a later lecture he clarifies that "it would have been better to qualify the signifier with the category of contingency" (40).

2   I add *discursive* here.

3   Žižek uses the term "intersubjective" rather than "transsubjective" in the original text. I am almost positive that he means "intersubjective" in the way in which I have

defined and am using "transsubjective." To avoid confusion of terms here, I have replaced the original term.

4 Chapter five will explain and develop what it means to be wholly and not wholly subjected to the Law. For now, I hope that ascribing these two relations to the Law with the respective sexuated positions will suffice.

5 The imaginary drama the child undergoes in the mirror stage that relies on the future anterior – which brings the *I* formation into a "will have meant" in the present – or, more specifically, the "orthopaedic" corrective function of this drama is more of an orthopsychic function brought on by and repeated through the gaze of the other *I*. The way in which the subject is displaced along the signifying chain in the Symbolic determines the subject's signifieriness as "masculine" and "feminine" to another subject.

6 Similarly, white people's lynching of Black folks provided the same affect of guilt-enjoyment. The institutionalization of unreasonable and unjustifiable hate – racism – provided the method for white subjects to release built up anxiety over the status of their own identity.

7 Earlier in *The Psychoses* Lacan explains Freud's anthropological purpose for working through his ideas while writing *Moses and Monotheism* and *Totem and Taboo* – specifically in terms of his writing the primal horde myth and Oedipus complex – as that which defines our very humanness in terms of guilt and debt: "Man is in fact possessed by the discourse of the law and he punishes himself with it in the name of this symbolic debt which in his neurosis he keeps paying for more and more" (SIII 242). Both Freud and Lacan are indebted to Nietzsche's work, particularly in *On the Genealogy of Morals*, because that is where he establishes the correlation between debt and guilt.

8 Here I am building upon Freud's notion that there is only one libido, the masculine libido. Guilt is the affective response written into and insisted upon by the dominant law. Moreover, Lacan's Seminar VII: *The Ethics of Psychoanalysis*, aims to explicate this notion of guilt, which, in the end, leads him toward the path of shame, as I will try to show below. Lacan asserts at the seminar's outset, "If there is, in fact, something that psychoanalysis has drawn attention to, it is, beyond the sense of obligation properly speaking, the importance, I would even say the omnipresence, of a sense of guilt" (3). And as he begins to wrap up the year's seminar, in a brief musing on Jules Dassin's film *Never on Sunday*, he explicates:

> If there is a dimension of social criticism in this symbolism [of the director playing the American as ironically the most American] – that it [*sic*] to say that what one finds hidden behind the brothel are the forces of order, so to speak – it is somewhat naïve to make us hope at the end of the screenplay that all that is needed to solve the problem of the relations between virtue and desire is to close down the brothel […] This shows us that *on the far edge of guilt*, insofar as it occupies the field of desire, there are the bonds of a permanent bookkeeping, and this is so *independently of any particular articulation* that may be given of it. (318, emphasis added).

9 For the scope of the project, I have no desire to delve into Kantian philosophy, so I will leave this here as such. Also, I will revisit Bersani's self-shattering later.

10 Epstein, Rob and Jeffrey Friedman, directors. *The Celluloid Closet*. Channel Four Films and HBO Pictures, 1995; Wyler, William, director. *The Children's Hour*. United Artists, 1961.

11 I mean not only that if a rape victim evacuated her/his bowels during a rape it could potentially save the victim from further violation, but also that a rapist most likely sees her/his victim as nothing but an object and to consider the object as a dynamic person, as a fellow subject, as one with a surface and a structure rather than a hole, would most likely prevent the rape impulse. I base this speculation on the common assumption that a rapist acts from anxieties about his/her own social disempowerments rather than directly upon the person who s/he violates.

12 Cf. Claude Lévi-Strauss, *The Elementary Structures of Kinship*. Beacon Press, 1969.

13 Cf. Levi Bryant's final chapter of *Democracy of Objects*, "The Four Theses of Flat Ontology," where he argues that the masculine side of the sexuation graph refers to "semblance" and the feminine side refers to "truth" (261–62). I will pick this up later and discuss it in detail with my own reading of the masculine and feminine.

Quilting point

I <u>AM</u> A MAN and the essence of Woman

It's not my job to make you a better man and I don't give a shit if I've made you a better man. It's not a fucking woman's job to be consumed and invaded and spat out so that some fucking man can evolve.

Jenny Schecter, L Word, 2.11 (2005)

To begin this quilting point, I explicate the sentence *I am a man*, a sentence that explicitly attempts to substitute the *I* with *a man*, a metaphorical declaration that "I" is "the same" as "a man." But since, as Lacan would have it, the enunciating and the enunciated *I* are not exactly the same, we can hardly equate either *I* fully with the substitution *a man*. Émile Benveniste, in "The Nature of Pronouns" from *Problems in General Linguistics*, explains that the *I* only has value in the moment of utterance, in the act of speaking it, which engenders a "combined double instance […] the instance of *I* as the referent and the instance of discourse containing *I* as referee" (218). He defines the pronoun *I*, then, as "the individual who utters the present instance of discourse containing the linguistic instance *I*" (218). Kaja Silverman recognizes this divided *I* as being related to what Lacan designates as the "barrier between reality and significa- tion," the difference between "'being' and 'meaning'" (*Subject of Semiotics* 46). Moreover, the term *man*, much like the divided *I*, is a metaphor for a discur- sive position that carries a variety of social assumptions. Man evokes the sex organ associated traditionally with the noun "male," as well as, say, the privileges and accesses assigned to and assumed by men historically. It also connotes varying ideas of masculinity, or even an idea of said masculinity in crisis. Also, it means through difference with *woman* or *boy* or *lion* or *dog*, for examples. Man functions metaphorically as substitution, but only by way of metonymical con- tiguity. *I am a man* is a metonymic chain of signifiers, a combinative sequence, that means not only in the connection of individual words with each other, but also, and crucially, through linkages with signifiers not visibly or audibly present in this utterance. Metaphor, as we have seen, depends upon the syn- tagmatic linear sequencing of the chain of signifiers that is associated with the metonymical. To privilege the metonymical function as metaphor's condition of possibility may be a crucial strategy for opening up ethical possibilities for intersubjective relations between subject and Other, as well as transsubjective relations for social change. Queering the patent metaphors of sexual difference, for example, will free up the constraints imposed upon the body.

Woman as metaphor (and the conundrum of the wisdom to pick one's battles wisely)

As metaphor, the statement or declaration "I am a man," is the articulation of an identity. Within the statement's historical use – that of the Black, male sanitation workers standing in the streets of Memphis in those early months of 1968 holding the signs that read I **AM** A MAN – whenever they hear the sentence uttered, it is a demand in that these men were not recognized as men by the white men who occupied the master's position. The image of the strikers' sign emphasizes the mode of being, **AM**, in bold and underlined. These men, fighting for labor and civil rights generally, declared subjecthood in response to the U.S. Constitution's declaration that "all men are created equal" so that they could be counted as men, rather than as a fraction of a man. The revolutionary moment was the demand, born out of desire, for recognition, which would provide them with a new identity status within society. Fortunately for these laborers, their demand was heard just enough, and they became counted as men. The social order provided a space for their meaning differently than previously. This provision as identity, though, is a lie, not only for these Black laborers, but also for the white men who had the power to carve out a space of meaning for their demand. The metaphor *I am a man*, which all the men involved declared, suggests that this is *the* identity, *the* explanation of their being, that which explains their existence, the place from where they assume privilege. In desiring and demanding to be recognized as men, the strikers want to occupy the masculine social position, which affords them an upwardly social mobility to be better than chattel, and, unfortunately, better than women. Even though my previous statement may seem callous, it is nevertheless a current structural truth. To be recognized as a man in our patriarchal society means that one gains dominance over women. Obviously, *man*, just as *laborer*, just as *Black* or *white*, is not an ontological Truth, as there are none; rather, almost like a catachresis, *man* is an epistemological function, a categorical situating of the body. Looking at the sentence metonymically, the metaphoric substitution becomes much more apparent, and the emphasis on meaning rather than being comes to the fore. To say I **AM** A MAN is to say in the moment of utterance that I am not something else within the domain of language: it is an argument based on the probable grounds that also includes/implies a contradiction that is suppressed, that implies I am not in the same place as I say I am, so I am not *really* a man.[1]

We can juxtapose the Black men's supposedly ontological demand for recognition as men to women's roles and (lack of) visibility in the 1960s civil rights efforts, as well as the 1970s women's movement. A quick scan of iconic images of Black women's protest signs during the 1963 March on Washington, reveals no declaration of being. For example, signs held by Black women during the march demand "Decent Housing Now!" and "Integrated Schools Now!" and "We March for Jobs for All Now!" The women even marched down a different street (Independence Avenue), separately from the men (Pennsylvania Avenue). Very few women were invited to speak and the ones who were said very little, e.g., Daisy Bates speech had 148 words. The 1970s Equal Rights Amendment (ERA) movement focuses on women's liberation mostly in terms of the right to choose whether or not to have children and to work, as well as the recognition that these choices are made only within a patriarchal system (and from a middle-class perspective). The difference between the Black, male laborer's famous protest and these women is that these women are not denied the right to a supposedly ontological representation of themselves within the category of sex. To declare ontologically is still to be within language; ontology is a function of the Symbolic, not the Real. For the Black men to demand to be men is to demand masculine privilege, to be seen as Black and as men, and the latter is the identity that they no longer want to lack, which they want to access for social power. Black women, as women, were (are) not as threatening to the white mind because they are women, and, as history shows, they are rapable, hirable, concubinable. Black men, as history shows, are considered, in the white mind, terrorists to white men's women and social safety generally. Differently from the Black men's protests, the women do not have to declare themselves as women.[2] Rather, the problem is that a very particular ontology *has been demanded for and of them.* They do not have to demand recognition of their status as women; *they do not have a choice but to be women.* "Being" a woman was (is) the very problem, just as being Black was (is) the very problem. Women today still struggle between one another over what "being" a woman means, as well as having to be a woman, as both occur within and through systemic male dominance, and many of the available meanings of "woman" are produced in and by that system to enable its reproduction.

Schlafly v. Johnson: the problematic of Woman as essence

The dominant controversy between white women during the fight for the passage of the ERA provides an example of this struggle between women regarding how to mean as women, that is, whether and how to redefine it or whether it is an ontology, an essence. To make my point, I consider two voices prominent during this period, belonging to women who are sharply opposed politically, Phyllis Schlafly and Sonia Johnson.[3] Schlafly, the leader of the Eagle Forum, an outspoken Christian conservative political lobbying group, founded the Stop ERA organization. Schlafly loudly, publicly, and persistently spoke out against all aspects of women's liberation – equal rights in the workplace, economic and custody rights in divorce, and rights to their own medical (read: reproductive) decisions – backed by her argument that women without husbands cause more government dependence, rampant homosexuality, and destroy the most important foundation of Christian American values, the heteronormative, nuclear family. For Schlafly, women need to raise children, happily, for the men who dominate and control their lives. Her unwavering, narrow stance disavows the realities of women's historically quotidian experiences of physical, verbal, emotional, and economic abuse in addition to systemic, institutional oppression. For example, her targeting of unmarried women and mothers shows her refusal to acknowledge the overwhelming fact that men often abandon their children and assume that the women will take care of them, hence the "dead beat dad" and the legal system's need to threaten absentee fathers with jail time due to their neglect to support their children. She refuses to acknowledge the overwhelming facts that many women flee their husbands because of violent abuse, which is easily substantiated by the abundance of shelters and organizations nationwide that house and provide services for these victims, and the even more overwhelming evidence that these services are still only capable of helping a fraction of women who need help. Simply put, she is an advocate for masculinist ideologies.

In her 2006 Eagle Forum online column post "Feminists' Double Standards about Child Care," she went so far as to call people who speak out against domestic violence and serve victims "agitators," and that the systems and people who help women and children in violent or inequitable situations a "big industry." In addition, as a white woman with a law degree and a privileged status in the social system, Schlafly disavows the hiring and wage inequality between women and men. Women in the 1970s not only were paid much less than men (59 cents to the dollar on average and even less for women of color), as they still are now, but were also still fighting to overcome previous institutionalized stigmas to hold certain positions within the workforce due to weight lifting constraints (30 lbs. maximum), the belief in their lesser intelligence in the fields of math and science, or because of the gender segregated architecture of the workplace. She uses a faulty logic to read feminists' desires for more choices in child rearing and careers and to have the labor of homemaking acknowledged as women not wanting to raise their own children or take financial responsibility for them. She even goes so far as to quote Freud – really, it is just too good – and asks, "what does a woman want?," which heavy-handedly implies that women should not want (for) anything.

On what seems to be the extreme opposite end of the political spectrum, Sonia Johnson, within the 1970s women's movement, represented the superiority of women over men and their spiritual and political revolution against patriarchy. She was excommunicated from the Mormon Church because of her outspoken feminist work in support of the ERA and against the Church. She even ran for president in 1984 under the Citizen's Party and was the first candidate of a third party and first woman to receive federal matching funds for her campaign. Once the ERA failed to pass and the media and other politicians failed to take her candidacy seriously, she turned radically anti-politics, anti-patriarchy, and anti-men and began living as a separatist, which she still does today. In her April 19, 2010 oral history, she explains her beliefs and position as to why – in opposition to Schlafly's insistence that all women require men – women and the world should be rid of men completely: "I knew that maleness was at the roots of all the misery in the world" (8). She continues with this essentialist viewpoint on patriarchy:

> what I was hoping is that we could get out of that mind. […] If we really understood that what it was was maleness, that men were made solid, made corporeal. […] that what paradigms do is that they come out of some-where, and since men had taken over the world by brute force and by being willing to torture and willing to kill those in their way […] they got to be on top. Because women were not willing to do this and are still not willing to do this. As a species, we are not willing to do this […] So out of them, when they arrived on this planet came all this.
>
> (14)[4]

For Johnson, men are *the* problem of the world. The very maleness of men is why the world is a violent and oppressive place. Johnson even goes so far as to argue that women are closer to a pure essence, and men's essence is incapable of such purity: "We don't do things, we are things. […] the difference between male and female. Men do. […] We can be. Men cannot be. And we remember being" (63). Johnson is an example of the extreme "man-hating" second wave feminist type who quickly became a mainstream anti-feminist arguing point.

Even though Schlafly and Johnson hold strongly oppositional political views as to the ways in which women and the world should be, they hold the same view as to what women *are*. Men and women are for both Schlafly and Johnson innately male and female respectively. Both Schlafly and Johnson see women within the scope of what I define as Woman as metaphor within the avail-able patriarchal scripts, which is to say that women are essentialized as the idea(l) of Woman as bounded entity. (They, of course, do not think of women as metaphors.) Schlafly metaphorizes women in that she promotes the identity of "Woman" as child bearer and rearer, as needing a man and men, and without these two basic, fundamental groundings, women will be the vehicle for the "right" society's destruction. When in her proper place Woman is the vehicle to manifest society correctly. Johnson metaphorizes women as essentially primary and superior in the world. Men are but a defect, are deviance from essence. She learns from Shenai, a Hopi elder woman, the myth that in the beginning there were only females, and after an enormous explosion, men began to appear in most species as a consequence (65). Both women, in taking part in this metaphorization of Woman, assume and promote an *identity* of women *as such* – even in Johnson's attempt to separate herself from patriarchy completely – and thus fail to stand outside of the patriarchal master's discourse.[5] We see this pro-motion of woman *as such* throughout the history of feminist and women's movements in the reduction of women to the gender symbol also equated with the female sex and sex organ, ♀. In using the symbol to represent feminist and women's agendas, the participants conflate themselves with the gender con-struction of the feminine and the female sex. The gender construction and the sex become substitutions for each other. Between the two signifiers of feminine gender representations and the female sex organ a spark occurs that engenders Woman as metaphor within the master's discourse. This metaphor is exactly what activists like Johnson try to disrupt, but a tack such as Johnson's serves to reinforce the metaphor, just with slightly different content.[6]

Notes

1 Of course, any claim to an identity is a lie, an impossibility.
2 Indeed, in 1851 Sojourner Truth delivered a now renowned speech subsequently entitled "Ain't I a Woman?"; however, this speech, in its earliest documentation has little to do with her implying that her blackness keeps her from being a woman and everything to do with the women's rights convention at which she spoke, where women were asking for more equality in general. Of course, by the very nature of her blackness, her speech would inherently imply that her womanhood and her blackness were both entwined and opposed, depending on what (white) lens the audience listened from. Given the racially volatile context that is always at work in the U.S. and the ways that white women silenced women of color during this first wave of women's rights, though, it is no wonder that she did not explicitly address her blackness for fear of being ostracized from the movement. Her brief speech has more equivalences with Mary Wollstonecraft's lengthy "A Vindication of the Rights of Women" than with the racially motivated civil rights marches that occurred over a century later. Cf. Kay Siebler, "Far from the Truth: Teaching the Politics of Sojourner Truth's 'Ain't I a Woman'," *Pedagogy*, vol. 10, no. 3, Fall 2010, pp. 511–33; Matthew K Samra, "Shadow and Substance: The Two Narratives of Sojourner Truth," *Midwest Quarterly*, vol. 38, no. 7 Winter 1997, pp. 158–71; Roseann M. Mandziuk and Suzanne Pullon Fitch, "The Rhetorical Construction of Sojourner Truth," *Southern Communications Journal*, vol. 66, no.2, 2001, pp. 120–38.
3 For the record, Johnson makes it a point to articulate her admiration for Phyllis Schlafly: "She is admirable […] I mean, well, she has some admirable qualities" (33). I think Johnson, who loves all women no matter what, thinks Schlafly's perseverance and intellectual capabilities are admirable, not her ideas or the way in which she necessarily goes about introducing those ideas to the public. Of course, perseverance and intelligence are ambiguous characteristics.
4 Oral histories are transcribed as closely to the speech of the interviewee; therefore, grammatical conventions are almost impossible to adhere to.
5 In referring back to my brief explanation of resistance and opposition, I want to point out that Johnson's seemingly oppositional stance is one of resistance when looked at through the lens of Lacan's discourse formulae.
6 Academic feminism and Women's Studies has canonized the point I make above *via* Audre Lorde's "The Master's Tools Will Never Dismantle the Master's House," in *The Bridge Called My Back: Writings by Radical Women of Color*. Anzaldúa, Gloria and Cherríe Moraga, Kitchen Table Women of Color Press, 1983; rpt. in *Sister Outsider: Essays and Speeches*, Crossing Press Feminist Series, 1984.

5   Woman as metonymy

Or, I am not your *manqué l'être*

Because it seems to me that, why think and do the same old stuff? It's so boring. I'll tell you the worst thing about patriarchy is that it's boring. It is so incredibly boring. Oh my gosh, oh my word. Nobody says anything different ever, you know that? It all fits in that same paradigm. It all fits together. I'd just, I'd just come to the place where I just am dying of boredom.

Sonia Johnson, April 19, 2010

This chapter addresses and complicates the necessary ambiguity within this project between the idea of Woman and women as subjects. I consider the notion of Woman as metonymy in order to forward a shift in consciousness through political acts. In doing so, I subsequently address Luce Irigaray's theory of the idea of Woman and feminist renderings of that idea in relation to metonymy.

Woman as metonymy

How are we to stop writing Woman as metaphor, as the identity of certain socio-discursive objects through our subjectivization to the master's content? In order to begin considering this question, I want to look briefly at the difference between the phrases *Woman is metonymy* and *Woman as metonymy*. The basic, literary difference between them is metaphor and simile. Perhaps more conceptually significant, the first can stand alone as a sentence and, therefore, can demand an ontology, a contradictory lack of movement even in its declaration of metonymic movement. The second is a phrase that cannot stand alone as a sentence and, therefore, provides almost (restricted by linguistic possibilities) infinite possibilities that would have to qualify what the *as* means. So, even in the implied metaphor of *as if* that the *as* may connote, movement is always needed within and from the phrase's incompleteness and its implied directionality of metonymy.

The first, *Woman is metonymy*, just as we saw in I **AM** A MAN, substitutes Woman for the trope metonymy and thereby declares an identity. To replace Woman with metonymy is to say that Woman is both a part to a whole, as we see in Shklovsky's "Butterfingers!" example, and a chain of signifiers. Just as Schlafly and Johnson essentialize women into Woman as metaphor, an attempt to declare *Woman is metonymy* makes the same essentializing mistake. One would merely be replacing *Woman is metaphor* with *Woman is metonymy*, one trope for another. In this phrasing, Woman stands in as a defining part of the larger patriarchal structure, which could not exist without the fantasy of Woman *as such* because men need to suppose such a difference from themselves in order to organize the structure. The idea of Woman, whether it is in terms of what Woman is or what Woman stands in for, is complicit with patriarchal ontologism in that Woman *is* only in its difference from what Man wants to be (and what Man wants her to be). Woman *means* only as *différance*, as that which allows the differing from what man means and the deferring, that is, the retroversive causality of the way in which sexual difference becomes scripted. Scholarship from Lévi-Strauss to Monique Wittig to Irigaray and many others demonstrate variously the ways in which women, condensed and denied under the signifier Woman, serve as that which men traffic as the link for their organized structure.

The second, *Woman as metonymy*, brings forth an analogy that does not assume identity but forwards the idea of a method for possible avenues of iden-tification. By the phrase *Woman as metonymy*, I mean to forward a contingent and temporary identification – rather than a stable identity – that functions to rupture our metaphoric conception of Woman. If we situate our thinking somewhere between actual, empirical realities of women – e.g., systemic abuse, alienation by the pedestal, the disposability of third-world women laborers, and femicide[1] – as well as the ways in which women resist these realities through covert and overt activism – e.g., the ERA movement; *Ni Una Más!* (Not One More!), *Mujeres de Negro* (Women in Black) and *Nuestras Hijas de Regreso a Casa* (May Our Daughters Return Home) fighting in Mexico for their murdered daughters, the *maquiladoras*, piled in mass graves in Ciudad Juárez;[2] *Madres de Plaza de Mayo* (Mothers of Mayo Plaza) standing every Thursday in the square to demand back their abducted children; Asmaa Mahfouz's vlog that helped begin the Egyptian revolution; and now #metoo – and recognize that nei-ther the abuses nor the resistances are the "identities" of these women, then we can begin to imagine *Woman as metonymy*. For example, *Ni Una Más!* is an activist movement started in Mexico to bring awareness to and fight against the rampant, endemic violence against women in their country. In line with the common formula for activist and revolutionary formations, the women form a common link around an issue that is part of themselves, and then organize into one mass to stand up and make their argument. Gayatri Chakravorty Spivak explains this separating out of the self and forming a unity outside of the self as metonymic: "I put aside the surplus of my subjectivity and metonymize myself, count myself as the part by which I am connected to the particular predicament so that I can claim collectivity [...] A performative contradiction connects the metonymy and the synecdoche into agential identity" (480). Spivak's prescrip-tion for the development of active agency in the production of collectivity calls for a setting aside of our surplus identifications. The very performance of splitting ourselves into parts (synecdochizing) allows for an active aspect to emerge (metonymic collectivity) for the purpose of larger socio-political agendas.[3]

More than just setting aside other parts of themselves in order to create this collectivity in *Ni Una Más!*, these women strategically compile a metonymy of symbols from their Catholic, Hispanic culture both to bring guilt to the foreground of men's consciousness, as well as to safeguard themselves from *machismo* attacks on their legitimacy to march and speak in public; the men cannot shame them back into public exile if they present themselves strategically as the acceptable metaphors of woman (but with a difference). The women carry large pink crosses on black backgrounds (or vice versa) that say *Ni Una Más!* often with the face of a missing or murdered *hija*, daughter. The women dress in black mourning gowns and either cover their faces with black veils, paint their faces as sugar skulls (invoking dead ancestors), or wear traditional (and here is the subversive kicker) politico campaign hats to cover their heads, and sometimes the mourning gowns are sown together as one giant drape that covers all the bodies with holes for their heads to fit through. They march through public spaces, sometimes just within a city's borders, and sometimes for hundreds of miles throughout Mexico to bring awareness to as many towns and cities as they can. The marchers create a symbolic chain of meaning by putting together the color of femininity, pink, the major religious icon, the cross, and the traditional expectation of women in mourning, the black drape and veil.

Within the culture of *machismo*, women have only three metaphoric identities, the mother who leads a private life in the home, the virgin who stays at home until marriage and transitions to the mother, and the whore who lives a public, unrespectable life.[4] The *maquiladoras*, the women who work in the factories (*maquilas*), fall into this latter metaphor of Woman, and it is the *maquiladoras* who often disappear or are found murdered and dumped. The women standing up to this violence play the role of the mother in order to demand respect and protect themselves from public attack, as the men would hesitate to cross the boundary into shame by defiling the symbol of the mother or the cross. At the same time, these women also transgress the metaphor they embody in these acts by the very public-ness of their movement. While donning the garb of the Catholic mother, they occupy the place of the public whore with their bodies, their voices, their movements, and their spectacle of feminizing the crucifix.[5] They take cultural metaphors that seem so utterly sedimented (S_1s, master signifiers) and combine and use them differently, thus highlighting their polyvalence within the Symbolic, and this act begins to remove the essentialized Imaginary function these metaphors have served for centuries. The differential troping of the idea of Woman serves, on the one hand, as a sedimented ideal that provokes violence but, on the other, by virtue of being a *trope*, shows its Imaginary formation as not fixed, not static, and, therefore, changeable. By forcing the desires of those validated masculinist subjects who make and enforce these S_1s into the feminist contexts of resistance, articulating them as *other* desires, pushes them out of that seemingly sedimented Imaginary categorical and more into the space of the empty Symbolic. The *Mujeres de Negro*'s protests in *Ni Una Más!* can be read as straddling the hysteric's and analyst's discourses in that they work to create new S_1s from which may be issued a different kind of master and master signifier. *Las Mujeres* publicly disrupt the reification of themselves and their *hijas* within patriarchal narratives, even though they may fail at the disruption of masculine privilege. This disruption of Woman narratives provokes the interrogation of the master signifiers that naturalize these narratives, which opens up the space in the template of identifications. And, for a time at least, the capacity to produce new S_1s is crucial during the fall of the fantasy of the consistency of previously understood master signifiers. The activist movement is metonymical, and as soon as that movement is static, it is reified back into metaphor.

Given the public, political acts such as those performed by the women who comprise *Ni Una Más!*, the content that stabilizes the Imaginary fixation of these specific Symbolic components as a structure becomes conspicuously contingent and revisable. Perhaps, in order to re-stabilize social structures or re-orient cultural systems, metaphors will always arise anew, but the sustaining of metonymy for longer periods of time allows for the Symbolic multiplicity of contingencies and revisions, for a building up of differentiations that cannot be denied, and with which we must deal. As we see in the wake of the "Arab Spring," particularly in Egypt, one of the two earliest Arab Spring revolutions to occur, we are witnessing a very slow, fraught period of governmental re-figuring. These periods of sustaining patent metonymic systems refuse the easy reification that metaphor, treated Imaginarily, provides. The pay-off for a persistent and continuous disruption and refusal to occupy any one of the boringly similar, to borrow from Sonia Johnson's words, Woman metaphors is not only the exposing of the falsity of these identities, but also those of the men's identities who insist upon them.

Woman as metonymy is not a completely novel idea; however, the way in which I develop it here is, as far as I know, more pointed than others have dealt with it in the past. For example, feminist scholars, such as Diana Fuss, who I discuss in the section below, have forwarded briefly a thinking of Woman as metonymy by using Irigaray's work. In the following section, I offer a critical review of this scholarship and argue the differences in the rendering of Woman as metonymy for this project.

Contiguity and refiguration: Irigaray and her critics

In *Essentially Speaking: Feminism, Nature & Difference*, Fuss constructs an argument of "Woman as metonymy" through her reading of Irigaray's "two lips." Fuss thinks that a reading of Irigaray grounded in "the problem of an idealism based on the body, on an essential femininity, is fundamentally a misreading of Irigaray" (56).[6] Fuss criticizes "American feminists" for misunderstanding the body as discussed in French theory. American feminists "have difficulty accepting the metaphoricity of the body; they demand that metaphors of the body be read literally, and they then reject these metaphors as essentialistic" (62). Some feminist scholars have criticized and all but dismissed Irigaray's work because they understand her focus on the "two lips" as a reduction of women to the metaphor of a part of their genitalia. This reduction is essentialist, as it assumes the sexed body, based on the possession of a vagina or a penis, and the assumed gender as a one-to-one identity – the vagina means woman means feminine, the penis means man means masculine – rather than as a (word-to-word?) contiguity.

Fuss looks to a passage in the closing section of *This Sex which Is Not One*, "When Our Lips Speak Together," that reads as a creative, philosophical attempt at *parler femme*, written in order to complicate the essentialism with which critics often quibble:

> How can I say it? That we are women from the start. That we don't have to be turned into women by them, labeled by them, made holy and profaned by them. That that has always already happened, without their efforts. And that their history, their stories, constitute the locus of our displacement. It's not that we have a territory of our own; but their fatherland, family, home, discourse, imprison us in enclosed spaces where we cannot keep on moving, living, as ourselves. Their properties are our exile.
>
> (212)

Fuss reads Irigaray's meaning, her intention, here as a kind of strategic essentialism in that her claiming we are "women from the start" prevents us from being wholly and forever defined by a masculine discourse and allows us to always have something that resists the identity definitions inflicted upon us. Referring back to the contrast between the men's and women's protest signs from the 1960s civil rights movement, I have already argued that the women protesters did not protest from the place of identity as the men did because they did not have a choice but to be women. I make this argument from the position that women are women because of how they are placed within "reality" as a construct of patriarchal ideology – a system where certain Symbolic components through an Imaginary fixation come to act as S_1s, and thus not that they are women in spite of this patriarchal construct, which is quite different from Fuss's reading of Irigaray here. Fuss takes Irigaray out of context in order to figure a strategic essentialism when, in fact, Irigaray, put back into context, is critically noting Woman as an essential part of the symbolic structure. Irigaray, just before the above passage, disrupts women's mere reduction to the metaphor of (not-yet-) Woman as virgin by defining the virgin as "one as yet unmarked by them, for them. One who is not yet made woman by and for them. Not yet imprinted with their sex, their language" (211). For Irigaray, the virgin is not the virgin whom patriarchy empedestals as most desirable so much as it is she who has not been subsumed into the system at all.

As I read her, Irigaray's categorization reads more like the Lacanian pre- and mid-mirror stage *infans* who knows nothing of language or sexual difference.

The virgin does not have to be relegated to the position of woman or female – although we can see stark systemic oppression upon women under this category – but can be any (not-yet-) subject who ultimately succumbs to socio-discursive positioning. On this view of Irigaray's definition of the virgin, the category is the pre-subject, but always feminine. Yet, the very meaning of the position of woman, of *being women*, within this structure is that of at one and the same time standing in as the other's desire for purity and filth, for life giving and death bringing. I cannot help but hear Irigaray echo Lacan's comment about the siblings on the train destined for the same homeland, even though they think they are different; "their fatherland, family, home, discourse, imprison us in enclosed spaces" and displace all subjects, all objects even though they are displaced differently. Is this not the "ideological warfare" to which Lacan refers in his summation of the consequences of the siblings' bathroom choices?

There is a twinge of new age utopianism here – just a Butler's slipping (unknowingly?) into a nostalgic desire to return to the Real – in that Irigaray is in danger of trying to argue for a place for women outside of the Symbolic. There is confusion in the above passage that Irigaray has not worked out, and perhaps does not want to work out. Masculinist histories are the "locus of our displacement," she says, but we do not "have a territory of our own." From where are we displaced? From where are we exiled? What would it mean to have a territory of our own? Is not the idea of territory, of boundaries and property, a masculinist discourse? Is that territory from which we are exiled the quasi-desert of the Real as we see in *Code 46*'s reversed depiction? Or is Irigaray, like Butler, guilty of desiring the pre-linguistic? If she is guilty of the latter, then her fallacy involves relegating this exile only to *her* women, and her argument for a woman's place and a woman's *langue* disappears in her own sexism. If she is reproducing such an exclusionary logic, then she is repeating the guilt-enjoyment of the phallic apparatus discussed earlier.

How does Irigaray manage to complicate the definitions of *women* and *Woman*, then, if, as I try to show above, it seems that she does not distinguish clearly the literal corporeality of women and the idea of Woman? Fuss contends that the "debate over Irigaray's essentialism inevitably comes down to this question of whether the body stands in a literal or a figurative relation to language and discourse: are the two lips a metaphor or not?" (62). She continues, "What I propose to argue here is that, for Irigaray, the relation between language and the body is neither literal nor metaphoric but *metonymic*" (62, emphasis in original). I have defined the body for this project as a complexly constructed and ongoing lived relationship between psychic perception and physicality, a relation often impinged upon by unconscious, specifically hysterical, inscriptions. To think of the body as such a construction is to have to think of the body metonymically as a chain of all these component *moments* of body; however, the body, in that it is always somewhat inaccessible to signification, is largely occulted from the signifying chain itself, becoming the locus of that "spark" (of jouissance) that occurs between the "flash" of all these signifiers. The body, in that sense, cannot avoid becoming a metaphor in that it will stand in for something at some moment, but cannot be grasped *as such*. Yet, the body as metaphor does not have to embody simplified and oppressive scripts, such as those that underwrite the "gender identity" binary. The unary trait taken from the Other that marks the body as the desire of the Other "marks the body through inscription (a tattoo, for instance)" and "eroticizes the body and turns the body into an erotic object," (Libbrecht 35). So the S_1 does not necessarily have to be tattooed as the gendered binary. The body, thought of as a contentless dynamic of the relationships between the psyche, the corporeal, and the unconscious, is a wide open investiture. I do not think that the body, defined thusly, is either literal or figurative in relation to discourse and language, as Fuss asks. Rather, the body is a *literal figuration*, and Irigaray's "two lips" are, at times, a contiguous figuration of the complex construction of the body. I provide the "at times" caveat to this claim because I also do not think that Irigaray has a clear way of articulating or delineating what she means by the body or woman, and I do not think that she intends to provide us with one. For to make a clear articulation or delineation would be, like the great categoricist Aristotle, to serve the master's discourse, which is exactly what Irigaray does not wish to repeat.

Irigaray distinguishes a feminine syntax apart from the masculine syntax found in dominant discourse. Although she is not sure what exactly a feminine syntax is or might be, she imagines that it is repressed and censored because "it is necessary to *become* a woman" and take up "the *masquerade of femininity*" (Irigaray, *This Sex*, 134, emphasis in original). Differing from my argument above that women do not have a choice but to be women, Irigaray argues that "a man is a man from the outset. He only has to effect his being-a-man," (134) but women only become visible within discourse by taking up man's affectations. Said differently, men, according to Irigaray, do not have to do anything to be men, which is a bit like the fact that a puppy needs only to get larger with age to be a dog. Women, though, must learn to be women for men, which is to say that they must be very conscious of their feminine performance, and some women excel at this performance (e.g., Marilyn Monroe), some are good enough (e.g., most women who fit the "woman" paradigm), and, well, some fail wonderfully (e.g., butch lesbians) at the masquerade of femininity. I disagree that little boys only have to grow up and they just become men. If that was the case, the Oedipus complex/phase concept would have evaporated a century ago, or, perhaps, Freud never would have thought of it. Plenty of men, particularly in our 21st-century milieu, find themselves not quite successful at the *masquerade of masculinity*, or more consciously rejecting that masquerade.[7] Also, many men of the baby boomer generation and some younger people are having a very hard time with the popular shifts in gender performance and are terrified of the masculinity crisis they perceive around them. We see this difficulty in coping with shifts in masculinity most evidently in the American governmental policy backlash against women's rights that have been legislated in the past 40 years, and especially most recently in 2019, such as the new restrictions on abortion laws and the taking away of reproductive rights. The men who never had to think of their place as men, who fit into Irigaray's description, are now forcefully performing the oppressive masculine discursive position of master as a defense against this masculinity crisis.[8]

Through this deliberate attack on women's rights occurring in American state and federal legislatures, I write "women do not have a choice but to be women," which is different from Irigaray's claim that women must grow up and learn to be women, because the circumstances into which women are forced directly affect their corporeal and psychic body even if they do not identify within the parameter of the *masquerade of femininity*. In the feminine syntax, though,

> there would no longer be either subject or object, "oneness" would no longer be privileged, there would no longer be proper meanings, proper names, "proper" attributes … Instead, that "syntax" would involve a nearness, proximity, but in such an extreme form that it would preclude any distinction of [identities], any establishment of ownership, thus any form of appropriation.
>
> (*This Sex* 134)

Irigaray undoubtedly is describing the contiguity of the metonymic function within language. The sustaining of approximations that this syntax makes while keeping at bay identity and the metaphoric function's appropriation of its signifiers suggests that the feminine, apart from its masquerade within masculine discourse, is devoid of metaphor. For Irigaray and as a transition point for this project, this privileging of metonymy in its capacity to preclude metaphor is one way to begin thinking outside of subject formations that demand a figural mimesis.[9]

Speaking as ~~Woman~~: the discursive limitations of enjoyment and the discursive enjoyment of limitations

Turning to Irigaray's claim that "by *speaking (as) woman,* one may attempt to provide a place for the 'other' as feminine" (*This Sex* 135, emphasis in original), Fuss explains that "*Parler femme* appears to be defined not so much by what one says, or even by how one says it, but from whence and to whom one speaks. Locus and audience distinguish a speaking (as) woman from a speaking (as) man" (Fuss 63). As I have tried to show in the introduction to Lacan's four discourse formulae in Chapter 2, for all subjects it *only* matters from whence and to whom one speaks. The hysteric's discourse, to reiterate just one example, shows that the one who speaks *speaks from the place of* the barred subject, $, and she *speaks to* the master signifier, S_1, who is (assumed to be/demanded to be) the subject-supposed-to-know. Fuss is onto something when she reads Irigaray's notion of the two syntaxes, masculine and feminine, "not based on similarity but contiguity," as "they 'touch upon' but never wholly absorb each other" (63). Lacan tries to show in his sexuation graph, which I discuss thoroughly later, this contiguity and near miss that the occupation of a sexed position entails.[10] In any subject's discursive positioning, one means and enjoys as sexuated. "Woman," Irigaray describes, "always remains several, but she is kept from dispersion because the other is already within her and is autoerotically familiar to her," and Woman enjoys "from what is *so near that she cannot have it, nor have herself*" because she is in "a ceaseless exchange of herself with the other without any possibility of identifying either" (*This Sex* 31, emphasis in original). Woman, for Irigaray, always embodies the other from which she finds pleasure, but she can never fully have or be submerged in this pleasure; rather, she only comes near it, in its proximity. Irigaray's conception of woman's enjoyment seems very close, if not the same as, Lacan's notion of *extimité*. Woman, in her embodiment of the "two lips" and her capacity to find pleasure in this constant proximity, for Irigaray, is able to identify with this "intimate exteriority" (SVII 139). She can identify more closely with the Other as herself. Even though Lacan does enjoy focusing on the extimacy of the feminine subject, all subjects embody *extimité*. Yet, continuing to conceptualize feminine jouissance may provide different logics we can extract and put in to play.

Fuss turns to Lacan in order to question the usefulness of Irigaray's work: "Lacan writes that the play of both displacement and condensation (metaphor and metonymy) mark [...] the laws which govern the unconscious," and she asks, "Is it possible that the feminine neither has an unconscious of its own nor represents man's unconscious but rather articulates itself as a specific operation within the unconscious: the play of metonymy?" (Fuss 66).[11] Fuss does not follow up with answering this question, at least not satisfactorily. I find her question salient, though, because it implies that the unconscious, or rather everyone's unconscious, structured like a language, has this "feminine" play of metonymy. And if everyone has access to the metonymic function as such, then not only do Lacan's four discourses, specifically the hysteric's and the analyst's, provide the path to more deliberately open social relations, but they also allow us to map other possibilities of discourse formulae and to reorient both subjectivity and objectivity.

In situating Irigaray's essentialism into Aristotelian philosophy, Fuss, referring to Irigaray's meditation on essence and privation in *Speculum of the Other Woman*, explains that "Only man properly *has* an essence [...] Because only subjects have access to essence, 'woman' remains an unrealized potentiality" (Fuss 71, emphasis in original). Irigaray, in an odd Augustinian-Hegelian hybrid, muses that woman "can *never* achieve the *wholeness* of her form. Or perhaps her form has to be seen − paradoxically − as mere *privation*" (*Speculum* 165, emphasis in original). Irigaray gives us a paradox of subjecthood. On the one hand, remaining within the confines of what is now traditionally postmodern theory, no subject can "achieve the wholeness of her/his form," but, on the other hand, the idea of woman as privation, and the possibility of the "feminine" metonymic function within every unconscious, carries a way around the figural demands inscribed on subjects' bodies. Of course, Irigaray is specifically referring to males and females, but, as I am trying to argue, these biological designations matter very little; what matters is the place the subject occupies within discourse.

A metonymic disfiguration of masculinist syntax

In her admirable effort to think woman as metonymy, though, Fuss fails to develop the idea fully and slips back into using the functions of metaphor to describe Woman without explicitly acknowledging the slippage: "Woman is the ground of essence, its precondition in man, without herself having any access to it; she is the ground of subjecthood, but not herself a subject" (Fuss 71, emphasis added). As man's "ground of essence," Woman, here, serves as the vehicle within metaphor's operation, and simultaneously as the substitution of essence.[12] This metaphoric function of Woman is a common problem in women's and feminist movements. In light of the contrast between the male and female protestors in the 1960s, I argue that these women's protests take on a more pointedly policy-driven tack because they assume the very ground and substitution we see in Fuss. Having assumed an identity, it is a part of their inherent bodily inscription, making it difficult if not impossible to think and speak from the place of another discourse.

In "Woman Is One of the Names-of-the-Father, or How Not to Misread Lacan's sexuation graph," Žižek elaborates upon this idea of woman as privation to argue against feminist attempts to define woman "in itself" rather than "for the other" (i.e., for man). He reduces both arguments – the "in itself" versus "for the other" – to the same in that the male clichés of femininity and those claimed as essential by some feminists, and the way to distinguish them is to understand them topologically as different modalities. Turning to Hegel's movement from consciousness to self-consciousness in *Phenomenology of Spirit*, Žižek argues that the feminine "in itself," regardless of the characteristics that comprise the idea, designates a *Beyond* that "is not some positive content but an empty place, a kind of screen onto which one can project any positive content whatsoever, and this empty place is the subject. Once we become aware of it, we pass from Substance to Subject [...] In this precise sense, woman is the subject par excellence" (Žižek n.p.). Here, I understand Žižek's rendering the concept of woman and the feminine through Hegel as similar to the way in which I understand Copjec's rendering of the "two positions" that a subject must occupy via Lacan's conception of the emptiness of the Symbolic, as I discussed earlier. After all, the feminine is a Symbolic concept to which we have attached the Imaginary idea of Woman.

Similar to my own critique of Fuss, Drucilla Cornell, in *Beyond Accommodation: Ethical Feminism, Deconstruction and the Law*, criticizes Fuss's attempt to forward an idea of woman as metonymy as "too neat, since the refiguration is inescapably metaphorical" (184). Cornell also sees usefulness in Fuss's attempt at a refiguration of woman, and she adds that a "refiguration through the feminine body is necessary for a carnal ethics" (185). It is important to emphasize Cornell's use of the "feminine body" rather than the "female body." Cornell criticizes the feminist "strategy of showing [woman's] disfigurement within patriarchal society,"[13] as the imaginarily situated "Woman as 'fuckee,' in all its supposed diversity" that is "only their myth of Woman" (166).[14] Cornell, though, thinks it is impossible, and perhaps undesirable, to get beyond another or other ideas of the feminine and woman. The refiguring she desires always gets contained and constrained once again back into metaphor:

> And what tool or literary device do we use to bring women's "reality" into view if we cannot simply "unveil" it as inherent in maternity or women's reproductive capacity more generally? I want to suggest that the tool is pri-marily – and only primarily, because it is a mistake to think we can com-pletely separate metonomy [*sic*] from metaphor – metonomy. Metonomy, as Jackobson suggests, is frequently employed in "realistic" narratives. [...] For Jakobson, metonomy has the connection with "realistic" narratives precisely because it involves the contiguity that is dependent on contexture. But, at the same time, because metonomy moves along the axis of contiguity, the "reality" of women's difference is never consolidated. Contiguity disorder allows for the exploitation of the contextual aspect of language. The com-bination and recombination of words along the axis of contiguity is crucial to the practice of consciousness-raising.
>
> (62–63)

To privilege or emphasize metonymy allows a disordering to occur, a disfig-urement of naturalized syntax, a denaturalization of the metaphors we live by, and provokes confusion regarding identities and identifications, which in turn elicits critique. Yet, Cornell is correct, too, in a sense that no one up to the present has been able to escape being folded back into yet another metaphor (into one of the same old metaphors in all likelihood). In a some-times purportedly post-feminist milieu, our popular culture representations of women either remain within the boundaries of the Woman myth, or when the narratives do attempt to complicate or tear representations of women out of the myth, women are often merely multiplied along the tri-part structure of virgin, whore, mother. For example, the main character (Toni Collette) in the 2009-11 TV series *United States of Tara* has dissociative identity disorder (a.k.a. multiple personalities), but each of the four main identities is a caricature of the three categories – T is a drug-abusing, sex-addicted teenager, Alice is the epitome of the 1950s imaginary housewife, Tara is the modern mother and lover, and Buck is a drunkard, womanizing redneck. Buck may not seem like he fits into the category, but he provides the viewer with the lesbian sex fantasy in that he occupies a woman's body, and, paradoxically, he is an overt represen-tation of misogyny, which provides the viewer a phallic jouissance through guilt-enjoyment. Simply put, even when women purportedly are written to have more dimension than one of the three categories, the dimensions are often hyperbolic representations of the categories and provide the audience with the fantasy of them all at once.

Somewhat differently, Quentin Tarantino's 2007 *Death Proof* depicts the interaction of four women, all of whom occupy a metaphoric place of being the phallus. Zoë Bell (herself) and Kim (Tracie Thoms) play "gear head" stunt actors who are very confident and liberated in terms of self-perception and sexual encounters. Abernathy (Rosario Dawson) is in a relationship with a film director and will not have sex with him because she believes in the "good girl" romantic notion of commitment and marriage. Lee (Mary Elizabeth Winstead) plays a ditzy, naïve actor who wears her costume, a cheerleader's uniform, for the entire film. In a panoramic shot of the women's conversation over a meal at dinner, we begin to understand the problematic antagonism that occurs between women over their own phallic presence. Zoë and Kim, who are more like men because of their interest in all things gear related, treat Abernathy and Lee condescendingly. Abernathy, in turn, gangs up on Lee and tries to be more like Zoë and Kim. Lee, the most ditzy and girly of the four, barely has a place from which to speak for the duration of the film, and she becomes the trading commodity (read: trafficked). Zoë and Kim find a white 1970 Dodge Challenger, an explicit reference to the cult classic *Vanishing Point*, to test drive, and they trade Lee as collateral for the car. Abernathy, rather than staying with Lee, as two is often better than one when left with an ogling man, deliberately insinuates that Lee is a porn star and abandons her so that she can go be one of "the boys" too. On the car ride, Zoë takes the figurative position of the penis, or strap on, on the hood of the car that Kim embodies and controls (and now that I think of it, it could be a clitoris, instead). Abernathy looks on, desiringly from the rear. As they are attacked by Stuntman Mike (Kurt Russell), Kim shoots him; the only man in the film is penetrated by one of the women who we can read as a masculine representation, and they ultimately beat him to death. On the one hand, the fetish shots of their bodies – e.g., the long pans and zooms on Abernathy's feet and neck (often through Stuntman Mike's eyes), the view through Stuntman Mike's camera lens and the quick stills of the shots he takes of the four women, the cheerleading uniform – the denigrating way in which the women treat one another (and how Lee is never seen again), and the way in which they all come to stand in as and possess the phallus at varying moments fold each of them back into a metaphoric fantasy of Woman. On the other hand, Tarantino's film depicts feminine power and provides some other kind of jouissance for the viewer. The viewer is at once told to identify and enjoy the Woman as a kind of guilt-enjoyment while the female characters simultaneously subvert that enjoyment. Rather than the stereotypical horror flick tension building of fear for these women's impending demise because of their lack of common sense or female vulnerability, Tarantino's women – excepting Lee who, again, is an explicit, purposeful character installation that serves as a contrast to the others for a highlighting of masculinist enjoyment – are relatable; we can see ourselves and our friends in their characters. They are not dumb or vulnerable, and they toggle between the guilt-enjoyment of phallic jouissance, as we hear in their conversation about sex, their treatment of Lee, and the playing of ship's mast, and a refusal of the masculinist gaze upon that jouissance, as we see in their pursuit and bludgeoning of Stuntman Mike. Moreover, Stuntman Mike is the epitome of masculinist phallic desire: he is an old, washed up, out of work stuntman who is ridiculous in his desirous pursuit of younger women, which explains his perverse psychopathy. Stuntman Mike's supposed death at the end narratively points toward an eradication of the perverse, filmic gaze paradigm.

To return to the refiguring and disfiguring of naturalized syntax, the feminist focus on metaphorizing and remetaphorizing women and Woman perpetuates the erasure of writing about men and masculinity. More pointedly, it pushes to the background the argument that all subjects function as masculine subjects within masculinist discourse in that, as Freud claims, there is only one libido and it is masculine. At the nearest Imaginarized position, the "normal" subject desires masculine-ly, but I think that Freud's claim may be a bit short-sighted in that he only knows one libido: Lacan's entire 20th seminar, after all, is an inquiry to an *other* manifestation of the libidinal drive. My arguing that the masculine and the feminine are identificatory narrative manifestations of subject positions in discourse goes against Freud's libido theory in that the libido, as a drive riddled with anxiety, can manifest in various ways, but we only know of the masculine manifestation. The Buck character in *United States of Tara*, perhaps, is a hyper-representation of this masculine desire, so in that sense, the show may fail to write the feminine, but does write the masculine. Each of the four characters in *Death Proof* desire masculine-ly (phallic-ly) - some more blatantly than others, and all are boy crazy - want to stand in as the phallus for men. However, Stuntman Mike is a psychopath arguably because his Imaginary masculinity has failed him. When Kim shoots him, his Imaginary breaks down very quickly, and he begs for forgiveness before getting beaten to death. Of course, the extreme violence that he experiences just before dying is the very thing he fetishizes: he does not mind getting a little banged up, as we see in the hospital scene just before the transition to the film's second scenario, but this violent beating can be that destructive encounter with the Real, the literal shattering of what is often thought of as a figurative shattering, which occurs with an experience of jouissance.

Cornell reminds us, finding recourse in Lacan, that gendered subjectivity fails, is unfixed, and malleable: "The Lacanian story [...] demonstrates that women, as well as men, are masculine insofar as they enter the symbolic. Genderized subjectivity, as it is produced as a system, is produced imperfectly. Gender identity is only ever bounded by historically contingent circumstances" (63). The apparently always (already?) gendered subject is a lie in that every subject, given the terms we have to work with so far, embodies, is constituted by, both feminine and masculine properties and tendencies. Cornell assumes that the Symbolic is masculine. Whereas I suggest it is empty yet full of content that can be organized and constructed in various ways. Masculine only exists as a difference from feminine. Every subject functions contiguously as a set of signifiers. The default figuration just happens to be what we call the masculine, but it does not appear to be the paradigm (no matter what Freud and Cornell want). The masculine, rather, is perhaps the reactionary figuration to its fluid, syntactical alternative. Of course, to think of the masculine as a reaction is merely to place the feminine as the paradigm, and that is not what this project aims to do.

Irigaray conceptualizes figure and syntax as she argues against metaphorical figure(s) of Woman under the patriarchal lens and highlights the metonymic syntax of the feminine and woman's displacement within masculine discourse in order to show that women too are not impoverished.[15] The way in which Irigaray demonstrates, or performs, this feminine, I argue, is through the structure of her writing, as well as the turning of the content with which she engages.[16] In *Speculum* she goes to great pains to rewrite Freud from the book's first sentence, and she dedicates an entire section to the rewriting of Plato's "Cave." Her scholarship in *Speculum* is at one and the same time a refiguration of the metaphors that ground our culture and a performance of the hysteric's discourse in the "feminine" syntax. We see the same writing and discursive positioning in Kathy Acker's controversial novels where she "plagiarizes" literary theory and canonized authors and rewrites cultural classics like *Great Expectations* and *Don Quixote*. Irigaray and Acker, because of a need to catch the wider audience up to speed in terms of their anti-misogynistic, anti-patriarchal ideas, must use the texts that so strongly inform our cultural content. They must engage with these texts, argue with them, rewrite them to make apparent the problems inherent therein. They must use the master, approach the master's texts from the place of the hysteric. Irigaray and Acker, by introducing a new syntax for old language, begin to refigure old "identities" to show that they were just identifications all along. Their rewriting of the foundations of Western culture is exactly what must occur in order for us not to identify as impoverished metaphors or demand that identification from others.

In "An Ethics of Transsexual Difference: Luce Irigaray and the Place of Sexual Undecidability," Gayle Salamon turns to Irigaray's use of place in order to queer sexual difference: "Were that boundary [of the divide of sexual difference marked by male and female] not mapped onto the body in strictly determinative ways, we might be able to theorize sexual difference between women, between men, or between bodies and psyches who do not find easy home or place in either of these categories" (133). Salamon, in her close reading and interrogation of Irigaray's adaptation of Aristotle's philosophy of place, notices, as do I, Irigaray's consistent "collapse of the feminine and woman" and hopes to "coax those two categories apart" (136). Rather than parsing sexual difference morphologically, across bodies as substitutable, Salamon extracts the emphasis of place to allow for the parsing of sexual difference relationally. In focusing on the relationality of one body to or against another we avoid falling into the substitutions of any male for another or any part of a woman for Woman (137–38). Ultimately, she argues that if we can find a place for any body in its relation, then that body exists, and if there is no place, then what is imagined is impossible (139). Dean begins an endeavor similar to Salamon's by delineating the phallus within each of the psychic realms (Symbolic, Imaginary, Real) and re-emphasizing the Real in order to remind us that the unconscious does not "get" sexual difference (*Beyond* 82–89). He explains that "Whereas the uncon-scious endlessly proliferates meaning, the dimension of the real points to an impossibility of meaning, a fundamental resistance to sense," because, void of a signifier for sexual difference in the unconscious, "*sexual difference does not organize or determine sexual desire*" (87, emphasis in original). In thinking the body as a metonymic relation between psychic perception, corporeality, and the unconscious, then, we can begin to think, along with Salamon, Dean, et al., that there is a place, there are places, for contingent and indeterminate sexuated identifications.

Salamon emphasizes the boundaries of the body, the skin, and the unsubstitutability of bodies within space, which creates place in that boundaries are determined through the unsubstitutability. Following through with Lacan's claim that all sex is merely people masturbating in the same room, the vagina is substitutable by the mouth, or the anus, the hand, or an apple pie, and the penis is substitutable by, well, pretty much anything that will fit in any of those places. Even more, the physical body is, now more than ever, substitutable by the image (witness the proliferation of free internet porn and the subsequent addiction issue with it). Žižek uses an American beer commercial to illustrate this image substitution:

> Its first part stages the well-known fairy tale anecdote: a girl walks along a stream, sees a frog, takes it gently into her lap, kisses it, and of course, the ugly frog miraculously turns into a beautiful young man. However, the story isn't over yet: the young man casts a covetous glance at the girl, draws her towards himself, kisses her, and she turns into a bottle of beer the man triumphantly holds in his hand … For the woman, the point is that her love and affection (signaled by the kiss) turn a frog into a beautiful man, a full phallic presence (in Lacan's mathemes, Phi); for the man, it is to reduce the woman to a partial object, the cause of his desire (in Lacan's mathemes, the objet petit a). On account of this asymmetry the relationship is impos-sible: we have either a woman with the frog or a man with the bottle of beer; what we can never obtain is the natural couple of the beautiful woman and man.
>
>   ("Woman Is One of the Names-of-the-Father" n.p.)

Narratively, there is a redirection of pleasure and a re-inscribing of the body's sensors, its understanding of its limitations and capacities: if we can under-stand sexual pleasure normalized/localized to the genitals as a masculinist logic, then the redirecting of pleasure and re-inscribing of the body's inter and transsubjective stimulations have the potential to demand new narrative cat-egories of subjectivity. Salamon disagrees that "the most productive response to this [...] embodied difference is to close it up. Indeed, we might think 'corporeal surveying' as a method of apprehending not only the difference of the other, as Irigaray suggests, but also as a way of taking measure of the difference that inheres in my own flesh" (140). I would not go so far as to counter Lacan's claim that there is no such thing as the sexual relationship, because he means that it is an impossibility in terms of the discursive ways in which the masculine and feminine fail in "*nearness*," or to come in close proximity, in their relation. However, I would argue along with Dean and Salamon that we can redefine subject positions in ways that allow for a redefining of relations in general.[17] Salamon articulates this quite clearly as she addresses, in alignment with the same engagement I am trying to work through presently, the common critique of Irigaray's short-sightedness when it comes to sex and gender formations:

> For if we do not restrict our scope to the categories of male and female as they are most strictly conceived, and extend our consideration to the myriad ways in which gender is performed even within the category of, for example, femaleness, we can begin to discern differences, perhaps even difference itself. These are differences that are emphatically bodily, and undeniably material, even as they are also psychic, emotional, and relational differences.
>
> (142)

I hear an echo in this final sentence of the way in which I conceive of the body as material, psychic, relational. My main departure with Salamon's exploration is her focus on the function of gender performance for transsexual subject-ivity, whereas, even though I think that transsexuality is a very provocative and useful object for the study of sexuation, this project focuses more on discursive positionalities of the subject that the perceived body certainly influences, but only as one input to a multi-dynamic relation. Salamon peripherally touches on what I try to work through here in her discussion of the various ways in which queer practices and trans bodies can relate. The relationship between a trans man and straight woman is "that the difference between them is decidedly bodily and resolutely 'sexuate'," and "[r]ecognizing that movement is possible across the borders of male and female means that the bodily envelope cannot only be understood as the symbolic marker of the absolute otherness of sexual difference," but also "as a means of 'reclaiming the skin'" (Salamon 143).

Notes

1 Again, I am trying not to include specific arguments about transsexuality to this project as it will open up the floodgates of nuances and force me to begin com-pletely anew; however, the persistent global violence against trans women (even though this happens to transsexuals in general, e.g., Brandon Teena) is testament to the fact that this is an issue of "femininity" more so than isolated as violence against women. I suppose I can forward the claim at this point that femininity, from the

perspective of conservative, masculinist ignorance and fear, is enough to incite violent policing of norms.

2 For a compelling, Marxist reading of the Ciudad Juárez mass murders, see Melissa W. Wright's chapter "The Dialectics of Still Life: Murder, Women, and Disposability" in *Disposable Women and Other Myths of Global Capitalism*. Routledge, 2006, pp. 71–89.

3 I am not denying that these agendas and collectives become metaphors, and even metaphoric paradigms, but I want to focus here on the temporal moment of the event or act. This temporal focus is my attempt to try to suspend, for the purposes of analysis, the metonymic moment.

4 Of course this trinity metaphor of woman is a cross-cultural patriarchal phenomenon, not unique to *machismo*.

5 For a spatially themed, Marxist reading of *Mujeres de Negro* in their protest with *Ni Una Más!*, see Melissa W. Wright's "Paradoxes, Protests, and the Mujeres de Negro of Northern Mexico." *Gender, Place, and Culture: A Journal of Feminist Geography*, vol. 12, no. 3, 2005, pp. 277–92.

6 Fuss's chapter on Irigaray serves also as a literature review of Irigaray's critics. For a thorough literature review on the feminist and psychoanalytic criticism of Irigaray's supposed essentialism, see Fuss.

7 Tim Dean, following Lacan, distinguishes between the "feminine masquerade (appearing to be the phallus for the one who lacks it)" and the "masculine parade (appearing to have the phallus)," but notes that "Lacan insists that 'virile display in the human being itself seem[s] feminine' (*E* 291)" (*Beyond* 83). At the Imaginary level, which is where this masquerade occurs and is recognized, I see no reason to distinguish between one as masquerade and the other as parade. In upholding the idea of masquerade and always attributing it to the feminine (and most often women), we are only sustaining an idea of mysteriousness attributed to women and the feminine that patriarchy uses in order to claim false identities. As a New Orleanian, I cannot help but make an analogy here to Mardi Gras, where Krewe participants wear masks to parade, and, perhaps more pointedly, the Krewes were all male for the majority of Mardi Gras history. As I will discuss in the next chapter, Levi Bryant makes a similar point.

8 Jacques Rancière contends that an explicit display of power only displays that one is not in power. For an insightful exploration of Rancière's ideas on politics and power, see Žižek's "For a Leftist Appropriation of European Legacy," at www.lacan.com/zizek-leftist.htm, originally published in *Journal of Political Ideologies*, February 1998.

9 Dean argues that psychoanalysis challenges what he calls "business-as-usual" in gender studies, specifically in gender studies *a la* Butler as mimetic representations: "the concept of mimicry situates identification at the level of imaginary representations, excluding the real from consideration. [... .] Lacan's concept of the real can help us grasp that cross-gender identifications are motivated by something that cannot be seen or imagined – a place beyond sexual difference where gender would not be simply questioned or subverted but completely transcended" (*Beyond* 71–72).

10 In "Love and the Signifier," Lacan coins the neologism *par-être*, para-being, as a way to explain this always near miss: "It is in relation to the para-being that we must articulate what makes up for *(supple au)* [supplements] the sexual relationship qua non-existent. It is clear that, in everything that approaches it, language merely manifests [itself in] its inadequacy" (SXX 45).

11 Fuss errs on the syntactical placement between displacement with metonymy and condensation with metaphor.

12 Cf. Dean, *Beyond Sexuality*, 182–87; Grigg, *Lacan, Language, and Philosophy*, 156–69 for a discussion of metaphor's vehicle and tenor and ultimate linguistic function as ground, as well as the complicated relationship between metaphor and metonymy.

13 Entire bodies of feminist criticism across various disciplines focus on this disfigurement of women, and these critiques have become very common, so much so that perhaps posthumanism and cyborg studies could be considered an offshoot or consequence of it. Jean Kilbourne's *Killing Us Softly* lecture series is an example of how the feminist disfigurement strategy has become a mainstream commodity. Kilbourne, Jean, *Killing Us Softly: Advertising's Images of Women*. Margaret Lazarus Renner, director. Cambridge Documentary Films, Inc., 1979-2010.

14 The idea of Woman as "fuckee" is the underlying foundation of the categories of Woman I named above when talking about *machismo* but which are really categories of Woman under patriarchy generally. The rest of the quote for the *L Word's* Jenny Schecter, which I use as an epigraph to the previous quilting point but did not include, describes well Woman's experience in terms of the world's "fuckee":

> What I want is for you to write "fuck me" on your chest. Write it. Do it! And then I want you to walk out that door and I want you to walk down the street, and anybody that wants to fuck you, say, "Sure! Sure! No problem!" And when they do, you have to say, "Thank you very, very much." And make sure that you have a smile on your face. And then, you stupid fucking coward, you're gonna know what it feels like to be a woman.
>
> (2.11 2005)

15 In *Beyond Sexuality*, Dean adds figure and syntax to the metaphor and metonymy chains of association respectively (182).

> Paradigmatic → substitution → metaphor → similarity → condensation → figure
>
> Syntagmatic → combination → metonymy → contiguity → displacement → syntax

On his view, and in alignment with Lacan and Griggs, metaphor is posited as the impoverished trope, and metonymy is not seen as merely an impoverished metaphor (184–86).

16 I choose the word *turning* rather than, say, *transformation* here deliberately in order to evoke Lacan's turning of the discourse formulae, my later turning of the sexuation graph, and the emphasis on tropes. Her "turning" of the content with which she engages is at different times a response of the hysteric to the master's texts or an interrogation by the analyst.

17 Even though Dean argues that "relationality, as such, fails," he is nevertheless interested in the reorientation of relations.

Quilting point

The masculine symptom in *Brief Interviews with Hideous Men*

Poe's Queen illustrates the masculinist metaphor of Woman as that which signifies the King's and the public's Imaginary ideas of masculine legitimacy. The Woman metaphor repeats, but always with a remainder, with each of the letter's possessors, just as a signifying chain. This "symptomatic" interpretation, to use Žižek's term, of the Queen as metaphor is modernist in that it conveys the "ideological content" of hierarchical power roles and games; yet, Lacan's and subsequently my own reading of Poe's story that focuses on *la lettre*, which stands in for *objet a*, carries this over a century-and-a-half old narrative into the postmodern. Žižek distinguishes the postmodern as that which has "an obsession with the Thing [Freud's *das Ding*], with a foreign body within the social texture" (*Enjoy!* 140). David Foster Wallace's *Brief Interviews with Hideous Men* is ingeniously postmodern in that the "relationship with the Thing," that is, with the subject's and the other's sexual difference, "becomes *antagonistic*" (Žižek *Enjoy!* 141) while delivering seemingly modern, traditional masculinist perspectives on sexual difference. Žižek explains that the shift between modern and postmodern "theoretical antagonism" is that between "the axis of Imaginary-Symbolic to the axis of Symbolic-Real" to focus "on the traumatic Thing which resists symbolization (symbolic practices)" (141). Through laying bare the masculinist Imaginary against a silent Other, the Imaginary idea of Woman fades into the background. What comes to the fore is the affect (always anxiety) of the trauma of sexual difference, that which, recalling this project's introduction, Pluth defines as not an "answer or solution" to sexuality as such; rather, it is a "repetition and inscribing of that real impasse in a symbolic impasse, without its having any claim to being right or accurate" (Pluth 76).

The vignettes in Wallace's collection of fictional interviews unveil the masculinist perspective of Woman as metaphor in the modernist sense, while they simultaneously provide the reader, via the collection of vignettes, with a metonymical experience of the affect of sexual difference and the Thing that escapes symbolism. Each interviewee speaks of Woman – the repetition – but they are really speaking of their own trauma of sexual difference – the stain – and Woman stands in discursively as the symptom of the excess, that which escapes their frame. Each of the interviewees, whether consciously or not, thinks of and acts toward women as an other and as an object in order to cover over their own extimacy. Situated within the discourse formulae structure, the idea of Woman, for these "hideous men," is the metaphor product of their lack, the symptom of their *objet a*. Their discussions of women always revolve around the sex act, sometimes overtly and sometimes implicitly.

The interviewees, except for perhaps one, all speak from a masculinist discourse position, as the master, S_1. The structure of *Brief Interviews'* text are interviews only because of the number, date, and place ascribed to the interview as well as the not-too obtrusive but guiding "Q." that interrupts the men's monologues. This silent presence manages to account for the raw data of the interviewer and to represent ethically the research subjects' voices. But this format also illustrates how distanced the masculine subject is from the subject/object, and the Real Thing, in question. Ironically, the "feminine" subject position becomes that which props up the entire collection, and the reading experience becomes situated there. The heavy-handed way in which the "symptomatic reading" is unavoidable, which I discuss below through textual analysis, carries the reader into the postmodern, the reading experience as the other and with the sinthome: the masculinist narrative position becomes absurd and difficult to sustain, which provokes an ethical approach to the text.

The ways in which the interviewees relate their experiences with, and thoughts about, women often fit the "men are dogs" stereotype and show the hideousness of the traditional masculine subject. In "brief interview #30", for example, the interviewee confesses that he "always had this major dread of marrying some good-looking woman," who after having a child "blows her body out" and he still has "to have sex with her" (Wallace 27). Fortunately for him, he married this particular woman because she already had a child and so "she was pre-tested – the kid didn't blow her body out," so he knew "she'd be a good bet" (27). We get the unfettered version of the same focus in "brief interview #3", a conversation that the interview collector overhears between (presumably) two men, who are also (presumably) carpet salesmen. One of the men is telling the other about his sexual encounter with a distraught woman who he met as he was coming off a flight. She was abandoned by her lover, and he stepped in to offer solace in order to sleep with her. He sees her broken-hearted, on her hands and knees, "all bent over slapping and gouging at the product with the nails, bent over so you can you know just about see her tits," and he approaches her to "get a better shot of I have to tell you some pretty fucking incredible tits" (23). The man calls her the "girl with the tits" (23, 24, 27) throughout the anecdote and adds imaginative details about her preparing to meet her lover that resemble old 1940s boudoir-style burlesque shows where the performer often sits in front of a vanity in a bedroom setting and gets dressed, or undressed, to finally end the set with a brief and partially revealing dance: he imagines that she "gets her hair done up all big with spray like they do and dribbles perfume on her you know zones and all that business like the usual story and puts on her best pink jeans did I mention she's got on these pink jeans and heels that say fuck me in like myriads of major world languages" (24). He and his friend even refer to the lover as a "shitheel" (25), and they both admit that "Men mostly are shit" (26). In the end, the carpet salesman who tells the story also becomes a "shitheel" (27). The irony is not in the fact that the anecdote teller and the lover are both shitheels; rather, the irony is located in the way in which the anecdote functions as foreplay between the two carpet salesmen and there is no payoff, no climax. In telling the story to his friend, he is at one and the same time trying to legitimize his masculinity by his shitheel-ness and seducing his listener only to refuse him the happy ending. Reminiscent again of the old boudoir burlesque shows, his story ends with only a partial reveal – just enough information to get the audience going, but not enough to get the audience off. The teller simultaneously tries to legitimize his masculinity (read: heterosexuality) while seducing his male friend.

"Brief interview #3" provides a scenario that lends almost too easily to a feminist reading of the way in which men stereotypically think of women. The everyday feminist can read this transcription as, say, "see, men only see women as sex objects." This interview sets up a deceptive precedent: from this over-heard story, we think we are going to read a number of interviews similar to this one, that is, similar to the mainstream narrative that represents men as focused on sex as a visual and unemotional event and women as emotionally tied to the sex act. In the above two examples, both men focus on the woman's body and the way they can or cannot find enjoyment in its company. In the first example, even the mother must also always be a sex object, and in the second example the speaker thinks the "girl with the tits," in all of her affective display, is absurd for feeling anything because she is only a sex object.

But these brief glimpses into the masculine psyche also reveal the desire for the Other's desire, the failure of these men's masculinity, and the subject's lack mapped onto the idea of Woman. The subject in "brief interview #72" has put women, or Woman, at such a great remove that he speaks of them similarly to how a closeted bigot speaks of someone outside of her/his "identity" group: "Some of my best friends are women," he says and follows immediately with "I love to watch them move" (225). Almost in the same breath he attempts to claim women within his proximity and makes known the distance and fear he has of them. He proclaims their otherness, their object status for him. He both infantilizes them – "I love to hear them giggle, the different little sounds. The way you just can't keep them from shopping no matter what you do" (225–26) – and is fascinated by them – "I love how different they all are. I love how you can never understand them. [...] When it comes to women I'm helpless" (225–26). This talk of "love," though, makes his fear of the Other all the more apparent. Woman, who giggles and shops, enjoys in a way that is foreclosed for this interviewee. He wants to understand this enjoyment, but he cannot, and so he maps onto Woman, that is, his naïve and inexperienced idea of women, an infantile kind of *jouissance*. They enjoy without him, in spite of him, even. And he is perhaps not only afraid of this enjoyment, but also afraid of his desire for it. Just before the interview comes to an unexpected halt – "oh no not again behind you *look out!*" (226) – the detail he provides in terms of what else he loves about women – "bat their eyes or pout [...] Those teeny red bumps from shaving [...] little dainty unmentionables and special little womanly products at the store" (226) – imply an envy for what defines, for him, femininity and woman-ness, a femininity that he desires *to have and to be*, but cannot. In short, he desires the woman's body not for sex so much as for identificatory enjoyment. Yet, somewhere between masculine guilt – "some of my best friends are women" – and feminine shame of liking these small things too much – "those teeny red bumps" and "special little womanly products at the store" – he occupies a space between the master's and the hysteric's discourse. He tries to position himself as the S_1, the phallic subject in the dominant position, who speaks to S_2, the interviewer as subject of knowledge, in order to produce *objet a*, the object cause of masculinist desire, as we see in the stereotypical guilt statement that "some of [his] best friends are women." However, his repetition of the word "love," which he repeats ten times in the short span of a 186-word paragraph transcription, brings his position/status as (an) S_1 into question. "Love" here signifies an ingenuous twitch that fails, similarly to the Minister's queening, to repress (read: hide) discursively his lack of identification with masculinist scripts and desire for feminine identification. His sharing the details of the "teeny red bumps" and "womanly products" reveal too much attention paid to the art of femininity as object. Interviewee #72's focus on these details differs from Interviewee #3's (the "shitheel") Imaginary fantasy of hairspray and perfume application in that #3 relates the details of hairspray, perfume, and pink jeans to illustrate Woman as a prop for the masculinist story about his own prowess and virility. #72's hysterical symptom, his lack of surety in his placement as a "man," is much more apparent. The abrupt end of interview #72 – "oh no not again behind you *look out!*" – is that moment of the symptom as the materiality of the Real, the arrival of the letter. Although we do not know what occurs "again," we do know that it has occurred at least once before, that it has had a kind of traumatic effect on #72, and that it has a physical consequence ("*look out!*"). The symptomatic "love" he has for "all women" has not only discursive affective manifestations, but also physical ones.

In "brief interview #48," the interviewee shares his fetish of asking women if he can tie them up so that he can ultimately curl up next to them and cry, and he makes overtly significant the discursive element of his interactions with and about women. He divides women into two categories, hens and cocks, and it is impossible to tell by appearance into which category any woman falls, as "their response to [his] proposal," which determines them as one or the other, "depends on factors internal to them" (103). This detail is all too easily fit into the Lacanian categories of sexuation based on discourse rather than sexual difference or gender. He makes clear that he knows some of the women are not available to him as the phallus – that is, *to be the phallus* – for his fantasy because they are cocks, i.e., they *have* the phallus. He relates deliberately his memory of his mother with the fantasy that he plays out with these women. Moreover, he positions himself as speaker in the university discourse, S_2, grounded by the latent master, S_1. He delivers the fantasy scenario to the interviewer, *a*, as if he is a textbook teaching the correct information for how the fantasy is to be interpreted. His Freudian fantasy about his desire for his mother, and a phallic-mother at that, to provide "reassurance and affection" (110) is a mirror memory to his current sexual fetish. #48's mother, a "professional clinician, a psychiatric case-worker who administered tests and diagnostic exercises at a sanitarium" (111),[1] would often send him to his room while his fraternal twin sister would "enjoy unconfined freedom of movement about the house" (110). He has educated himself on some form of psychology – "Marchesani and van Slyke's theory of masochistic symbolism" (104); "*I cannot believe that this possibility is now originating from a point external to my consciousness*" (108); and he refers to the women as "subjects" where he corrects himself once the interviewer apparently questions him about it, saying, "I meant woman or young woman, not [f.f.] *subject* per se" (108) – and so deliberately connects the fantasy to this childhood experience with his mother, who, after keeping him in his room for a period of time would:

> open the door and embrace me warmly and blot my tears away with her sleeve and would claim that all was forgiven, all was well again. This flood of reassurance and nurture would once again seduce me into [f.f] *trusting* her and revering her and ceding emotional power to her, rendering me vulnerable to devastation all over again whenever she might choose to turn cold and look at me as if I were some sort of laboratory specimen she'd never inspected before. This cycle played itself out repeatedly throughout our childhood relation, I am afraid.
>
> (111)

The "[f.f] *hot* and *cold*" (110) that he perceives as his mother's "erratic" (110) temperament is clear, I think, in the above description.[2] What #48 describes could be nothing more than a mother putting her child in time-out and then taking him out and smoothing over the situation once he has served his time. His memory and assessment of these incidents are surely subjective, and I assume that he has repressed quite a bit of information due to lack of detail about his own actions that frame the memory.[3] We can begin to assume that #48 not only began to pursue and enjoy this game, but also that he replicates the game by playing both the mother and the child parts with the women. He makes clear that he shows the women no affection and that he sizes them up constantly, similarly to being "cold" and observing them as if they are new "laboratory specimen," until the end of the third date when he offers the proposal to seek the "flood of reassurance and nurture." His mother is both cock and hen, and in his fantasy he plays cock and looks for his hen.

There is only room for one cock in his fantasy. He determines their hen or cock status by reading metonymically both their body "language" and words in order to place them into his binary metaphor. In order to determine whether or not a woman is a hen or a cock, he toggles back and forth between the ways a woman uses words and her body; he pieces together a collection of signifiers and arranges them into a chain that means either hen or cock. The "true cocks," #48 explains,

> will yield the briefest of these shocked pauses. They will smile politely, or even laugh, and then will decline the proposal in very direct and forthright terms. No harm, no foul [Laughter.] No pun intended – [f.f.] *cock, foul.* These subjects' internal psychological maps have ample room for the possibility of being tied up, and they freely consider it, and freely reject it. They are simply not interested. I have no problem with this, with discovering I've mistaken a cock for a hen.
>
> (108)

Two aspects seem to determine that a woman is a cock: she speaks directly and is open to (read: has a sense of self-possession) possibilities. He even speaks of these women as "subjects." He understands them not as the laboratory object of his fantasy anymore, and, arguably, not as a woman anymore either. They are "chicken-sexed" as not-women, as unavailable to his fantasy of Woman/hen. He has in fact made a mistake in his discursive comprehension of the sexual relationship, as these cocks have made it to his ottoman on the third date. He read their ever-so-important-and-revealing body language incorrectly, or, really, body language, like all language, is fluid, non-absolute, and dips below the bar to mean *as if* differently than what it is. Moreover, regardless of the success or failure of his meticulous scrutiny, he assumes that these women, cock or hen, will fit into one of his created categories, that these women can and will be a metaphor of his reality. He hopes that the letter, *as he perceives it*, will arrive at its destination; that is, the hen will play along so that he can have a moment of guilt-enjoyment that ultimately, as the fantasy goes, breaks down. His hens are less sure of themselves, vulnerable. Even though he proclaims that his proposal and the game that leads up to it is not about "forcing or cajoling or persuading anyone against her will," (108) like the "shitheel," he has a target, an agenda, and sets up the scenario to accomplish it. How is the third date plan, the ottoman scenario, and the proposal not a persuasion or a cajoling? In his very meticulously planned fantasy, from the first date he tries to occupy the role of the cock, a personal interpretation of his phallic mother, as he only lets out the slightest hint of "hot" toward these women on each of the three dates, never touching or kissing them, but maintaining niceties to continue the plan. He takes great pains to be in control and stay in control in order for his fantasy to play out until the very last part; in the end, he does not have to be the cock anymore, does not have to force the fantasy. In the end, he tries *to turn* his guilt-enjoyment, but he is left only to repeat it. And enjoyment, as Žižek clarifies, is what this tension is all about: "The ultimate variation on the theme of a letter that always arrives at its destination reads therefore: 'you can never get rid of the stain of enjoyment' – the very gesture of renouncing enjoyment produces inevitably a surplus enjoyment […] the 'object small a'" (*Enjoy!* 26). At first blush, one may read the hens as his *objet a*, but upon a closer look, his *objet a* is the fantasy, the culmination of his fantasy labor, and the hens are merely a vehicle therein.

In reading the collected volume, the reader slowly pieces together metonymically a broader portrait of the masculinist idea of Woman and the way in which that idea spotlights the irony of the interviewees' masculinist identity/identification. Each of interviews is not about the sexual relationship and not about women, but about the "hideous" men and their preoccupations with their failure to have the phallus, as well as the failure of sexual difference, that thing that tries to bridge the gap between "sex and sense." The interviewees' inability to see women not as Woman, not as the Other, but as a satellite to their own fantasy and desire points out the irony of their symptom as affective manifestations of this anxiety over sexual difference.

Somewhat differently, in "brief interview #42," a man shares the detailed story of his father's career as a bathroom attendant at a "top rated historic hotel," (Wallace 86) and after a lengthy derogatory description of the hideous White men who occupied the stalls, he turned on not only his father's work, but also his father. Interviewee #42 could not reconcile his father's shitty career and the love his father must have had for his family to do the work. At the time of the interview, #42 had not seen or spoken to his father in almost 20 years (89), and since his father's uniform was all white, he "wear[s] nothing white. Not one white thing" (90) to separate himself from a loving father and the home in which he grew up. #42's father, arguably, is the epitome of love's absurdity, and #42 rejects his father and the absurdity of love.

#42, in his refusal to love, embodies a desire for guilt-enjoyment: he wants to be seen, to be a part of the larger ideological content, to be a part of the patriarchal/masculinist *hegemony of guilt*, to *have* the phallus. In order to join these ranks, he must refuse his father, the "anal father," to sustain an Imaginary-Symbolic subject position that fits into the master's discourse. In "Phallophany of the Anal Father," Žižek explains that this anal father "is the subject's double who accompanies him like a shadow and gives body to a certain surplus, to what is 'in the subject more than subject himself'" (*Enjoy!* 143). Just as #42 has not seen or spoken to his father in almost 20 years, the "subject must renounce, sacrifice even" this anal father "in order to start to live as a 'normal' member of the community" (143). Different from the Name of the Father that serves to provide an Imaginary "semblance of the sexual relationship" (143), the anal father is a "stumbling block" to this Imaginary "normalcy." #42 chooses the desire of the Other in the form of phallic desire, or, rather, he wants to have the phallus, the thing he perceives his father as lacking. He cannot come to terms with the obscenity of his father's occupation in its continuous close encounters with the fundament of the body, the real effect of the body's surplus. For him, this is a sacrifice of dignity, an inferior position on the margins of the master's discourse, which bars access to phallic *jouissance*. Ironically, though, Lacan locates morality in this anality. "The anal level," Lacan explains, "is the locus of metaphor – one object for another, give the faeces in place of the phallus. [...] the anal drive is the domain of oblativity, of the gift. Where one is caught short, where one cannot, as a result of the lack, give what is to be given" (Lacan SXI 104). In his renunciation of his real father, who he perceives to be the anal father, he hides from himself, or perhaps guards against, a fundamental truth of himself.

Part of his father's job required him, dressed in all white, to be unseen, invisible: "In the sonic center [...] In the crafted space between the end of the sinks and the start of the stalls. The space designed for him to stand. The vortex. Just outside the long mirror's frame" (Wallace 88), and "His task is to stand there as if he were not there. Not really. There's a trick to it. A special nothing you look at [...] Being there and yet not there" (90). In this silent and invisible occupational position, #42's father illustrates Lacan's gaze in the L schema. He sees that "you can never see me at the point from which I gaze at you." Yet, he recognizes his father in this position as shameful and as a horrifying double, because he sees the possibility of his own reality – and a persistence of the Real – in his father. He refuses his father in order to shy away from the horror of the Real: "As a rule, one focuses on the horror of being the object of some invisible, unfathomable, panoptical gaze," i.e., the big Other as *out there*, "yet it is a far more unbearable experience to find oneself at this very point of a pure gaze" (Žižek *Enjoy!* 145).

The relation between this "pure gaze," as Žižek calls it, and desire is more complicated than just a shying away in horror. Lacan explains that "the relation between the gaze and what one wishes to see involves a lure. The subject is presented as other than he is, and what one shows him is not what he wishes to see" (SXI 104). Our glimpse into the silent interviewer/researcher of the interview collection in "brief interview #46," when the interviewee warns the interviewer "to be careful of taking a knee-jerk attitude about violence and degradation in the case of women also" (Wallace 116) in order to argue that the devastating violence a woman may endure can essentially make her a better person, or, at least, know herself more securely. Thanks to #46, "Q." is not just a passive data collector; rather, he reveals her as performing a biased panoptic gaze, which he returns to her in an inverted form that she may not wish to see. We cannot know what the interviewer thinks or feels about this accusation upon her character or #46's ultimate claim about trauma, but we can assume there is a reason why #46 would so passionately assault her character. This assault places the silent "Q." within a canonized feminism born out of both second wave, white feminist hegemony and the stereotypes of feminism proliferated by patriarchal discourse as a way to combat it. In this way, "Q." is in the position of the master's discourse as S_1 via the university feminist discourse. Simply put, "Q." is not queer, but a conservative feminist who demands the recognition of women as subjects, but also paradoxically victimizes women's subject position.

#46 suggests that to know oneself as a thing, to be an object to oneself is a powerful knowledge, one that makes possible what, prior to that ability, seemed impossible: "What if I told you she could because she's had this happen and she totally knows it's possible to be just a thing [...] that every minute from then on minute by minute if you want you can *choose* to be more if you want, you can *choose* to be a human being and have it *mean* something?" (122–23, emphasis in original). The interviewer is called out as not so much discriminating against men, but more so for the irony of not considering that anyone can be the sufferer of such violence and the various ways in which the victim may adjust to the experience.

> what if I said it happened to me? Would that make a difference? You that are all full of knee-jerk politics about your ideas about victims? Does it have to be a woman? You think, maybe you think you can imagine it better if it was a woman because her external props look more like yours so it's easier to see her as a human being that's being violated so if it was somebody with a dick and no tits it wouldn't' be as real as you? […] What if I did it to you? Right here? Raped you with a bottle? Do you think it'd make any difference? Why? What are you? How do you know? You don't know shit.
>
> (124)

Here we have the gaze hysterically turning on "Q." as he asks, "What are you? How do you know? You don't know shit." Instead of asking the fundamental hysterical question herself, the interviewee does it to her. To boil what she presumes her knowledge to be down to nothing – that she doesn't even know the most elemental thing, shit – jerks her out of her comfortable zone of the other in the master's discourse. Having a "dick and no tits," the marks on the body that matter little, mean "shit" at the level of trauma. The irony here, which comes across well in the film version of *Brief Interviews*, is that the interviewer is so saturated in her "knee-jerk" feminist assumptions and desires that she forecloses two possibilities – the love of the self and the manifestation of ethical affect from a hideous act. In this regard, the interviewer/researcher shares a level of hideousness with the men who agree to participate in her project. Ideally, she recognizes at this moment how definitively masculine her consciousness is, the way in which she foreclosed possibility to this interviewee's claim, the unethical approach she may be taking with her collection of hideous men.

On the other hand, however, we should not take #46's accusations and attack on the interviewer at face value. As I have intermittently insinuated throughout this analysis, #46 is suddenly trying to articulate a personal experience of feminine subjectivity. He implies that it was him who experienced the rape, or has, at the very least, become intimate by proxy with the trauma of such violence. In accusing the interviewer that she does not "know shit," he assumes, as hysteric's do to their chosen master, that she finds guilt-enjoyment in her exemption from the other's shame. Because we can trust, from the apparent completeness of the other interviews, that this interview is transcribed in full, there is no evidence that #46 sees the interviewer as a comrade, a fellow feminine subject; rather, in his (naïve) attempt at feminine subject understanding or experience, he speaks to her – a life-long female who has likely been made into various objects of masculinist desire quite often – as if she has no knowledge of feminine subjectivity, as if she cannot understand that men can also embody shame.

Yet, the interview project is specifically about *hideous* men, not men in general. In comparison to #72's feminine slippages and the interruption that points to his own shame, #46's outward assumptions about masculinity and inadequacies at feminine shame place him into the hideous category. The interviewer takes his hysterical accusations silently, both performing and refusing simultaneously the masculine subject for this interviewee. She does not confirm nor correct his attack. In doing so, she both allows us to see his hideousness as well as help him along the hysterical path to (hopefully) an ethical subject position in relation to other subjects. The bottom line here is that #46 has encountered a disruption or invalidation of his masculine subject position, and he is downright angry about this traumatic loss: we see the hideousness of the assumption of masculine privilege, of guilt-enjoyment, through the shame of losing it. In this way, the subject undergoes another castration, one that severs traumatically the hegemonic security of one's place as masculine subject.

Of course, we never hear from the interviewer; we never see an analysis of the data; rather, we only get a compilation of seemingly unorganized interviews, like loose sheets of transcriptions found by someone else, and many of the interviews are missing – not only are they out of order, but they are not all there. Nevertheless, the laying bare of this masculinist narrative, the way in which the data lends itself to us, the readers of the data, allows for the idea I am forwarding of discursive possibility to occur. The discursive evidence of the metonymical ways in which we create metaphors of sexuation becomes even more absurd as we sift through the data. Our relationship to the postmodern Thing (*a la* Žižek) remains antagonistic, but we cannot necessarily "disown" (Žižek *Enjoy!* 141) it; rather, the hideousness revealed in that which is uncannily present (read: ironically and paradoxically central) with all the interviewees and the researcher herself is "a particular traumatic kernel" where "various universals […] function as a series of specific, ultimately failed attempts to symbolize […] and thus 'neutralize' the traumatic core of the Real" (141). The hysteric core of each of these subjects becomes apparent in their symptom, in their attempt to situate themselves within the absurdity of sexual difference.

Notes

1 He describes his father as "kindly but repressed and somewhat castrated" (111).
2 The "[f.f.]" stands for "finger flexion," or what we popularly know as scare quotes or rabbit ears when people use the double-finger movement in the air to imply an emphasis on a word or phrase. Interviewee #48 uses finger flexions in almost every other sentence he speaks, and this is one of the rare moments we see the interviewer, as she comments on how annoying it is.
3 Chris Kocela was kind to point out to me that "passive-aggressive mothering is such an overwhelming focus of all Wallace's writing that, by this point, [he is] not willing to abstract the portrayal of woman in this case from Wallace's deeply troubled depiction of mothers and motherhood throughout his work." Clearly, this comment is absolutely correct; however, I want this reading to also take into account the unreliability of the narrator, as well as his complicated, discursive fantasy structure of sexual difference.

6   Jouissance and ethical extimacy

*Assuredly, what appears on bodies in the enigmatic form of sexual characteristics –
which are merely secondary – makes sexed beings. No doubt. But being is the
jouissance of the body as such, that is, as asexual, because what is known as sexual
jouissance is marked and dominated by the impossibility of establishing as such,
anywhere in the enunciable, the sole One that interests us, the One of the relation
"sexual relation."*

Lacan, SXX, 6–7

[W]oman is not a fixed reality, but her body is a place for her to pursue possibilities.
Elizabeth Wright, *Lacan and Postfeminism*, 53

The monstrous ~~Woman~~: symbolic failure in *Antichrist*

Lars von Trier's 2009 *Antichrist* is the story of a married couple, He (Willem
Defoe) and She (Charlotte Gainsbourg), whose son falls out of a window and
dies while they make love in the next room. He, an established psychologist,
decides to treat She, a stay-at-home mother writing her thesis, as she becomes
more and more traumatized from the loss of her son. Her discipline is not clearly
stated, only her subject matter, which we find out in the narrative's climax is
gynocide/femicide. After a period of treatment at home, He decides to move
them to their cabin deep in the woods, which they call Eden. Once at Eden,
He employs various psychological strategies to cure his wife of her trauma and
symptoms. He eventually finds She's thesis work on gynocide, which shows
evidence of serious psychosis. The film turns from drama to horror when She
attacks He during sex, mutilates his genitals, and impales his leg; he makes an
escape attempt, she monstrously pursues him, catches him and returns to the
cabin, castrates herself, and he strangles her to death. The film ends with He
presumably burning She on a pyre and walking out of Eden dishevelled and
alone. As He leaves the woods, a mass of what seem to be apparitions of women
dressed in white with blurred faces rush past him and He pauses seemingly
reflectively.

Building up to the film's climax, She asks He upon waking, "Did you have good sleep?" He replies, "I've just been having a lot of crazy dreams." She says snarkily, "Dreams are of no interest in modern psychology. Freud is dead, isn't he?" He agrees but does not seem to detect her sarcastic tone or to reflect upon the exchange; rather, he just accepts the textbook demand that Freud not enter his consideration. This brief dialogue summates his approach to her both as husband and therapist. If we juxtapose Freud's talking cure approach to that of He's, which consists mainly of games and exercises, She has little to no voice in her own healing process. Toward the end of the film, He even goes so far as to lecture her on the history of women's suffering, which is her thesis topic, and then to conclude his lecture saying, "You don't have to understand me. Just trust me." He infantilizes She and assumes father-knows-best, the subject-who-knows approach. This textbook approach, as we see from He's practice, is a master discourse that approaches the female subject from a traditional masculinist narrative of the feminine. He only recognizes She as the metaphor of Woman and feminine subjectivity defined within a paternalistic Symbolic, which fails consistently in his attempts to comprehend, pathologize, and cure her after their son's death. The layers of contradiction and impossible relation within the myth of Woman as metaphor in which He categorizes her will inevitably become monstrous discursively, psychically, and materially. He's failure both as husband and therapist to identify and understand She as a subject, rather than as Woman, and She's progressive disintegration as subject/object within the Symbolic are connected directly to the inevitable failure of myth in Imaginary-Symbolic structures; that is, the inevitability of the Real's materiality and the inherent extimacy of the subject.

Language is material, and "words themselves can suffer symbolic lesions" (*Écrits* 248): in fact, we can only know the Real though indices that mark a moment (either of negativity or time) between it and the Symbolic (255). In *The Excessive Subject: A New Theory of Social Change*, Molly Anne Rothenberg's reading of the significance of extimacy for purposes of social change is salient to how She is monstrous both because of, and in spite of, this extimate causality. Rothenberg explains that "social relations depend upon retroversive signification," (10) which means that subjects always mean to other subjects informed by other established meanings after the fact of signifying. In this sense, it is extimate causality that generates every subject, but this always "leaves a remainder or indeterminacy" that is an "unspecifiable excess within the social field" (10). This indeterminate excess both within, as part of the interiority of the subject, and without, as part of the social field, is both how we have meaning and also what blocks meaning of, and for, us (10). It is this indeterminate excess of She as subject that makes her monstrous to herself, to her husband/therapist, and to us. She cannot embody the myth of Woman as metaphor, which at first she mourns, but later refuses. He's attempt to signify She retroversively within his Symbolic structures fail because it is her indeterminate excess that has surfaced, which both fascinates and horrifies him; to encounter this excess on the surface is monstrous because the subject, who is only a subject as signifier to another signifier, has no recognizable signifying index for itself or the other.

What is most horrifying both for He and She is that Woman does not exist. She begins to understand this, but He refuses to do so and continues to hold on to the myth of Woman as metaphor. He needs to feel safe in his own narrative identifications, so He silences and erases She literally through strangulation in order to sustain them. In merging Lacan's claim that "Woman can only be written with a bar through it" (SXX 72) and "is the only [signifier] that cannot signify anything" (73) with the understanding that all subjects embody inde-terminate excess, She embodies the queer monster through the demand of ~~Woman~~, i.e., through the excessive subject, which opens up both the terrifying inconsistency of the Symbolic, as well as queer possibilities in the social field. Woman does not exist, according to Lacan, because Woman is a myth. This metaphoric structure is the fundamental foundation of the Symbolic Law as we know it.

Starting out as a hysteric monster and then shifting into the psychotic mon-ster, like the Lacanian Real knows nothing of its lack, I think that *Antichrist's* She gradually comes quite close to a psychic and bodily space without lack. In fact, it is in the Symbolic, as mother and wife, that she is overwhelmed with literal lack – He is always distant, and She loses her son. Perhaps, what is most compelling about She as monstrous is that She is not masked in the way in which the horror genre typically does so. At the film's outset, She is very real to us as a grieving Woman. (The film depicts her as a grieving Woman wholly as mother and not as a complexly suffering subject.) But we come to realize that mask is She as Woman, which is our interpretation both/and perception of what traditional narrative expects from us. Once we recognize She as ~~Woman~~, we understand the horror, the monstrous, first as a hysteric and then as a psych-otic disruption of the Symbolic, as an interpretive encounter with the Real. She first embodies the abject through a refusal to perform as Woman; She forces the viewer into the abject by this refusal; She shows us the horror of the Symbolic's failure, but She also makes us all too aware of the oppression mapped onto Woman in the patriarchal structure and the necessity of her disruptive act.

The film's "Prologue," when She and He make love as their son, Nic, falls from an open window, shows the first sign of a lapse in the Symbolic, but we do not know we are looking between the Symbolic limit's perforations upon a first viewing: as Nic climbs out of his crib, we see his shoes placed inverted and his feet turned outward. In "chapter 2: Pain," He looks at a couple of Polaroids of Nic sitting with his feet turned out in the photo's foreground, but neither He nor we know how to read this. Once He reads the autopsy report and finds out about the deformity, He finally sees the oddity in the photos. When He tells She about the autopsy and shows her the photos she clearly does not rec-ognize that she has done this either. He, She, and we all discover this together. Something as simple as placing one's shoes on the correct feet has escaped everyone involved: shoes are made quite symbolically in that they match up shapes, one of the earliest symbols we learn – and learn by way of how it affects our body – as children. Prior to the film's temporal framing, She is already partly outside of the Symbolic in that she cannot recognize this simple disruption of reading rudimentary signs; He is also absent from playing his part in the Symbolic and Imaginary because he does not recognize that this lapse in signification is right in front of his eyes, presumably, every day. He fails to embody the Law because he assumes himself as subject-who-knows, as well as assumes that She succeeds to embody mother/Woman. Once He decides that they need to move to Eden – which not only is both a metaphor of the return to a mythical paradise governed by the Law-of-the-Father and the prohibition of knowledge *par excellence*, but also the materiality of the Real – Symbolic security begins to break down both materially and psychically. The Symbolic fails He at every turn – animals as living death, ticks on his hand, and his refusal to hear She's realization about the death drive apparent in nature that she articulates in her story of the acorns.

There is an excess bubbling up in her materiality that he cannot comprehend because it is an excess that does not register in the Symbolic. There is no language for this excess. He has no way of interpreting it/her. In the early stages of her therapy under He's direction, she says, "Perhaps I'm not supposed to talk about these things" when discussing how she feels about him. He replies, "There's nothing you can't talk about." Recalling Freud's talking cure, this exchange is significant: with the usage of *perhaps* and *supposed to*, She recognizes her expected role as Woman, but also positions herself as hysteric – the subject position in discourse that questions the master's position. He's response is one of negation. He could have just as habitually responded with "you can talk about anything," but he did not; instead, his response reads more as "you can't talk about nothing" both/and "there exists a nothing that you can't talk about" and, ultimately, perhaps, "you talk about nothing." In other words, her therapist does not want her to talk. Similar to his "just trust me" and his therapeutic doctrine that exposure is "the only thing that really works. Everything else is just talk," He has no interest in considering She as anything outside of his own fantasy, and his goal is to place her back within that fantasy. And when language is what defines us as people, and we are prohibited from access to it, no doubt the monstrous appears.

On the way to Eden, He and She are on the train, which I cannot help but link to Lacan's siblings on the train that exemplify sexual difference. Yet, what occurs between He and She is, again, significant: even though dreams have no place in modern psychology, He constructs (and conducts) her dreams through a hypnosis exercise. He commands her dreams instead of faces them, and once She begins to enter the Real, he cuts her off, wakes her up, and imparts a lesson of "mind over matter." The separation of matter and mind brings the monstrous to the fore. The forcible covering of She as subject's matter with the Other's mind always fails in Symbolic constructs. Her most horrific, monstrous acts, the rape and genital mutilation of He and her own clitorectomy, are a material performance, perhaps an almost necessary physical violation of the matter which is most fundamental to signification for the mind in the Symbolic structure by which He abides and within which She is prohibited to mean agentially. As monster, She must perform the cut that makes Symbolic failure apparent; *the horrifying cut toward jouissance that answers Symbolic castration.*

She's physical collapse at the beginning of "chapter 1: Grief" also marks the psychic collapse of the Symbolic for her, as there is nothing holding her to it as Woman anymore. He diagnoses her state as grief over the loss of her child. However, he is not accurate: She is using the grief just like she used Nic as a Symbolic anchor. Grief, as a chapter title, is He's perspective, not hers. He reads it as a symptom of loss, but it is really a symptom of overall prohibition as agential subject. She's inability (and unwillingness) to articulate her trauma coupled with her gynocide research mark indices of presences of absences in the Symbolic. He's attachment to the fantasy of She as Woman juxtaposed to her excess in the Symbolic (e.g., their son's deformed feet) and her self-castration mark the Real materially through her extimacy as un-gendered monster.

Antichrist builds on the horror genre, what Daniel Vilensky terms "cineliminal" (n.p.). For Vilensky, *Antichrist* "is an 'exception film' which, though using elements from a range of genres, deals with a different form of narrative, which might be called a cinema of the border line, an invocation of the liminal, of a process of becoming" (n.p.). These films "are centered on the thematic of the question: what is it to be human?" (n.p.). *Antichrist* also falls in the postmodern horror genre, but it does so hysterically in that both characters are monstrous, rather than just one monster who threatens the other normal person. Jody Keisner summarizes that postmodern horror "relies on the man/monster who already threatens an already violent and untrustworthy social order [...] does away with binary logic by blurring the distinctions between good and evil," and "resists closure, with the man/monster rising from the dead/undead or the protagonists' systemic deaths" (412). She, burdened by the violence of the patriarchal structure in her stay-at-home motherhood, unfinished thesis, absent successful husband life, becomes a violent monster who threatens that structure. As we see the inequities in He and She's relationship, we begin both to empathize with She and understand her psychic break, as well as He's both demanding to and failing to succeed in caring for her; there is no way to distinguish clearly a good and evil between the two characters.

Antichrist's He abandons sound logic to hold onto his Symbolic-Imaginary ego and to justify killing She. Finally, only one of the monsters dies, and the other rises from beside her pyre leaving Eden, but the remainder of ~~Woman~~ lingers there in the aphanisis of women who He sees as he turns back to look once more. *Antichrist* forces the audience to face the horrific unveiling of ~~Woman~~. Amber Jacobs, responding to Mark Fisher in their conversational essay "Debating Black Swan: Gender and Horror," asks:

> there must be many thousands of films that could qualify as an "Irigarayan *horror*." Is there something about the horror genre which structurally prevents it from having a sense of a beyond? Wouldn't it be so much more

interesting to imagine an *Irigarayan* horror, where the source of horror would not lie in the body of the hollow female subject or her "distanceless proximity" (as Irigaray calls it) to her abject mother – but in what truly threatens the achievement of her subjectivity?

(Jacobs and Fisher 62, emphasis in the original)

"Irigarayan *horror,*" Fisher explains, is the projection of "Irigaray's negative images of female subjectivity under patriarchy but without laying open any possibility of an alternative" (61). Woman will continue to be monstrous until it is no longer a hysteric concept; that is, until it is part of the Symbolic and no longer a fear as index of the Real's materiality. Yet, *Antichrist*'s She is both a strong example of the ways in which the phallus as master signifier is replaced by the empty signifier (or *point de capiton*, as the S_1 is and will always be already filled with something), and is a cautionary tale of the ways in which S_1 as empty signifier can go awry from a lack of Symbolic and Imaginary support for whatever the subject's desire is that turns into a desperate demand.

Woman and extimacy

Whenever the Woman question arises, the interrogation is not really asking what does Woman want, but what is Woman enjoying that the questioner does not know. (Nevermind for now that, as I pointed out earlier, the question is about *a woman*, singular, not all women generalized as Woman.) Parveen Adams, in "The Art of Analysis: Mary Kelly's *Interim,*" asks of this question, "What does the question want with us? Who does the question want us to be? How does the question want us to answer? What relation to truth does the question demand of us? […] There isn't one world in which the question is posed" (72). Woman, for the masculine subject, enjoys something outside of his purview, but he cannot provide it, have access to it, and her enjoyment is often unrecognizable as such to him. (I must complicate this by also arguing that most if not all subjects are, functionally, most often masculine subjects and engaged with phallic jouissance.) The enjoyment assumed is the impetus for so much political, social, domestic, and personal oppression. What is Sonia Johnson enjoying? Why would Sonia Johnson be considered a dangerous woman? What is the threat of these women's separatist communities? What has *Antichrist*'s She accessed? Why must She be "fixed" according to the masculinist pathology and its methods?

Paul Verhaeghe succinctly describes Lacan's concept of jouissance as that which "indicates the limit between a pleasure arising from the drive that can be controlled and one that cannot, thus threatening us (in our imagination) with the loss of our sense of identity" (13 fn 4). The threat that subjects like Sonia Johnson and She pose is one of phallic jouissance disruption. Johnson, who is asexual and does not live in the world of men, enjoys, and she enjoys without sex, without thinking like a man, and without being defined by what men want from women. Von Trier's She did not enjoy being a Woman, as his depiction of her unconscious foot binding of her son and her obsessive demands for sex indicate. Phallic jouissance is acceptable, expected, institutionalized, but the presence of another jouissance, and an active participation in it, threatens to dislodge the stable identity of the phallic subject and the social system that provides it with identificatory signifiers. If there are subjects, specifically women, who do not function discursively in relation to the master signifier, or, at the very least push up against it, then that means the discursive positions that prop up the dominant social structure are not necessary, are not the Truth.

In this making obtuse the hegemonic demands upon the body, the hysteric serves perhaps the most significant discursive role in transsubjective relations. Žižek warns us to avoid the two typical ways to understand the hysteric's importance, both of which deflate her position. The first is exactly what He does to She: "the dismissive treatment of the (feminine) hysterical subject as a confused babbler unable to confront reality." The second is "the false elevation of hysteria to a protest, through woman's body language, against male domination" ("Woman Is One of the Names-of-the-Father" n.p.). Rather, he argues, "Hysteria has to be comprehended in the complexity of its strategy as a radically ambiguous protest against Master's interpolation which simultaneously bears witness to the fact that the hysterical subject needs a Master" (n.p.). In other words, the hysteric, the subject in hysteria, serves as one of the vehicles that makes the subject in language's sedimentation impossible. The hysteric, speaking as $, pokes so as to lay bare (unconsciously as *objet a*, as lack – perhaps, as privation) Symbolic possibility through the interrogation of the Imaginary content that fills it.

Returning to Rothenberg's "excessive" or "Möbius" subject, this is one of various ways that scholars are beginning to rethink subject identifications, positions, and relations, a thinking beyond that is made possible by the hysteric's interrogation. The excessive or Möbius subject is "*already* a function of otherness – a subject of extimacy – that an identification with an other can help sustain the conditions of existence for the subject. The subject seeks to maintain the interior exteriority that is the ground of its existence in the first place" (Rothenberg 199 fn 10). The formulation of the Möbius subject is founded on the Lacanian idea that all subjects are subjects of extimacy. I explained earlier that extimacy is the grounding of the alterity of the Other in a nonphallic jouissance, a jouissance that has no signifier. More specifically, extimacy, "invokes that peculiar blend of being both inaccessible and intimate, but also stresses the Thing's ambiguous position with regard to in- and outside," and the "real Thing of the drive is jouissance" (Libbrecht 156). The Thing, in Lacan's reading of Freud, is what "human experience is organized around" (156). Its "paradoxical nature is that it never existed as human experience, but was installed retroactively," meaning that which human experience must exclude to become *human* experience, as we find in the incest prohibition that "bars access to an object that was never available in the first place" (156). The social field, comprised of subjects driven by their extimacy, is characterized by the excesses exuding from the subject and by the transsubjective relations between subjects, what Rothenberg terms extimate causality.

[S]ocial relations depend upon retroversive signification, which is one way of saying that the social dimension of subjectivity is irremediably *excessive*. Extimate causality names the operation that gives us social identities, properties, and relationships. In producing the social subject, extimate causality also leaves a remainder or indeterminacy, so that every subject is an "excessive" subject. [...] the "Möbius subject" because the topology of the Möbius band (with its apparently impossible configuration of two sides that turn out to be the same) provides a convenient model for understanding how, at every point in the social field, an irreducible excess attends social relations.

(10)

The way in which social relations, the "specific modes of relationality" within the social field "make different properties" of those who comprise the social field "*signify* differently" across relations and subsequent interpretations of those relations, and "these varying signifying modes articulate differentially with one another" (17, emphasis in original). The social field, despite hegemonic desire for stability, refuses sedimentation. These differential relations, which are unpredictable and always susceptible to varying significations, "are always both fluctuating and creating flux, stabilized and stabilizing," yet also always "mediated" (17). The Möbius subject, whom all subjects are, is a "site of nondeterminate 'sidedness' or switchpoint [...] which lends to the social field its character as non-orientable object" (32). The social field, created by the subject's excess, is a kind of floating object. I want to add here, and what I hope to make clear in the following chapter, is that the Möbius subject, as a conscious signification of ethical extimacy, also becomes a non- or trans-orientable object in transsubjective differential relations.

A psychoanalytic feminism does not need a penis-phallus relation

Above, when discussing masculinity, I at times conflated masculinity with phallic jouissance. I also conflated the phallus and the penis when reading Tarantino's *Death Proof*, and used the muscle car as a metaphor for the male body.[1] I also begin using Lacan's discourse designation of the master signifier, S_1, to talk about what is usually discussed as the phallus or phallic things. My deliberate conflations and terminological shifts are a strategy to push emphasis on the phallus to the margin, to argue for its insignificance. Simply put, the phallus has caused too much confusion, too much apartheid, and has stifled further developments of Lacanian psychoanalysis. Not to say that the argument around the phallus has not been productive, but the phallus as *the* master signifier and *the* quilting point of Symbolic and Imaginary reality contributes nothing to develop my feminist desires for social change and the reorientation of subjectivity and subjectivization. I am tired of having to argue that the phallus is not the penis or the clitoris. I find this signifier that causes such a deadlock unproductive, and, frankly, easily and desirably replaceable. Part of me says, "you can have your one-to-one phallus equals penis relation." I have no trouble with this logic anymore. Why not let it be so? After all, Lacan most likely (if not admittedly somewhere in his seminars) chose the phallus as master signifier because he is reading, that is, analyzing, patriarchy. What do we gain from demanding a separation and difference between the penis and the phallus? Let the critics win this one. I want to pick a wiser, more productive battle. If the master signifier in one narrative is the phallus, then what prevents it from being *objet a* in another? In terms of the mapping of the discourse formulae, the interaction between $ does not necessarily have to be directed toward an *objet a*, an S_1, or an S_2, but can between an $ and $. If the person speaking speaks from the place of *objet a* to someone who is in the same place, *a*, then they are both standing in a position of object and service to each other. As well, both entities positioning themselves as objects, and specifically the object that functions as *manqué la lettre*, have the potential to create together in that transsubjective moment how and with what to fill the particular moment's lack. I simply argue here that it can be some other signifier that serves as quilting point, and, well, that it is high time that we use some other signifier or signifiers. After all, how are we to "think beyond the phallus" if we do not refuse its primacy? Remove this primacy, and eventually down it falls from dominance.

Here, and throughout, I am depending on the distinction between the Symbolic and Imaginary as different orders or registers. As language is always the first exemplification of the Symbolic, we tend to assimilate texts, utterances, and discourses to the Symbolic and likewise in understanding our engagement with them as critical, perhaps deconstructive or historicist, wherein we seek to show how they are used for certain (suspect, political) ends. But when one contests the meaning of a term, one targets the place where the Imaginary overlaps with the Symbolic and where, consequently, the incessant slippages of signification which the Symbolic always threatens can be fixed (at least in the realm of fantasy, and fantasy surely becomes operant when collectively held), or perhaps "stabilized" and crucially heavily cathected as S_1s, or master signifiers.[2] When I speak of the Woman as constructed by the subject of *machismo*, with the connotations provided by language and culture, religion, and politics, I imply therein the sense of context specificity or, perhaps more productively, that the concept is situated in a regional Symbolic. If we return to that tripartite, fixed and coded set of S_1s, mother/virgin/whore, then begin to chart the ways that these S_1s are used by those who appear as subjects of *machismo*, a dispersion would result as an enormous net of connection crossing many discourses (in the looser, everyday sense of the word) and found seemingly everywhere in the culture. The Symbolic here, in this example, would be not so much the signifiers themselves but more the set of all the ways that they are currently articulated, as well as all the ways that they are implicitly or potentially able to be articulated.

I can recall the day when my child finally figured out how to read (not out of the thin air, of course, but it finally "clicked"). Prior to this seemingly epiphanic moment, however, he lived in a world of infinite texts, but the vast majority of them were unreadable, containing gibberish or unidentifiable sequences that he wanted to mean, and only now and then a word or an intelligible phrase reached him. This universe on the precipice of Symbolic coherence is an Imaginarization of the Symbolic. All the unreadable text reduced from its own signifieriness to a mute a-signifying mark is a measure of "empty space" or spaces that could still be occupied, but they are (for the most part) already implicated by the Symbolic as articulated thus far by the regional ideological apparatuses of Patriarchal Masculinity Inc., as only there could those signifiers be found. We do not exist in the Symbolic. Rather, we are subjects of a montage, the admixture of the Symbolic and Imaginary, of "reality." Thus, when we are oppressed by meanings – just as when we assert meanings that allow us new and more livable ways to understand our lives – we are dealing in fixings, in problematic stabilizations of the Symbolic arrived at through Imaginary means. To argue that Lacan's theory of the Symbolic and Imaginary is misogynistic and/or patriarchal is to refuse the potentiality of the emptiness of these psychic realms. As psychic realms, they are not inherently or innately misogynistic and patriarchal. We only know them as such because that is what they have been filled with for so long. The only requirement, I argue in fear of utopic idealism, is that we must make these empty spaces mean; i.e., they cannot become part of our identifiable Imaginary if we do not fill them with content. Otherwise, these empty spaces function as indices of the Real, or, at the very least, as generally unrealized.

What is at stake in what I forward here, and what scholars such as Rothenberg imply, is the power dynamic as we know it, even (perhaps, especially) after Foucault. If we understand the barred subject as the subject in language, barred from bodily jouissance because that particular language relegates enjoyment to the erotogenic zones (Adams 73), then reprogramming and reorienting this enjoyment disrupts the subject's stable identifiers. For example, the silencing and silence that culminates in She's genital mutilation of He and herself and, ultimately, She's murder are dynamical acts of this reorientation met by its refusal.

In consciously synecdochizing oneself *a la* Spivak and forming (or joining?) a metonymic collective by harnessing the excess of one's subjectivity – for, after all, excess moves both back into the social field from that which the subject does not use, as well as into the collective as that which is removed, repurposed, from the subjectivity for the collective – and relating differentially to others in the effort to bring about social change indeterminately, as Möbius subjects, one begins to allow discourse dynamics to shift into forms that are yet to be determined. In an effort to safeguard myself from my own critique of utopianism, I will say that the "yet to be determined" is at its core an indeterminate thing; the "shifts into forms" potentially can go in any direction and take any form.

Rothenberg's differential relation is a tad less pointed, it seems, than what I intend to mean here. I turn to Chela Sandoval's definition of the term *differential* in order to support more clearly my intention. She uses the term differential to designate an aspect of resistance and a mode of consciousness. As a mode of social movement, the differential "represents a new kind of generative activity, the step outside of [Althusserian] ideology into the realm of movement – *the place from which language is generated*" (3 fn 3, emphasis added). Differential consciousness, for Sandoval, is

> *composed of difference and contradictions*, which then serve as tactical interventions in the other mobility that is power. […] I defined differential consciousness as a kind of anarchic activity (but with method), a form of ideological guerrilla warfare, and a new kind of *ethical activity* that is discussed here as the way in which opposition to oppressive authorities is achieved in highly technologized and disciplinized society. Inside this realm resides the only possible ground for alliance across differences. Entrance into this new order requires *an emotional commitment within which one experiences the violent shattering of the unitary sense of self as the skill that allows a mobile identity to form takes hold.* […] Within the realm of differential consciousness there are no ultimate answers, no terminal utopia (though the imagination of utopias can motivate its tactics), no predictable final outcomes.
>
> (63 fn 61, emphasis added)

I emphasize the moment of "shattering" that "allows a mobile identity" in order to push the idea that this transformation must be required of all subjects, not just those who suffer from societal oppression upon whom Sandoval and Butler tend to focus. Sandoval's call for a "shattering of the unitary sense of self" is akin to Bersani's *enbranlement*, or "self-shattering," which is a jouissance where the "subject is momentarily undone" (100). In this sense, Bersani's jouissance is not phallic, as phallic jouissance reifies the subject within the same Symbolic-Imaginary content. Bersani's self-shattering, in alignment with Sandoval's activist call for subject change, "disrupts the ego's coherence and dissolves its boundaries," which removes the ego as privileged point of conscious identification: "Psychoanalysis," Bersani reports, "has justifiably been considered the enemy of anti-identitarian politics, but it also proposes a concept of the sexual that might be a powerful weapon in the struggle against the disciplinarian constraints of identity" (101).[3] Sandoval recognizes and develops a methodological strategy, based on Barthesian, Derridean, and (without her fully acknowledging it) Lacanian theory. The requirement for the subject to undergo a self-shattering and develop a "mobile identity" in order to become ethically active toward a movement of social change is no small demand. Yet, similar to the ethical Möbius Subject, which must also relinquish an Imaginary stability, there seems to be no other way to imagine ethical social change: the subject must give up being a subject in the way in which we understand the subject.[4]

Within current popular discourse, to assume subjectivity seems to be a mode of assuming an occupation of a position of oppressive power. To assume subjectivity as we know it in hegemonic terms is also to assume a position within sexuation as either masculine or feminine, to enjoy most often phallic-ly, or in

relation to the phallus. Yet, this assumption is also based on the false presump-
tion that the subject finds an identity in either having or being the phallus
for other subjects. To relinquish such presumptions, to not assume a (singular)
subjectivity, allows for differential discursive positions and, therefore, social
relations of mobility, for indeterminacy via the refusal to present oneself as
an identifiable metaphor in the social field. Dislodging oneself from a (pre)
assumed subject identity, one can potentially engage in transsubjective relations
more equitably with others by removing oneself and others from masculinist
positions. (Of course, this dislodging does not guarantee such equitability, as
new methods of oppression can always arise.) This potentiality for decision and
creation can only occur if subjects are willingly and knowingly functioning via
indeterminacy and working ethically with its excess, if the subjects act as the
"switchpoint" rather than merely filling the allotted positions within already
scripted metaphors of "identity."

Parveen Adams, in "per os(cillation)," explicates the connection between the
symptom and hysteria in Freud's work, discovers the contradictions therein,
announces that he did not follow up on his hypotheses of conversion, and
concludes that "*the relations between the woman, the body and hysteria have shifted*"
(11, emphasis in original). If we agree that the hysteric's question "Am I a man
or am I a woman?" is symptomatic of bisexuality and its identifications, then
the hysteric's question is indicative of a heteronormative sexual desire because it
seeks to situate the subject in one of two positions for the desire of the opposite
position. However, if we begin to consider the hysteric's question as the articulation of discursive positionality and identification, then we understand that the
hysteric's problem is one of straddling both/and misidentification with access
to phallic and non-phallic jouissance. If most (if not all) subjects subscribe to
the hegemonic masculine position, or identify in relation to it – i.e., having or
being the phallus – then we can think of the hysteric's question, in consideration of the hysteric's close proximity to the unconscious (Adams 6, 8, 10), as
one which is a symptom of knowing the fluctuation between masculine and
feminine identification. If the subject was not in a sort of metonymical contiguity with that fluctuation, then the hysterical question could never even arise.

The hysteric symptom(s) to be attributed mostly to women and femininity,
when thought of as a mark of knowing the identificatory fluctuation, make(s)
sense in that patriarchy signifies the feminine as secondary. The accoutrements
of the feminine masquerade weigh down our skin, our muscles, strain our
tendons and bones, clutter our bathrooms, vanities, and bombard us in images
and store aisles. The little girl who identifies "successfully" with a mother is just
such a performance and understands the performance as that which attracts her
desired "daddy" love-object in the oedipal stage is likely to grow up a psychotic,
as the Symbolic has an opening, or unravels, and the Imaginary takes precedence
without the Law. The psychotic is determined by the foreclosure of the Name-
of-the-Father; that is, by a lack of reliable determiners ascribing the subject to
"normal" social structures. The little girl only understands her role as dressing
up as Woman, rather than embodying Symbolic-Imaginary identifications,

and, therefore, her dominant psychic mode is that of the psychotic, lacking transsubjective ethicality, or lacking assimilation into Symbolic Law (*Écrits* 217). "In the hysteric," Adams explains, "the gap between subject and object is most visible and she raises the question of the object which resists interpellation" (75). Let us recall that the left side of the hysteric's formula is $/a$, that which she and the master, S_1, both do not know, and the master never will know, as we see in his question "what does a woman want?" Adams points out, though, that the analyst's discourse "hystericizes the analysand" (75). If the aim of analysis is for the subject to identify with the sinthome, but in doing so disrupts the discursive positions as to make the analysand the object spoken to from *the* ~~object~~, *objet a*, then analysis, in a slight turn of logic, brings forth an identification of self as that part of the self that is object, not subject. Analysis "detaches the subject's signifiers" from their cozy places in the subject's past history and "reinforces their symbolic weight," (77) that is, not their Imaginary weight that turns a girl into a Woman or a boy into a trans woman. No matter what, as speaking beings, "the signifier offers shelter to humans. Signifiers supplied by social apparatuses yield humans the relief of identity," and even if those signifiers are detached, they are always reformulated, reoriented, reprogrammed (77).

I have tried to address the Woman problem by arguing that the Woman problem is the manifest content of a latent oppression general to all subjects that is particular to what we do in and with the Imaginary. In reconsidering Woman as metonymy, in an almost unavoidable relation between Woman and the feminine position, I try to provide a tactic for reorienting our transsubjective relations so that we can begin working differentially, cutting across and displacing oppressive power dynamics. As well, I have tried to argue for a focus on the master signifier, S_1, as a general replacement for the phallus in order to begin forwarding more specific and varying signifiers that can occupy the place of this quilting point. I will develop this replacement in more detail next, as I replace all instances of the phallus, ϕ, with the general designation of the master signifier, S_1. I dedicate the following chapter to a reading of Lacan's sexuation graph in order to reconsider first metonymically, and then discursively, different relations of subjectivity and objectivity and suggest other trajectories that result in giving up Woman as metaphor and the phallus as master signifier.

Notes

1 I am now rethinking this morphology and wanting to go with the game as a clitoris and the car is a woman. Either way, as this paragraph keeps going, it does not matter which one it is.
2 Or, alternately, "quilting points," all these ideas at different moments take over, usually with greater abstraction or figural-fidelity, conceptual functions previously accomplished by the phallus in its Symbolic version. Just as Dean argues for the object as a better replacement for certain functions of the phallus in Lacan's theory, the notion of master signifiers, or S_1s is an updating, a pluralization and further abstraction of other functions of that seemingly always fraught term.

3 Tim Dean explains that:

> There is a different kind of pleasure involved in violating one's self-image […] a pleasure in tension with that of secure boundaries and self-recognition. Since the pleasure of self-shattering or self-loss tends to be experienced as more intense than that of self-recognition or security, we refer to the former as jouissance; jouissance isn't merely a stronger pleasure but exists in tension with it. In standard psychoanalytic terms, we could say that the tension between the pleasure of recognition and the jouissance of self-shattering is figured by the conflict between the ego and the unconscious, or, in other words, between identity and desire.
>
> (22)

Dean, Tim. *The Unlimited Intimacy: Reflections on the Subculture of Barebacking.* The University of Chicago Press, 2009.

4 I realize this takes an ontological turn. On the one hand, it is a matter of semantics, and on the other hand, I am working toward an emphasis of the object rather than the subject.

7   Myth, truth, and non-phallic sexuation

Meaning (sens) indicates the direction toward which it fails (échoue).

Lacan, SXX, 79

The very notion of a quarter turn evokes revolution, but certainly not in the sense in which revolution is subversion. On the contrary, what turns – that is what is called revolution – is destined, by its very statement (énoncé), to evoke a return.

Lacan, SXX, 41

I began to discuss at the end of the last chapter the notion of ethical jouissance in connection with Lacan's theory of extimacy and my desire to replace the phallus with a general S_1. As a feminist and a Lacanian, I want to argue that we do not need the phallus to represent the master signifier or *point de capiton*. Even though Lacan's early theory of the phallus often dominates, an understanding of sexuation as discourse eliminates the phallus as *the* master signifier. In this chapter I will develop my conception of ethical relations both for the subject with itself and between subjects. First, I explicate Lacan's sexuation graph. Second, I revisit the hysteric's discourse in order to explain desire as labor and to delineate desire and the drive along the lines of "masculine" and "feminine" logics. I replace the phallus symbol, ϕ, in the graph with S_1, which serves as the general master signifier and can take on any content that can become the *point de capiton* for transsubjective relations and identifications with the signifier. I replace ϕ with S_1 in order to illustrate what I mean by an ethics of the body – always for this project as a complex compilation of the corporal, psychic, and unconscious – and social relations.

The significance of the first epigraph above – "Meaning indicates the direction toward which it fails" – should be clear at this point in the project. Meaning is an absolute only insofar as it is *the* human phenomenon; meaning, according to Lacanian psychoanalysis, is the manifestation of desire in language, that which always fails to wholly encompass an absolute, a One. The One can never be realized because it is founded on the sexed binary as complementary, on the attempt to reason sex within a mythical logic. Psychoanalysis argues that sex is the limit of reason, that which marks the index of the Real through sexual difference as a symptom of anxiety. The way in which the subject means discursively is always a failure of the desired direction toward either, to use Lacan's terms, the masculine or feminine position. However, there is an entire spectrum between and beyond these positions. Sexuated meaning is inherently ironic: to take the masculine position in discourse is to negate its possibility. Copjec, arguing cogently against Butler's desire for open *gender* categories, reminds us that sex and sexual difference are negations, that they mark difference, which is not a positive term or category (*Read My Desire* 209–212). Similarly, to take the feminine position in discourse is also to negate its possibility while simultaneously to bring to the surface, or return, an excess of the person outside of the Symbolic. The sexuated positions that, for now, discursively represent sexual difference are "misfirings," to use Copjec's term, that attempt to symbolically represent the unsymbolizable, the Real (207).

The second epigraph above describes the possibilities of movement open to the subject both intersubjectively and transsubjectively. I have argued, in keeping with Lacan's two theories on discourse and sexuation, that a subject can occupy any of the speaking and receiving positions of the four discourse formulae, and, as we have seen in the case of the hysteric's discourse, a subject can be the agent in either of the sexuated positions as well. A subject who identifies as agent in the master's discourse enters analysis, say, and moves into the hysteric's position only to come out the other side of it as an agent in the analyst's discourse. The goal of psychoanalysis is to revolve, to turn the master's discourse on its head. The analyst's discourse returns the master's discourse to the subject, but inverted, as evidenced in Lacan's L schema and the gaze. However, just as there is an inherent irony in sexuation (and meaning), the occupation of the speaking subject in the analyst's discourse will inevitably return that subject to a master's discourse, only the content will (potentially) differ from the old one.

Lacan's sexuation graph

In Seminar XX: *Encore: On Feminine Sexuality, The Limits of Love and Knowledge, 1972–1973*, Lacan further develops a system of identification to which the subject submits (is submitted?) through discourse, as the subject is a social entity and must function through discourse in (at least) one position. After laying out his theory of the discourse formulae in Seminar XVII, Lacan continues to develop his ideas on discourse in Seminars XVIII and XIX, and in the latter he introduces and explicates the formulae in the top two quadrants of the sexuation graph. Let us look at these formulae.

These formulae, through symbolic/mathematical logic, express the psychoanalytic concept of castration, understood not as a loss of genitalia but as a severing of the self from the Real, an initial scissoring/securing of the subject's position within the Symbolic. Both sides of this top quadrant of the graph illustrate the way in which the subject is castrated; that is, the reasons why and the way in which the subject may or may not have access to a jouissance that is not

$$\begin{array}{c|c} \exists x \ \overline{\Phi x} & \overline{\exists x} \ \overline{\Phi x} \\ \forall x \ \Phi x & \overline{\forall x} \ \Phi x \end{array}$$

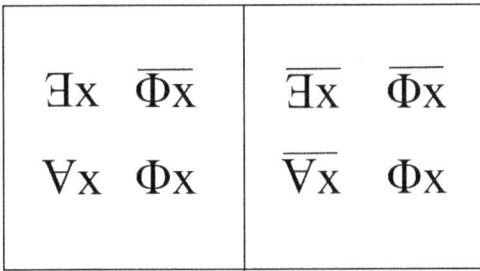

Figure 7.1 The upper quadrants of the sexuation graph

in and of language. The phallic function in the top quadrant of the graph, then, should be understood as the function of castration – similar to the inherent irony in the meaning of sexuation – and its effect on the subject as it determines the trajectory of the subject's desire.

The left-hand side, typically considered the "masculine" side, reads as two sentences horizontally. So reading horizontally with the first line as one sentence and the second line as another, the symbols read as such: Every man, except one (who is a mythological figure, e.g., God or the primal horde father), is subject to the phallic function; all of any man (and all actual men) is/are wholly subject to the phallic function. The bar above the phallic function in the first sentence signifies exception. The one who is not subject to the phallic function is the phallic father, illustrated by Freud's primal horde father as the patriarch *par excellence*, the Father whose law subjects internalize as they become subjects. This theory of the internalized (law of the) Father, of course, necessarily presupposes a patriarchal and paternalistic society, a society that is very real as our lived history shows us. This internalized Father is the signifier representative of the social system born out of fear of castration, but also represents the necessity of castration (or "alienation" from the mother, from the "oceanic feeling," from animal-ness) as one becomes a speaking being. For subjects who identify as masculine or situate their subject position wholly within a masculinist logic, their inter- and transsubjective reality is wholly phallic in its function; there is nothing that escapes this subjectivization. The way in which "men," or rather "masculine subjects" relate is through this phallic subject identification and, therefore, in a desirous trajectory toward phallic jouissance – the enjoyment of having the phallus.

The right-hand side, typically referred to as the "feminine" side, reads as such: There is no woman who is not subjected to the phallic function; not all of (a) woman is subject to the phallic function. The bar above the symbols in these logic sentences signifies negation, rather than exception as it does for the one mythic man who is not castrated. Feminine subjects, just as masculine subjects (as they are subjects too after all), are also subject to phallic subjectivization. Yet, unlike the masculine subject, part of the feminine subject escapes this subjectivization to phallic identification and, therefore, part of the feminine subject escapes or evades the desire for phallic jouissance. In other words, the only reason why we know that there is something else besides, or beyond, phallic jouissance is that subjects do in fact experience a jouissance that we cannot interpret (as phallic). These subjects seem to be able to access an *excess*, a pleasure that the phallic function does not account for, or cannot name. The excess, the "not all," that partially characterizes the feminine subject is exempt from castration, or, perhaps, the feminine subject is not fully castrated. This quadrant of the graph has been misinterpreted at times as claiming that women are "not whole" – as if Lacan was claiming that women are castrated, do not have penises (following up with Freud's *penisneid*), that they are missing some-thing – rather than that women are not wholly castrated. In understanding the symbolic logic correctly, as well as *reading* Lacan, we can shift from an emphasis of the "not all" that privileges phallic logic to one of possession, of *having an excess*, that privileges a *beyond* phallic logic. To refer back to Lacan's claim that "men, women, and children are but signifiers," (SXX 33) we can now begin to expand on the consequences of this collusion of sexuation and discourse, specifically the excess that becomes paradoxically evident, a positive term in its negation of a complete set: "A man is nothing but a signifier. A woman seeks out a man qua signifier. A man seeks out a woman qua […] that which can only be situated through discourse, since, if what I claim is true – namely, that woman is not-whole – there is always something in her that escapes discourse" (33).

The idea of a *beyond the phallus*, a phrase that has received much play and flak by Lacan himself as I quote him at the project's opening is one that brings forth much skepticism and resistance but also provokes curiosity and desire. Differing from Butler's (and possibly Irigaray's) slippage into a desire for a precastrated, prelinguistic "reality," the *beyond* suggests not a regression into infancy or uncastrated blissful idealism, but an excess that is a jouissance beyond (phallic) meaning.[1] Recall the two siblings on the train. Lacan laments, but also acknowledges the necessity of, the siblings' differing identifications and, hence, their trajectories of desire, that is, their directionalities. The siblings, headed for the "same homeland," seem to be forever on the track of phallic meaning, a meaning that always fails. Nevertheless, not all is lost in that at least one of them, the one who identifies as feminine, will not wholly stay on track. The feminine subject is "feminine" not because she is biologically female but by virtue of the fact that "she" is not wholly subject to the phallus. Parts of the feminine subject, particularly in the place of hysteric subjectivity, eludes the phallic function in her desire and enjoyment. The question "what does (a) woman want?" is geared toward this elusiveness, toward that which cannot be articulated, toward that which is outside of discourse.

Lacan uses the example of mystics who return from the experience of non-phallic jouissance and can say that "they have experienced it, but know nothing about it" (76). In other words, they can report that the experience occurred – "the idea or sense that there must be a jouissance that is beyond" (76) – but there are no signifiers to provide adequate detail of it because it escapes discourse.

Significantly for this project, Lacan asserts that it is not *women* (or females) who have access to this "beyond," but it is the non-phallic, i.e., the non-masculine subject who accesses it.

> Mysticism isn't everything that isn't politics. It is something serious, about which several people inform us – most often women, or bright people like Saint John of the Cross, because one is not obliged, when one is male, *to situate oneself* on the side of ∀xɸx. One can also *situate oneself* on the side of the not-whole. There are men who are just as good as women. It happens. And who also feel just as fine about it. Despite – I won't say their phallus – despite what encumbers them that goes by that name, they get the idea or sense that there must be a jouissance that is beyond.
>
> (76, emphasis added)

Here, Lacan makes a clear distinction between, on the one hand, male and female and, on the other, the masculine and feminine positions. More so, perhaps, he is also claiming that the subject has agency in the identification and/ or situating of the self in one of the two positions. Staying with Lacan's logic and language for the moment, we can say that all subjects are phallic in that they are castrated and function within a signifying system dominated by phallic signification. However, not all subjects *and* not all of any subject are required to identify as *wholly* phallic. Only part of a subject and only some of the time must a subject mean within the phallic signifying system as either having or being the phallus. As a masculine subject, one has the phallus; as a feminine subject, one is the phallus for the masculine subject. Of course, as all meaning fails, the subject can never really, actually, have or be the phallus in terms of the quilting point or signification absolute. One can only parade as such, as discussed earlier. In this parodic or "parodic" sense, all subjects are phallic by their very subject-ness; however, to a certain extent, subjects can choose, as did the two siblings on the train via happenstance, whether they identify in the having or being category, but the choice is always made under considerable duress. Given what Lacan says in the lengthy passage quoted above, though, we can read an indefiniteness, a mobility, in the situating of one's subject position within this *discursive* dynamic or relation. Unlike Copjec's claim that "within any discourse the subject can only assume either a male or a female position," (210) which is a definitive either/or and a poorly chosen biological terminology, the subject, even within discourse, does not have to locate itself or be located only and always on either only one of the (masculine or feminine) sides.

In *Revolution in Poetic Language*, Kristeva distinguishes and develops her concepts of the semiotic and the symbolic, the two necessary components present in every subject's signifying processes. The semiotic is the "modality" of the signifying process that "Freudian psychoanalysis points to in postulating not only the *facilitation* and the structuring *disposition* of the drives, but also the so-called *primary processes* which displace and condense both energies and their inscription" (25, emphasis in original). The semiotic is that part of the subject's "signifiance," her term for the "unlimited and unbounded generating process" of the drives "toward, in, and through language," (17) that propels the subject on the chain of signification, particularly as sexually differentiated, as we see with the siblings on the train.[2] Kristeva's explanation of this part of the signifying process – the inscription of the drives – within Freud's notions on displacement and condensation (read: metonymy and metaphor) is useful in my understanding of the complexly constructed body and the ways in which that discourse is written on the body. Sexual difference is the primary mark on this complexly constructed body that the unconscious censors, that escapes Symbolic language, and that we resort to covering over with the use of tropes. The semiotic "precedes the establishment of the sign," and can be "accurately elucidated only within a theory of the subject that [...] *opens up within a subject this other scene* of pre-symbolic functions" (27, emphasis added). The Symbolic provides linguistic space for the manifestation/articulation of the subject's Imaginary identifications, but the materiality of the Real, the pre-identification "energies," to use Kristeva's term, do not evaporate. We can best understand Kristeva's semiotic in relation to Lacan's unconscious inscriptions on the body: the semiotic shares signifying duties with the symbolic, and the subject's meaning-making process is partially constructed by that which escapes sense, by that "radical antagonism" to sense that Copjec discusses. The symbolic, for Kristeva's signifying process, is the "social effect of the relation to the other, established through the objective constraints of biological (including sexual) differences and concrete, historical family structures" (29). As a "social effect," then, the symbolic is that part of the subject's signifying process that induces castration.

Kristeva, perhaps implicitly following the connection between Lacan's theories of discourse and sexuation, associates the binary components semiotic and symbolic with his categories of the feminine and masculine respectively. In light of Kristeva's theory that every subject's signifying process is constructed by both of these modalities, every subject contains and, therefore, can access discursively both masculine and feminine positions. Moreover, I desire to shift emphasis from the overdetermined privileging of having the phallus to more consideration on the subject *having the excess*. Similarly to the way Fuss views Irigaray's discussion of woman's lack of essence as an "unrealized potentiality," I think Kristeva's efforts at sussing out the semiotic within the text in conjunction with her concept of the writing subject can be read as an effort to emphasize an excess.[3] The right, "feminine" side of Lacan's sexuation graph describes the subject's excess, the not-fully castrated aspect of the subject, namely, extending from Kristeva, that aspect of the subject's semiotic modality.

If we can look at the upper quadrants of the graph through the lens I have set up with recourse to Kristeva, then it is not only the possible representation of an either/or, as a subject only represented on one side and another subject on the other side, but also the representation of one subject's signifying process within a given discourse. In other words, we can think the possibility of each side of the upper portion as the symbolic and semiotic modalities of the signifying process, as well as the way in which a subject accesses different types of jouissance in the situating of the self. It is for this reason that the gendered terms "masculine" and "feminine" do not quite get at the potential of this discourse-sexuation relation and act as a kind of foreclosure in thinking *beyond* the phallus.

Copjec's Kantian reading of the graph's two sides in "Sex and the Euthanasia of Reason" re-categorizes them as the dynamical and mathematical antinomies for male and female respectively: the "male side" fails dynamically whereas the "female side" fails mathematically. We cannot read the two sides of the graph symmetrically, Copjec teaches us, because we cannot ascribe the logic of the "not all" of the feminine side, which as we will see below allows for a positing of Woman, to the masculine side; we also cannot posit Man (*Read My Desire* 227–28). The masculine side is Lacan's logic for that which is true of the world of subjects, the world of meaning, that which can be counted. The left side of the graph, then, is the inclusive logic of the limit (229–30). This side, as Copjec explains, "covers over" the lack of "the possibility of metalanguage" (230) because it cannot say anything about being, i.e., existence as such (231): "on this side it will always be a matter of saying *too little*" (231, emphasis in original).[4] The feminine side fails mathematically in that there is evidence of an excess that cannot be counted and which escapes the inclusive logic of our world, the covering over of the lack: "woman is there where no limit intervenes to inhibit the progressive unfolding of signifiers, where, therefore, a judgment of existence becomes impossible" (226). In other words, the feminine side illustrates the way in which the signifier of woman unveils the failing of all signifiers to account for the thing-in-itself and, therefore, that which escapes discourse, as well as the way in which signifiers can mean within the Symbolic differently.

The Symbolic is a limited register with limitless signifying possibilities, but we think of it as that which "guarantees our consistency" (227); however, the excess illustrated on the graph's feminine side is the constant remainder of the inconsistency of signifiers, specifically their inability to stabilize identities. Copjec's argument that sex and sense are diametrically opposed becomes clearer in light of her reading of the graph, and we can now get a better idea of the absurdity of trying to make sense of sexual difference in any one particular way. All subjects, regardless of the signifier(s) they present as the designation of their sexual difference, embody extimacy and, therefore, that part of them "remains inaccessible" (234). The significance of understanding sex and sexual difference through the inconsistency of signifiers and the always lurking excess of the subject is that "Lacan has allowed us to perceive the fraudulence at the heart of every claim to positive sexual identity" (234). Copjec sums up her reading by claiming that "All pretentions of masculinity are […] sheer imposture, just as every display of femininity is sheer masquerade" (234). The interconnectivity of sexuation with discourse, then, highlights the inconsistency and excess that all subjects embody. My aim is to bring to the fore the fluidity of transsubjective discursive relations. Our situating ourselves consciously among and between transsubjective discursive relations has the potential to manifest ethical relations that reflect a different understanding of power that is not based on the domination and oppression of other people to cover over our lack. Rather, we can manifest ethical power relations based on an exploration of our lack that emphasizes excess. Rather than claiming power via one's masquerade of masculinity and femininity, we can let our understanding of these identifications as masquerade compel us to relate to one another and other objects through dis-identification with the traditional signifiers and imagine new ones.

The sexuation graph's lower quadrants

In *The Democracy of Objects*, Levi Bryant's reading of Lacan's sexuation graph through an object-oriented ontology lens leads him to conclude, much as I have, that masculinity is a *sham*:

> If it is true that subjectivity is at root hysterical, if it is true that obsession is a subspecies of hysteria, and if it is true that hysteria is associated with feminine sexuation and obsessional neurosis is associated with masculine sexuation, we find that we are able to invert a fundamental characterization of woman through out Western history. Generally we hear that woman is characterized by masquerade, deception, semblance, inconsistency, and so on. However, in light of the foregoing, it would appear that in point of fact it is masculinity that is a charade, a semblance, a masquerade.
>
> (260–61)

Recall the discussion of the hysteric and hysteric's discourse from Chapter 2, specifically Lacan's theory that all neurotic subjects are at root/core hysteric, as the hysteric is that which constitutes the split subject. What Bryant claims here is that the so-called feminine subject often attributed to women/woman is the failure of the masculine masquerade to cover over the actuality of the split that characterizes and constitutes all subjects. In turn, the attempt to cover over the failure of the masquerade is Woman (as metaphor), which is to say, as a symptom of man. The agent of the master's discourse is $S_1/\$$, the feigning of a patent subject-supposed-to-know who represses his fundamental hystericism. The agent of the hysteric's discourse is $\$/a$, the patent split subject who asks "who/what am I?" from a repressed place of *objet a*, the object cause of desire/lack; that is, the nearest place to the subject's excess. *Objet a*, as we will see in the lower quadrants of the graph, is that which blocks the $\$$ from accessing that Other jouissance. The "masculine" or "phallic" $\$$ chases after that which blocks his excess, but in this case what constitutes *objet a* is trivial substitutions for the lack that *objet a* actually is. If the latent content of the agent is *objet a*, then the hysteric in some way knows of the core lack, and the jouissance the hysteric chases/experiences is one where various *objet a* substitutes do not matter.

Differing slightly from Copjec's mathematical and dynamical readings of the sexuation graph, Bryant reads the two sides of the graph as representations/illustrations of a philosophy of transcendence for the masculine, left side and a philosophy of immanence for the feminine, right side. Within symbolic logic, we can understand the left side of the graph as a logic of exception in that there exists for subjects wholly subjected to the phallic function a fantasy of a subject who is not castrated and only castrates (forcefully), and the right side of the graph as a logic of "not-all" or "not whole" in that there is no logic of exception or of universality. Therefore, Bryant names the masculine side as representative of a logic of transcendence because of the fantasy of He who is the exception to the rule. The feminine side is a logic of immanence because there is no exception or universality, but rather "a flat plane," (255) as well as a more democratic understanding of the subject position. This democratic turn is what Bryant reads into Lacan's declaration that *the* woman does not exist, definitive article emphasized as an articulation of the lack of an exception (255–56). So, rather than focusing as Copjec does on the way in which subjects fail, which only brings to the immediate fore the "deadlock," to use Bryant's term, of the Symbolic's untotalizability, Bryant focuses on the productive possibilities within the logic of immanence. Similar to my argument concerning the way in which the negative, empty space of the Symbolic provides libratory wiggle room in which subjects can create meaning, Lacan's claim that Woman does not exist, for Bryant, is also a positive function born out of a negation. The universality of castration and subordination on the masculine side of the graph has "no analogous instance on the feminine side of the graph of sexuation, therefore it is impossible to constitute a universal class of women" (256). Instead, women, Bryant continues, "form an open set without any shared or overarching predicate defining a universal identity, thereby undermining any pretension to essence or identity" (256). An implied essence lurks behind the claim of a lack of essence, but this lack constitutes subjects; the side of immanence simply lacks differently both in terms of place and affect.

Bryant's philosophical desire within his project is to remove once and for all the centrality and logocentrism of the human subject from the ways in which we seek to understand what surrounds us, as well as to restructure the categorical binary of subjects and objects as oppositional poles (249).[5] He reduces the gap of this inherent irony by reminding his subject-readers that subjects are a category of objects: "Within the framework of object-oriented ontology, there are not two domains of being, one belonging to the domain of the subject, the other belonging to the domain of the object […] but [subjects] are themselves a type of object" (251). And all objects, not just human ones, are agential actors and actants rather than passive objects (251). His philosophy, "flat ontology" or "onticology," aims to be "an ontology of doing justice to these strange non-human actors, capable of respecting these strange strangers on their own terms, and an ontology capable of doing justice to the phenomenological and the semiotic" (248). Lacan reminds his audience filled with amnesiatic subjects that we all forget that we were initially all – that is, "initially determined as" – *objet a*s (SXVII 160). Bryant's focus on the positive terms present in the symbolic logic on the right side through the logic of immanence is helpful in redefining an ethical understanding of inter- and transsubjective relations.

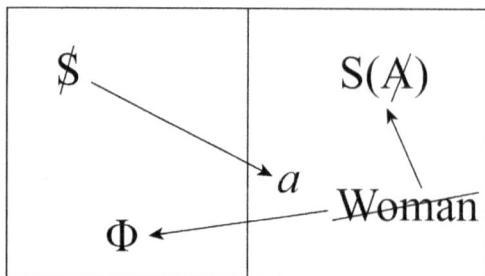

Figure 7.2 The lower quadrants of the sexuation graph

We can now begin to map the trajectories of desire and the phallic and non-phallic attainments of jouissance in terms of a logic of discursive (mis)identifications of the other. The lower two quadrants of the sexuation graph illustrate the directionality of the subject's desire in its quest and attainment of jouissance as an effect of the subject's castration.

On the left, masculine side of the graph, Lacan locates the split subject, $, in the top left-hand side of the box far from the line that separates the two sides. The $'s vector crosses over to the right, feminine side of the graph's *a*, that is, *objet a*. In the lower portion close to the line that separates the two sides, Lacan places the phallus, Φ. The split subject – the subject in and of language – desires the lost object, *a*, which is the object cause of desire and that which defines lack, that which is substanceless but can take on a temporary form. For example, the split subject, in desiring to fill his/her lack, will desire another person to "complete" him/her, or will desire a poodle or a Corvette or a meal at a certain restaurant or a powerful position, etc. The trajectory of that desire only fills a lack temporarily; or, rather, the fulfillment of that desire, that lack, deceives the subject, and s/he ultimately has the desire returned in another form. The phallus, Φ, is on the masculine side of the graph as the primary signifier, the quilting point, firstly, because the (greater hegemonic) social network as we know it is grounded in masculinist discourse and, secondly, because it is the primary signifier of sexual difference within this masculinist discourse. The subject in his/her sexuation, a discursive realization of sexual difference, has a relation of meaning to the phallus as "having" or "being" it.

On the right, feminine side of the lower boxes, at the top-left corner, close to the separating line, Lacan places S(Ⱥ), the subject's extimate relationship with the unconscious self, and the A, the big Other, is barred, or split, just as the split subject is on the left side. S(Ⱥ), in this way, is the signifier of the lack in the Other. In "Subversion of the Subject and the Dialectic of Desire," Lacan places similar content there as he does in ~~Woman~~:

> My definition of the signifier (there is no other) is as follows: a signifier is what represents the subject to another signifier. This latter signifier is

therefore the signifier to which all other signifiers represent the subject – which means that if this signifier is missing, all the other signifiers represent nothing. For something is only represented to.

Now insofar as the battery of signifiers is, it is complete, and this signifier can only be a line that is drawn from its circle without being able to be counted in it. This can be symbolized by the inherence of a (–1) in the set of signifiers. It is, as such, unpronounceable, but its operation is not.

(*Écrits* 693–94)

~~Woman~~ also cannot be spoken. In the middle of that box, he writes ~~La~~, translated as ~~Woman~~. ~~Woman~~ has two vectors, one directed toward S(Ⱥ) and the other crossing the separating line over to the φ. Unlike the $'s direction of desire toward *objet a*, one of ~~Woman~~'s directions of desire splits toward Ⱥ, which is the signifier that desire exchanges with the *objet a* of fantasy (697). Placed in the middle of the vectors and in between ~~Woman~~ and the separating line is *a*, or *objet a* that is the ending point for the $'s desired directionality on the masculine side. S(Ⱥ) is on the feminine side of the graph, rather than $ repeated, because, as I understand the distinction, the feminine subject's experience with desire and jouissance is in excess of, or outside of, the $'s *conscious* experience and access. The subject in this instance is not split or barred with itself in that jouissance; rather, it is in an extreme relation with the unconscious, which is what is barred/split within the intersubjective signifying process with the $. To clarify, I do not claim here that the subject on the feminine side of the graph is not barred, as all subjects are, but that the subject recedes and the ~~Other~~ takes precedence in this instance of jouissance.

For Lacan, ~~Woman~~ signifies that which is not true or real in the sense that the idea of Woman desired and idealized by masculinist discourse does not exist in the way I argued earlier that the three paradigms of Woman – virgin, mother, whore – do not exist, and that feminine subjectivity is non-universal. Unlike $, which is situated syntactically as the subject of a sentence, for example, on the masculine side of the graph, ~~Woman~~ lingers in the middle of the feminine box, *as if* it were a center, but the positioning hovers uncannily, similar to the pipe in Magritte's famous 1928-29 *The Treachery of Images* (*Ceci n'est pas une pipe*).[6] There is no universal Woman, and a discourse that centers on such a sham idea, such an impossible and absurd ideal, cannot hold. Because this center cannot (and will not) hold, Lacan interrupts the desiring trajectory of the masculine $'s vector with *a*, that which always marks and returns a lack, the lack. Rather than ~~Woman~~'s other vector reaching *a*, Lacan directs it toward the phallus, φ. He locates the other desire there because the feminine subject also is a discursive subject, must function in the larger social network, and does so by desiring to be that which the masculine (read: dominant) subject apparently has.

I see a correlation between the bathroom diagram in "Instance of the Letter" and the sexuation graph. I read the diagram of the bathrooms as a prototype for the later sexuation graph.

LADIES **GENTLEMEN**

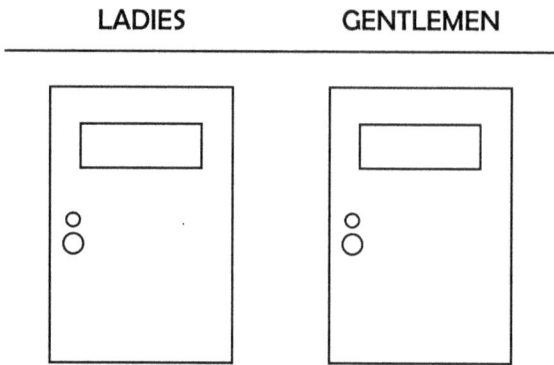

Figure 7.3 The bathrooms (again)

To recap what I discussed earlier, the bar of prohibition in this diagram is not situated between the bathrooms – remember the siblings end up at the "same homeland." Instead, the bar sits above the doors, the separation between the Symbolic designation of Ladies and Gentlemen and the identical doors, as well as in front of the bathrooms, horizontally between the siblings on the train and the doors. The bar that we see in the diagram is the textual prohibition we are quite acquainted with as that which designates sexual difference and the prohibition that, as Copjec argues, one must choose to signify to other subjects (read: signifiers) as one or the other; it is the prohibition within semiotics. The way in which we mean as ladies or gentlemen is always above the bar, always on the metonymic chain of signifiers. What goes on behind the bathroom doors does not correlate with that which the signifiers try to represent – that is, the signifiers above the bar demarcate us *as if* we are ladies and gentlemen – but what we do behind those closed doors is far from what it means to signify as a lady or a gentleman. The word lady and the socio-cultural accoutrements that accompany its signification, in fact, function to cover over what goes on behind that closed door (and even further behind the anteroom found in traditional, formal Ladies restrooms).[7] The bar that *we must imagine* between the siblings and the textual image above, that which the railroad tracks or the platform may represent, is the bar of prohibition raised against the Real: these children must become subjects and mean within the discursive paradigms illustrated by sexuation as discourse. They are at this moment split between becoming and being or having; they are developing what constitutes the upper quadrants of the sexuation graph. What goes on behind the closed doors for these two siblings and the directionality significant for them – according to the gaze allowed by where they are situated in their seats – correlates to the lower quadrants of the sexuation graph. They are identifying at this moment – the decisive and divisive moment which causes so much "ideological warfare" – the ways in which they will desire, as well as act upon the basis of that desire. Even though Lacan's tale is heteronormative, the way in which the siblings are situated on the train and their line of vision to the bathrooms is arbitrary. (After all, Lacan is not clear as to what these directionalities mean – whether it means that the little girl will desire men and vice versa for the little boy; his glossing of the tale allows for a discursive identification between the girl and gentlemen and the boy and ladies, too.)

The ways in which the siblings will desire, as well as act upon the basis of that desire, are fundamental to the important connection I see between the discourse formulae and the sexuation graph. The discourse formulae function in tension with one another: Lacan is quite explicit that the analyst's discourse is an inversion of the master's, and that the hysteric's discourse is a direct antagonism of the master's. The trajectories of desire, as well, are illustrated within a dynamic of tension, a way to work with and through anxiety. The horizontal line that separates the top and bottom quadrants of the sexuation graph correlates to the bar of prohibition between the signifiers "Ladies" and "Gentlemen" and the identical doors. The vertical dividing line that separates the two sides of the sexuation graph is also a line of prohibition. For example, on the left side of the graph the $'s trajectory of desire only goes in one direction, and it must cross the line of prohibition to get at that which it desires. However, that which it reaches, *objet a*, is never that which matches what it wants and especially never fulfills or completes the subject. *Objet a* literally stands in the way of $ getting at what $ wants, which is Woman, because "she" does not exist (W̶o̶m̶a̶n̶). This particular directionality only functions through an idea of metaphor, through an *as if* of desire, an *as if* that always fails: not only does the $ desire something that is blocked from access, but that which he desires does not exist, is not symbolizable, is only an imaginary, metaphoric construction of his desire.

W̶o̶m̶a̶n̶'s directionality of desire is plural, split in two directions, which is another element of the non-universality of this particular subject in discourse as it desires in more than one way, and one of those ways, as I try to explain here, is particularly unsymbolizable and, therefore, cannot be known as identical in its manifestations. W̶o̶m̶a̶n̶'s lower trajectory of desire crosses the bar to the ɸ on the left side of the graph. She must, in part, desire as such in order to be a subject, so as to be counted as a person, so to speak. However, her upper trajectory of desire does not cross the bar, but rather vectors towards S(Å), the (non-barred) subject's extimate relationship with the Other, which is barred. The Å, for Lacan, designates that there is no Other of/for the Other. In recognizing this lack, the subject's split and prohibition are transferred there in an accession of jouissance for which the Imaginary cannot count, and we find the Symbolic's limit. Bruce Fink explains that the Å designates that the Other is "structurally incomplete" and that S(Å) designates the "Signifier of the lack in the Other," which "is not always apparent to the subject, and even when apparent, cannot always be named" (*The Lacanian Subject* 173). The Other as complete is a myth, just as Woman is a myth, which is why Lacan writes Å.

The first revolution: towards a discursive signification of desire's metonymy

To understand the significance of Lacan's sexuation graph beyond the mas-culine and feminine paradigms, I use Lacan's tactic of his discourse formulae revolutions and turn the sexuation graph in order to look at it awry, as well as to focus primarily on the lower quadrants of the trajectories of desire. This prelim-inary move, rooted in the early ideas of semiotics *a la* Saussure and then Lacan, allows me to read the trajectories of desire and types of accessible jouissance as tropological functions, specifically the left (now lower) side as a function of metaphor and the right (now upper) side as a function of metonymy. What I am slowly working towards is articulating a theory of new subjectivities and will try to illustrate the progression or trajectory of what these new subjects might look like narratively through cinema in the quilting point that follows this chapter.

In looking at the lower portions this way, we can read the two sides as the semiotic Sr/Sd diagram. As I briefly mentioned earlier, we can read the $ → *a* syntactically as the basic sentence structure subject-verb-object: the barred subject wants/desires/trajects-towards an object. Even though the phallic signifier appears to be the likely direct object of the sentence, the $ fails to complete his sentence through his misidentification with himself and through the assumption that he has (secured) the phallus, and so he must let another object substitute for the phallus. The barred subject, in the position of the signified, must cross the bar in order to signify to himself and to other subjects. In other words, in chasing after whatever fills in the *a*, he presents himself as metaphor – as phallus possessor – and the *a* becomes a metaphor for himself, or his desire to complete himself in that it stands in for, signi-fies for, him in transsubjective interactions or recognitions. He substitutes his desire with an object and labors to have the object become a figural mimesis of this phallus possession (that always fails). We see this metaphor function in Lacan's shorthand notation of fantasy's structure, $<>*a*, where the lozenge

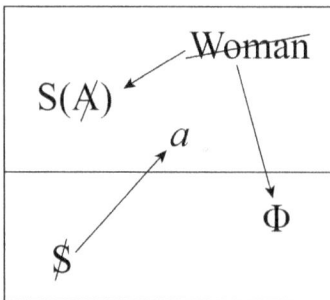

Figure 7.4 The sexuation graph's lower quadrants one counter-clockwise revolution

implies a structured relation that can be read as the $ and *a* as greater than, lesser than, or as we see in the vel and rim, which I discuss later, that they function symbiotically in a production and recursive return. Fink explains that the fantasy matheme can be read as "the subject in relation to the object" and that it "suggests that the subject tries to maintain just the right distance from that dangerous desire [of the traumatic experience of jouissance]" (174). In situating itself, to use Lacan's words, along this trajectory of desire, the subject represents (and, therefore, is defined inter- and transsubjectively by) this desire; the fully castrated subject functions as metaphor in that he replaces himself as "being" with himself as meaning, or desiring to mean, along the chain of signification. Desire is inherently metonymic in that the *objet a* only approximates, nears safely, jouissance, but the way in which that desire represents the signifier-subject discursively to other signifier-subjects in a standing-in-for lack is an operation of metaphor.

The now upper portion of the trajectories toward jouissance functions metonymically as ~~Woman~~ toggles between, on the one hand, the phallic signified that defines her as representing a metaphoric content within the Symbolic and, on the other, the relation this subject has with the incompleteness of the Other, the lack of full content in the Symbolic. This subject is ideologically interpellated into the Symbolic-Imaginary content already established by the Law and so "genuinely" wants to be a part of this transsubjective reality, hence the trajectory towards φ, the symbolic anchor of her anthropomorphism. However, this subject maintains access to an enjoyment, a knowledge, which does not fit into the Symbolic-Imaginary content that hinges on the phallus as the *point de capiton*. Whatever/whoever this subject is, it is not the Woman as empedestalled by the Imaginary, and, therefore, it does not exist within the phallic framework. Rather, this subject, ~~Woman~~, ex-ists, defined by her finding lack elsewhere, *on that other scene* rather than by her misidentification with the phallus. The trajectory of jouissance to the phallic signifier crosses the bar downward toward the signified, which is the metaphoric *as if*, the occultation of the signifier. The subject can never actually be the phallus because the crossing of the bar of prohibition is metaphoric. ~~Woman~~ will function *as if* she is the phallus, but only in so far as this function makes her subjectivity known (legible, readable, significant?). The trajectory of the subject seemingly backward (if we stay with the usual syntactical direction of the sentence) along the signifying chain is a metonymic deferral. This "backward" direction, as I read the subject's close relation to the Other, correlates with Kristeva's semiotic in that it is that modality of jouissance that cannot be named, that defines this particular category of subjectivity as "not-all" castrated, that is a residue of the knowledge of the empty Symbolic and its interdependence with the Real. In other words, the Imaginary, as psychic register, does not partake in this jouissance as it does in large part with the creating and sustaining of phallic jouissance.

These multiple trajectories illustrate the differing and deferring (*a la* Derrida's *différance*) of a specifically discursive and syntactical meaning-making.

The metaphor Woman is an Imaginary construction by which masculinist hegemonic discourse mobilizes sexual difference unethically (i.e., from an assumed position of dominance). Here, I refer back to Bryant's logic, following Lacan's discussion of the "sham jouissance," that the masculinity within the phallic economy as illustrated on the left side of the sexuation graph is all "charade, semblance, masquerade." The defining of masculinity through negation – that is, by the manifest Imaginary content of the metaphors of *objet a* and Woman, and the way in which these two metaphors fail in presenting a presence (without absence) of masculinity – make present the absence of sense, to refer back to Copjec's claim, in sexual difference. Rothenberg's retroversive causality – the unpredictability of meaning effects we can use to understand, for example, that the linearity of history shaped by specific events is a myth – is one of the ways we can understand the paradoxical discursive effects of Woman/Woman (Sr/Sd) within masculinist discourse. On the one hand, there is a very real oppressive order based on the sexually differentiated logic of this discourse, but, on the other hand, the unpredictability of this logic based upon an Imaginary metaphoric construction causes that very logic to fail. Woman's other jouissance, the subject's relation to the barred Other, is, I think, a more ethical function of inter- and transsubjective relations in that it refuses the totalization of any hegemonic logic by always keeping present the absence of Symbolic content, i.e., the emptiness of the Symbolic.

Notes

1 "An excess that is a jouissance beyond (phallic) meaning" is a close rendering of one of the definitions of the sinthome.
2 Kristeva's definition of the semiotic is closely related to Lacan's definition of discourse and the social link.
3 Later I will return to the text and the writing subject. For now, recall my brief explanation of the writing subject in the introduction. Her interests for her project on poetic language cover avant-garde literature, specifically and only that of Antonin Artaud, Georges Bataille, James Joyce, Comte de Lautréamont, and Stéphane Mallarmé in whose texts she finds "the prohibition of jouissance by language and the introduction of jouissance into and through language" (80). As well, she locates desire in the unconscious with her understanding of poetic language: "The theory of the unconscious seeks the very thing that poetic language practices within and against the social order: the ultimate means of its transformation or subversion, the precondition for its survival and revolution" (81).
4 As I will address briefly below, Lacan desires to situate himself on this side of the graph. In *Television*'s introduction he claims to always speak the truth although he cannot say it all, and in the first lecture of *Encore* he situates himself as the hysteric in the discursive dynamic between himself and his audience.
5 I cannot help but find an inherent irony is this endeavor: we, as human subjects, are still seeking out and representing the entities that surround us, so there is always at some level a human/subject centered logic at play.

6 Magritte's 1966 *The Two Mysteries* is more indicative of the S($\bar{A}$).

7 Calvin Thomas, in a conversation with me, rightly added, "Not to mention the fact that what goes on behind these doors, or what proceeds from behinds on the other sides of these doors, all ends up in the same place, since sewage is not subject to segregation." It all ends up at the same homeland. Also, I add, not all women are afforded the privileged designation "Lady."

Quilting point

Tapping into excess, or the feminist trilogies

Lars von Trier, a problematic figure often getting himself into trouble for apparent misogynist and racist statements, somehow, and perhaps unconsciously, creates a feminist film trilogy – *Antichrist, Melancholia,* and *Nymphomaniac* – that strongly critiques masculinist logic and portrays women acutely as full subjects in their own right, particularly in regard to the ways in which masculine discourses harm women. We have already discussed *Antichrist*, but, to reiterate, She's mental health was deteriorating long before the death of her son, and He's narcissism was a partial catalyst for her deterioration; that is, until his narcissism and paternalism became her destruction.[1] *Melancholia* depicts two sisters: Claire (Charlotte Gainsbourg) is highly obedient to her husband and Justine (Kirsten Dunst) is maybe manic-depressive, maybe bipolar, who literally and symbolically frees herself from marriage at her wedding party, falls into a severe depression, and then finds extraordinary emotional strength in the face of apocalyptic destruction by a rogue planet colliding with Earth. Claire's husband, the astronomy enthusiast who assumes the subject-who-knows, ultimately cannot handle the apocalyptic realization and kills himself, leaving the women and child to handle it themselves. In *Nymphomaniac*, Joe (Charlotte Gainsbourg) narrates her life's sex story to Seligman, a virgin hermit of sorts, who has taken her in after an assault, and who ultimately tries to rape her as she falls asleep. He obviously has not heard or seen her as a subject, but only as the signifier whore from which he can take for his own experience. She shoots him in defense and flees.

What is evident in this trilogy is the critical lens placed on patriarchy and misogyny alongside an emphasis on women as subjects. *Antichrist* is told from He's perspective, not She's:

> There are no scenes of She alone that are not revealed as narrated by him, but there are scenes of He alone. *Antichrist* is told as a series of memories divided into chapters (Prologue, Grief, Pain, Despair.) …
>
> *Antichrist* is not simply a misogynistic tale, but a deeply reflexive account that underscores the gaps, contradictions and cracks in the… emphatically male account. It is, in a sense, the story that a man might tell to himself just as that story is falling apart. If he finally "solves" the problem of She

by strangling her at the end, He is implicated in more than murder, but in gynocide.

(Geller, n.p.)

While *Antichrist* is told from a male POV with a clearly masculinist logic, the audience's POV of his memories cannot help but be critical of him. The other films in the trilogy shift to female points of view. *Melancholia* shares POV between Justine and Claire. We see Justine finding her autonomy in excess of masculinist logic and Claire juxtaposed to that excess as struggling to maintain a sense of identity within the oppressive logic. The male characters in *Melancholia* are unfortunate casualties in Justine's battle for autonomy – her brief husband, her greedy and dominate boss who is relentless about work at her wedding, and Claire's husband, who is condescending and controlling until his façade is destroyed and he kills himself. In *Nymphomaniac*, von Trier gives us only the female POV, which is vocally and actionably opposed to masculinist logic, particularly in regard to the control or regulation of women's agential pleasure. In the end, we are neither surprised by Seligman's rape attempt nor upset by Joe's act of self-defense, because he has clearly not heard Joe's story, is not capable of seeing her beyond the opportunity to use her as sex object. Von Trier's trilogy walks us through a critical narrative transition from a POV of masculinist logic to one of feminist agency upon typical interactions between men and women.

Similarly, David Lynch's *Lost Highway*, *Mulholland Drive*, and *Inland Empire: A Woman in Trouble* are a trilogy.[2] I contextualize the three films as a trilogy via POV, as this particular element of their narrative structures ties them together for a reading grounded in sexuation as discourse and the metonymy of woman based on aphanisis. POV is crucial in Lynch's films: the viewer cannot understand the narrative of these films without first figuring out from whose POV the narrative unfolds and from what psychic place(s) that POV originates at various moments. These three films offer a gradually shifting progression of the narrative's and the viewer's POV. *Lost Highway*, like *Antichrist*, depicts critically the consequences of violent misogyny within masculinist logics when those logics fail the male subject: Fred Madison's (Bill Pullman) transformation into Pete Dayton (Balthazar Getty) through a psychotic break brought on by his sexual insecurities and lack of trust in his wife lead him to kill her and then experience a fugue. *Mulholland Drive* similarly divides the narrative between dream and waking life: the first two thirds or so of the film are a dream and require the audience to interpret the dream against the details of reality in order to understand the narrative (Thomas). Diane Selwyn (Naomi Watts) wants nothing more than to be the Hollywood star, *the* Woman, as well as Camilla Rhodes' lover. But instead it is Camilla Rhodes (Laura Elena Harring) who succeeds at becoming Woman, and, more importantly for the narrative, not Diane's woman. Diane, like Fred Madison, reacts violently to her failure to fill successfully the part of Woman for masculinist Hollywood and to get the girl, and imagines a fantasy of herself as Betty and Camilla as Rita where everything works out the way she desires, until, of course, it does not. *Inland Empire* is a critique of masculinist narrative by way of forcing the viewer into the hysteric's perspective, not just as critical viewer of a master's or hysteric's perspective. The critique of masculinist narrative, though, is not the stopping point for Lynch's film; rather, I argue, that *Inland Empire: A Woman in Trouble* is also one of the emerging, innovative trends in creating non-masculinist narrative structures and presentations. This film and the leap into a narrative space outside the masculinist mode or logic of presentation is a move that also problematizes modes of interpretation dependent upon masculinist logics.

Anna Katharina Schaffner points out that some critical scholarship argues that Lynch's work is misogynist and does nothing to criticize violence against women or the metaphorization (my term) of Woman, i.e., he is not complicating the stereotypical objectifications and archetypes of women in narrative (270 fn 2). However, she offers a strong reading of the 'trilogy' as "decidedly feminist in outlook" and argues that "Lynch does not simply orchestrate Hollywood's male gaze, but in fact thematises and deconstructs it" (271). Schaffner, like myself, sees Lynch's work as a critical lens of heteronormative male fantasy, particularly that fantasy of Woman. She likens Lynch's work to Barthes' demythologizing in that he acts as a "deconstructor of clichés, someone who shows how myth works on the level of stereotypical cinematic representations. He repoliticises and rehistoricises these constructions and their underlying ideological functions by interrogating their presumed naturalness" (273). He does this by showing "us openly how and why both cinema and fantasy work by exposing their underlying structures and assumptions" and by telling "us stories but questions and problematises them at the same time, thus positing and deconstructing his propositions in one and the same gesture" (274). Typical cinema narratives are born out of particular ideological structures and content; they both reflect that ideology as escape fantasy and help shape and inform that ideology simultaneously. Lynch puts these structures and content into stark relief by dividing his films' narratives into moments of desire opposed to moments of fantasy (McGowan 18–21). Typical cinema allows us to escape into fantasy, specifically fantasy that often softens the normality of the everyday, the place of desire, that we endure. McGowan explains that "Our everyday experience allows our desire to remain unconscious: we don't see how our desire shapes what we see; we believe that we simply see what appears in the world to be seen" (23). But Lynch's film narratives lay bare that fantasy, implicating us as participants in and making us aware of that not-so-invisible ideology at work. Escape, if the viewer experiences it in a Lynch film, is an "escape into the trauma that remains hidden but nonetheless structures the outside world" (24). *Inland Empire* – as the final film both of this "trilogy" and of Lynch's film career apparently – serves up a forceful critique of the Hollywood cinematic ideological fantasy, the Woman trope, the blurry nightmare of the viewer's expectation of fantasy overlaid with normality, while delivering the aphanisis of the subject from the demand of Woman put upon her. This last element, the aphanisis, is probably the new fantasy he offers to those of us who are critical of Hollywood cinematic ideology. But his creating and delivering that fantasy both disrupts the problematic, violent tropological one and brings forth the possibility of new narratives. Lynch discursively turns the filmic narrative on its head; his critique of the master's cinema hystericizes the viewers expectations and analyzes what both cinema and the viewer do within that domain.

A few psychoanalytic literary and film theorists have proposed possibilities of necessary and ideal ruptures in narrative structure, possibilities that could re-define the functions and purpose of narrative structure and how narrative positions film viewers. More specifically, the fantasy distance afforded to and desired by viewers is a problem in which these critics invest; they consider this problem precedent in terms of how popular culture mediums can influence the ideologies to which various publics subscribe. If film, arguably the most popular entertainment medium in our culture, introduces new narrative structures grounded on unfamiliar or untraditional points of view, then viewers may begin simply to think differently. In "The Fear of Women and Writing in *Spellbound*," Robert Samuels suggests:

> Psychoanalysis, deconstruction, and poetry all provide strong tools for the dismantling and upsetting of the monological masculine discourse. Yet, these tools will go unused if they are not affirmed and put into play by people who are committed to heterogenous life-styles and methods of interaction.
>
> The first step to this affirmation of the multiple may be the acknowledgment that none of us are in control of language and that we are all alienated in the discourse of the Other. The next step is to be vigilant against the attempt to displace our own linguistic lack onto others through the process of abjection. We must reinterpret our world in order to free it from singular interpretations and not reestablish fetishistic forms of denial.
>
> (43)

The last sentence in Samuels' statement condenses, to a degree, the problem that serves as the exigency or impetus for this project. To think Woman is to think a "singular interpretation" and is an established "fetishistic form of denial," and it lends to the implicit trope Man, which is just as fetishistic and violent. Lacan's hysteric and analytic discourses function as persistent movements in ethical discursive practices that can keep monolithic discourses from becoming sedimented. Laura Mulvey argues further that the

> first blow against the monolithic accumulation of traditional film conventions (already undertaken by radical filmmakers) is to free the look of the camera into its materiality in time and space and the look of the audience into dialectics, passionate detachment. There is no doubt that this destroys the satisfaction, pleasure and privilege of the "invisible guest," and highlights how film has depended on voyeuristic active/passive mechanisms.
>
> (33)

McGowan suggests that Lynch's filmmaking style "departs significantly" from even current radical filmmaking (3). According to him, Lynch collapses the distance traditionally afforded to film viewers by complicating the "all-perceiving" position of the viewer. Mulvey's suggestion that productive radical film should evoke thought rather than mere identification on the viewer's part (6) is what Lynch forces us to do in *Lost Highway* and *Mulholland Drive*. *Inland Empire* not only evokes thought, but it also has the ability to propel the viewer into such proximity with a metaphoric abjection of the postmodern condition that normal channels of identification are in some senses precluded. The non-masculinist narrative structure of *Inland Empire* makes us simultaneously detached and involved in the film.

Following the POV from the first to the last of Lynch's trilogy, we notice the obvious shift from male to female main characters and points of view. *Lost Highway*'s main character's emasculation and fantasy of ideal masculinity clue the viewer in to the socio-cultural gender constructions and narrative representations of those constructions that are so prevalent in Lynch's work. *Lost Highway* is Lynch's introduction into the "dismantling and upsetting of the monological masculine discourse." He exposes quite blatantly the disturbing and harmful male fantasy of his desire based on impossible idealizations, a violent rejection of women subjects. His commitment to "heterogenous life-styles and methods of interaction" begins to surface clearly in *Mulholland Drive*, the trilogy's transitional narrative, where Lynch films from not only a female POV, but also from a lesbian POV. The jump from a traditional male POV, as psychically skewed as it is, to that of a lesbian subject, forces the viewer into a non-traditional discourse between women and alternative interaction with the film experience. The lesbian POV has the potential to exclude the traditionally masculinist male viewer from the sorts of identifications that Mulvey critiques, which opens up possibilities for non-masculinist and queer identifications. Even though the film problematically depicts lesbian desire similar to that of masculine desire at times – and recall here Freud's claim that there is only one libido, so the phallic jouissance that manifests in sexual relations is difficultly portrayed – the only points of view we have are from women, and queerly intimate women's psyches at that. In other words, even though we are viewing the intimacies between women, we are to recognize that they interact from two different discursively sexuated positions. The lesbian component of the film is significant because it is contrasted deliberately with the heterosexual stereotypes of Hollywood's demands of women.

Lynch maintains a female POV in *Inland Empire*, and, as I will discuss more later, the issue of sexual orientation is tabled, but the issue of sexuality is not. This shift from *Mulholland Drive*'s somewhat heavy-handed and shock value type tease scenes to make the lesbian POV matter to *Inland Empire*'s points of view of multiple women in similar, but seemingly different, oppressive situations, as well as the comradery we see between groups of women in different scenarios, brings to the fore the difficulty of women's ability to *situate themselves*, to use Lacan's terminology. Rather than allowing the viewer a non-traditional, familiarly alternative viewing experience, the film bombards the viewer with multiple and multivalent female points of view that do not follow an easily recognizable narrative template within traditional space and time structures. The film plays with space, time, and discourse so much that it propels the viewer into a different kind of distance than the distance typically experienced while watching a film.

Inland Empire

I am not so much interested in offering a film interpretation here; rather, I want to discuss the structures at work and the feminist lens. The film has multiple entry points and, therefore, lends itself to many interpretations. The film is nonlinear, the characters are not clearly explanatory, and, to make things even more subversive, it has a second disc which includes "More Things that Happened," acting as footnotes to the film. Its nonlinearity and persistent, feminist multiperspective carry the viewer through a range of variously connected scenarios and women-centered experiences with sexuality and agency.

As a summary of "linear" events in the film, we can deduce that the Lost Girl (Karolina Gruszka) lives in Poland. She has two men in her life, the Phantom (Krzysztof Majchrzak) and some variation of Piotrek (Peter J. Lucas). She is a sex worker and lives an oppressive life. She cries in a hotel room and watches a television on a fuzzy channel. Nikki Grace is an American actor trying to make a comeback in southern California. She lands a role in a remake film, *On High In Blue Tomorrows*, which was adapted from an older script, *Vier Sieben* (Four Seven, or 47). The older script never went into production because of an apparent curse and a terrible tragedy. Her film character is Susan/Sue Blue. The film promises Nikki's comeback. Susan Blue and Billy Side (Justin Theroux), *On High*'s characters, have an affair. Sue Blue runs for her life in the Hollywood streets from another woman (Julia Ormand) who is trying to kill her. All the while, Nikki/Sue and the Lost Girl are haunted by the Phantom who stands in, along with Piotrek, as a threatening patriarchal figure. In moments illuminated by the second disc's footnotes, we understand that the Lost Girl has made a deal with the Phantom in hopes of securing a better life, and Sue Blue delivers a long monologue in the form of a quasi-analytic session that pulls quite a bit of the story together and provides insight into minutiae of her character.[3] The film culminates in Sue Blue and the Lost Girl escaping from the hotel the Lost Girl is in, Nikki/Sue killing the Phantom, finding the Lost Girl, kissing her, disappearing into Nikki's parlor where a wild bunch of eccentrics from Sue Blue's monologue gather, and the Lost Girl walks out of her hotel room into the fantasy of "Smithy's House" – the house on the film set that Sue Blue had been stuck in for the majority of the film – to be reunited with her lover and child. In the end, Nikki breaks the cycle of the Hollywood Woman not only by freeing the Lost Girl, but also by killing and having the Phantom fade through her. Schaffner succinctly claims that "*Inland Empire* is essentially about a woman's struggle to liberate herself from the cultural roles and fantasmatic projections imposed upon her" (284).

Inland Empire's men

Between the first scene with the Lost Girl crying in the hotel room and when we first meet Nikki Grace, Lynch inserts one of his infamous rabbit scenes. Two rabbits are marked in pink and have feminine voices, and the third rabbit is marked in blue and has a masculine voice. He is the only rabbit who enters and exits the room where these scenes take place. The single room is large, dingy, slightly lit, etc., which can easily fit into a classic film style representation of the unconscious. Moreover, the conversation and the laugh track lack context, which also lends to an unconscious domain. Given what we know about the feminine subject's relation with the Other and extimacy, the pink bunnies who stay in the room, who want to know things from the blue rabbit – "when will you tell me?"; "I will find out one day" – and the blue rabbit's wanting to know what time it is and hearing someone also lend to the way in which we locate/situate dreams psychoanalytically. The Other's desire is the subject's desire, and the subject (just as the Other of the unconscious) tries to hide things from it. Also, the dreamer is often concerned about how long s/he can continue to dream, as the dream's desire is to keep dreaming, and the hearing someone "out there" can be the conscious as other to the unconscious. The feminine rabbits stay in the locus of the Other, while the masculine rabbit fluctuates between this space and the world outside it.

The cut, though, is significant. We see the blue rabbit exit the room, and on the other side of the door his silhouette fades into a long parlor occupied by two men. One is sitting quietly, as if he is the dominant of the two, and the other man is the Phantom who paces and talks frantically: "I am looking for an opening!" The Phantom begs the man – the Father? – to give him an opening into what? The man says, "That's good. You understand." The Phantom realizes something, something to which he desperately needs access, and he thinks this man can give it to him. The Phantom is killed toward the very end of the film, and his murder results in the Lost Girl and Sue Blue finding each other, almost mirroring these moments of the film's opening. The Phantom in the film's outset is the gap between these women, and he also sees a gap to which he wants access. Is it that other jouissance that he is looking for?

From the perspective of this film as the final installment of a conceptual trilogy that functions as commentary on the human psyche, this scene with the Phantom searching is arguably the masculine psyche, or even the Father myth, looking for a way into ~~Woman~~. Here, Kristeva's writing subject is helpful in understanding how a film-maker can both consciously and unconsciously produce a product that shifts narrative content over a period of time. The first two films are similar enough in the way in which we can find a psychic locus from where the action takes place, first in Fred Madison and then in Diane

Selwyn, as well as the progression from the masculine POV of Woman to lesbian POV of Woman. *Inland Empire*, though, is an even more intense, indeterminate exploration into the feminine psyche juxtaposed to women's experiences in masculinist realities. Lynch's project, then, is looking for an opening. An opening into what?

In SXVII and SXX, Lacan quibbles with the logic of masculinity via the hysteric's discourse, the pushing aside the psychoanalytic privileging of the Oedipus complex and the Father, and in the sexuation graph's narratives. The left side of the sexuation graph provides a narrative via mathemes of this same logic. I favor Bryant's renaming the masculine side of the graph the transcendent logic, because I think that Lacan's purpose for reducing the "masculine" side to a structural logic shows that the Symbolic has a fundamental structure within it that can be filled with content, such as the masculine logic. In other words, the left side of the graph does not have to be masculinist or phallocentric, as I try to show by replacing ϕ with S_1. Transcendent logic functions through the exclusion-inclusion binary – there is One that does not submit, but all must submit – while simultaneously functioning as all-encompassing, and, therefore, without exception. Paradoxically, an exception must exist as the difference that allows the identity formation of those who are included, e.g., heterosexuality needs homosexuality (or vice versa) in order to exist as a concept. And this exception is marginalized, debased, abused, oppressed – pick a term – by those who are included in order to claim a seat nearest to the mythic One who stands in as the Imaginary Law for the lot of those who submit.

Critique of the trafficking of women

Dern's characters and the Lost Girl are parallels in that they are both abused and enslaved by men in various iterations of their lives. The parallels allow for a feminist reading of the film as a critique of the trafficking of women, which is heightened by the hysterical and abject way in which their abuse is presented. As I discussed earlier, Lacan claims that all men's relationships with women are repetitions of prostitution. Nikki Grace is the property of her husband. He pulls her co-star aside to tell him threateningly, "she is not a free agent." Susan Blue is a married woman who has an affair, and she also seems to work for the character who her co-star plays, which doubles (perhaps triples) her status as prostitute. Finally, Dern's working-class Sue Blue character is married to an abuser and she often goes out "Screwin' a few [guys] for drinks." Each of the Dern characters is a different class-based representation of women who are all in trouble: they are all under the thumb of men who see them as their property, and, more importantly, as the increasingly abject embodied failures of these men's fantasy of Woman, which sparks the violence that they endure. The fact that all of them are played by one actor, Laura Dern, and the same man plays their oppressor, Peter J. Lucas, condenses tropologically this abusive phenomenon endemic to patriarchy and illustrated by the traditional way of reading the sexuation graph. In other words, whether a woman is wealthy and possesses her own talents for success and independence or is poor and lacks the education and access to resources for success, women often experience a forceful, violent positioning under masculinist discursive logics. The trope of violence against women saturates the plot.

Gruszka's Lost Girl, when we first see her, is in a room sitting at the foot of a bed watching a fuzzy television and crying. Naked, she has wrapped herself in the bed sheet and clutches it tensely. The opening of the film depicts a man and woman with blurred out faces entering a hotel room. The woman is obviously disoriented, as if drugged. She is told to undress and reduced deliberately to whore status – he asks, "You know what whores do?" She replies, "Yes. They fuck. Do you want to fuck me?" He snaps back: "You just take off your clothes. I'll tell you what I want." Then the film cuts to the vertical movement of his shoulder on top of her to insinuate fucking as she repeats, "Where am I? I'm afraid. I'm afraid …" Although we do not know whether the woman in the blurry scene is the Lost Girl, we can deduce that it may as well be her. When we see her later in the film, she seems to be the wife of the man we know later as the Phantom, who beats her because he knows she is trying to leave him for her lover. Finally, we see her on a Polish street along with a small crowd of other sex workers.

The parallels between the Nikki/Susan/Sue character and the Lost Girl's characters should be obvious at this point. Lynch condenses each of the women's characters into the metaphor of Woman as whore, as well as connects all six metonymically to show the parallels in their experiences. The metonymic function is present as a significant meaning-making trope in, among, and between the triple splits between both characters. This metonymic function of the triple split also subverts both the masculinist Woman as metaphor narrative, as well as the linear and tropological narrative expectations that viewers may instinctively have. In this subversion, the film offers up a non-masculinist narrative structure through the hysterical dimension both of film and the viewing process. Each character is inextricably linked to the others, as they are all women enduring masculinist violence, lacking a self-positioned place, and fighting to reposition themselves. This condensation of woman's plight within the most obtrusive patriarchal practices, though, is not what is most unique about *Inland Empire*'s multiplicitous points of view, although it is an important critique of a very real human view phenomenon. The unique depiction is the points of view that emerge from various aspects of these women's psyches; that is, their own inland empire.

The mere narrative depiction of women's oppression, although a feminist endeavor, does not necessarily mean that the narrative does not still fall within masculinist logic. Lynch's use of multiple points of view that not only overlap but also cannot necessarily be located by the viewer are layered psychically within and between the six characters. In a scene that occurs toward the temporal center of the film, one of Dern's Sues is dreaming that she is in a backyard at a cookout. The film cuts to the Lost Girl, genuflecting by lighted candles, and she prays, "Cast out this wicked dream that has seized my heart."[4] The use of superimposition for the Lost Girl and Sue Blue on a couple of occasions blurs the viewer's ability to discern which of the women is the guiding consciousness – here we are in one woman's dream that is accessed by another woman on the other side of the world at a different time. These superimposed moments in the film – and there are many – connect the women by way of a differential consciousness, to use Sandoval's terminology, which she defines as that which "operates as process and shifting location" to make possible the transformation and alliance of social movements through radical love (138). Love, as Lacan defines it, "has nothing to do with sex" (SXX 27). This differential consciousness "is linked to whatever is not expressible through words. It is accessed through poetic modes of expression: gestures, music, images, sounds, words that plummet or rise through signification to find some void – some no-place" (Sandoval 140). The feminine knowledge that Lacan tries to find in *Encore* is expressed well, I think, through Kristeva's semiotic, her readings of her men's avant-garde novels, and here in the way Lynch links these women metonymically and differentially.

Inland Empire has a consistent repetition of dialogue. The main four women actors repeat one particular line differently to one another. Either Sue or the Lost Girl or one of the other "whores," turns to the others in different scenes and says: "Look at me and tell me if you've known me before." In each case, the woman saying the line never gets a straight answer, if she gets a response at all. Keeping with the analysis that the film is itself a repetition of particular previous films, but also a critique of those films in terms of the Hollywood trope of Woman, we can say that this request to recognize the speaker is a request for this allusive connection of identification or common knowledge. Yet, in an immanent discourse, where subjects spread out along a flat plane equally, the recognition, or understanding of a differential mode of consciousness, could occur. Each time the request is made the two women who are asked the question are in submission to masculinist Law, and, therefore, cannot/ do not respond in a way that neither the one who asks, nor the audience can understand. The two women who at times act as parts of Sue Blue's psyche, or Hollywood sex workers, or Polish sex workers, or even imposing faces directly addressing us, the viewers, function as the Woman trope to each of the Sue and Lost Girl characters. In other words, the request is more intersubjective rather than transsubjective, a request more for recognition of the self than from others.

The Lost Girl, who is Sue's Other, A, connects her metonymically to the various signifiers of an intersubjective knowledge. Because the Other, here the Lost Girl, is always in the same position no matter her place, she is always just the Other, not the Other of the Other in one of her positions, so she is $Ⱥ$. As a kind of parallel, the Lost Girl who sits at the edge of the bed receives transmissions of clips of Nikki/Sue's life through the fuzzy television, as if they are screen memories. We could, on the one hand, deduce that the Nikki-Susan dynamic is a show that the Lost Girl watches in her prison of a hotel room and identifies with or dreams about, and that Sue Blue is one woman's reality of a failed Hollywood dream. On the other hand, though, the screen as access to pieces of Sue Blue's life can be the Other's view of consciousness. Regardless of who is what for whom in the film, the women are metonymically linked in a psychic struggle over the trouble they are in with the Phantom, the patriarchal Law *par excellence*. No matter the differential consciousness and access to something − a jouissance, a knowledge, a link between them − that they may have, these women are subjects and must pay their debt to language. They must toggle between two trajectories of subjecthood, one toward the φ and the Other, which they learn to do retroactively, to S(Ⱥ).

The symptom that drives the hysterical film and the hysterical viewer

Lynch's script sets us up in the third scene with the tension of sexuation as discourse. As the film cuts from the hotel room to the rabbits and the Phantom "looking for an opening" to Visitor #1 (Grace Zabriskie) walking up to Nikki's home, we find ourselves in the film. Visitor #1 imposes herself under the guise that she is new to the neighborhood and stopping around to get to know her neighbors. Unprompted, in a heavy, seemingly Polish accent, she tells Nikki an "old tale":

> Visitor #1: A little boy went out to play. When he opened his door, he saw the world. As he passed through the doorway, he caused a reflection. Evil was born. Evil was born and followed the boy.
> Nikki: I'm sorry, what is that?
> Visitor #1: An old tale. *And* the variation: A little girl went out to play, lost in the marketplace, as if half-born. Then, not through the marketplace, you see that don't you, but through the alley behind the marketplace, this is the way to the palace. But, it isn't something you remember. Forgetfulness, it happens to us all. And me, why I'm the worst one, "Oh, where was I?" Yes … Is there a murder in your film?
> Nikki: Ah, no. That's not part of the story.
> Visitor #1: No. I think you are wrong about that.

This sexed tale tells of the difference in the directions that the little boy and the little girl take, similar to the siblings on the train. But instead of explaining in what direction their libidinal desire will go, it explains the way in which the two sexuated children will situate themselves discursively and the different social and psychic effects the binary creates. The little boy, in a patriarchal discursive system, will only see a representation of something similar to the image he sees in the mirror and grow up to represent that representation, a necessary and persistent trope of masculinity, which perpetuates a particular Imaginary-Symbolic signifying system. The little girl, though, is "lost in the marketplace," which refers to the trafficking of women (*a la* Lévi-Strauss and, later, Bourdieu), as well as the way in which women must accumulate products in order to mimic the Imaginary concept of Woman and thereby lose themselves in that construct – "you just can't keep them from shopping no matter what you do" (Wallace 225). Moreover, she is lost "as if half-born," which harkens back to both the *as if*-ness of metaphor, and particularly the metaphor of Woman, and the "not-all" of woman within Imaginary-Symbolic relations that we see in Lacan's right, immanent side of the sexuation graph.

The little girl eventually knows that it is "through the alley behind the marketplace" that "is the way to the palace." I read two allusions here. The first is again the running thread of prostitution, which is most often conducted behind the scenes, and the unfortunate hope of prostitution paying off in the long term (*a la Pretty Woman*). In the second allusion, though, we can think not of a literal marketplace but more the marketplace as psyche, a wonderland of signifying possibility. In this way, the "alley behind" carries an element of extimacy, a link to the unconscious, and the palace does not refer to a rich man's bed but a knowledge of that other jouissance. Schaffner reads the marketplace as Hollywood and "the palace is self-fulfillment, reaching a higher state of being, spiritual rebirth" (285). The "evil" that is born in the little boy is the trap of the S_1 as ϕ as *the* way to understand one's position in transsubjective relations, as phallic desire and a seeming demand to have the phallus. And "it is not something you remember" because one's sexuation occurs upon one's entry into Imaginary-Symbolic consciousness. If we remembered this traumatic kernel (to use Žižek's term), we would be devastated, perhaps propelled into psychosis. Visitor #1's following the tale with a whimsical "Forgetfulness, it happens to us all" is ambiguous in that she is talking about both the fact that we all come to forget in our old age, and that in general we just can't remember everything, but also that we forget, we have that primary repression of our lack, and it is something that does happen to us, not something we do as active agents. And again, with the ambiguity, she transitions, saying, "Oh, where was I?" Of course, this is a typical transition for someone who has lost her train of thought, but this is also reference to the forgetting that happens to us all, the loss of the *I*, the *I* that is an Other.

We can explicate the previous films in the trilogy using the university discourse in which S_2, knowledge, addresses *objet a*, the student or reader on behalf of a hidden master signifier S_1, which is here equivalent to the always absent but nevertheless always semblance interpretation of the master. No interpreter could truly have this absolute interpretation, but one can approximate it by virtue of having the more successful interpretation. *Inland Empire's* multiplicity and indeterminacy do not lend to the same interpretive mastery. The film humbles us as interpreter, first hystericizing us as we search for a key or any sort of S_1 to cling to, then addresses us in the thick of our hystericized desire as being just as divided as its characters. Thus, it suggests, or perhaps embodies, the discourse of the analyst, in which *objet a* (the film) addresses $ and requires that we produce our own S_1s (our interpretations, lacking though they must be). This lack of a perfect interpretation is an effect both of this film and of any S_1, which always tries to cover over through repetition that lack that we try to forget.[5]

The reason, at least in discourse terms, why the film is globally uninterpretable is that it makes us aware of our symptom as viewer within a specific mode of logic. The film's characters, cuts, temporal and spatial distances, nonlinearity, etc. all force us into an abject and then hysterical non-identification with this subversion narrative mode. Schaffner, pointing up Walter Benjamin, observes that "with distance, whether spatial (from foreign countries) or temporal (from tradition), comes a kind of authority which cannot be achieved by that which is familiar and close at hand. The tale of the curse … draws both on otherness and on distance for its effectiveness" (283–84). The obvious conflations made between characters and definitive relationships represented all point to a critique of the violence of masculine logic, but the production around and out of these little critical markers haunt us with repetitions of dialogue among and between disparate scenarios of possible realities and possible dreams that we cannot identify. We cannot provide a "normal neurotic" interpretation of the film if we cannot identify its parts; rather, we are forced into a relational and relative interpretation situated between the hysteric's and analyst's discourses. The film and the film within the film serve as symptoms: the film within the film is a symptom of the film, and the film is a symptom of a radical desire for non-masculinist narrative.

So at least two layers of hystericization occur within and around *Inland Empire*. The film exposes the viewer's hystericized desire to their self as divided, which may create in the viewer various identifications within the film, whether with a character and/or with a desire found in the film's lack of coherent narrative even if it does induce misery. Arguably, each of the characters we glimpse reveal symptoms – e.g., the Phantom's "looking for an opening" quite hysterically, and the various requests to be known by the women. Nikki Grace, as Schaffner summarizes, "embarks on a long and perilous journey of self-discovery" where "she becomes whole, sheds her masks, witnesses the death of her other, inauthentic selves, and fully emancipates herself from the influence of shadowy male forces" (285). Apart from the claim that she "becomes whole," Schaffner's description of Nikki's experience sounds like the analytic experience of the hysteric liberating herself from her symptoms.

The fading of masculinist logic: aphanisis and metonymic identifications

The Sue trapped and living in Smithy's house leads a quotidian existence. She cooks, cleans, grocery shops (surely at a marketplace), takes out the trash, watches television. If Lynch made a film documenting Sue Blue's life, it most likely would not hold our interest. Other than the occasional presence of the erotic women who engage in a comradery of girl talk, a Sue Blue narrative would lack all the elements that make narrative structure what it is – situation, conflict, struggle, outcome, and meaning. Sue's life does, in fact, embody very little of anything interesting except for a few small details.

Sue Blue has a heavy drawl, her verbs are grammatically incorrect, and she curses often. Sue Blue tells her story to the frumpy man in the burlesque club's upstairs office where she takes refuge as she runs for life from Ormand. We receive Sue's story in mixed-up flashbacks (read: hysterically) according to how she unfolds her story in the monologue. Sue appears to live alone in Smithy's house, but from the flashbacks we know that at one time she lived there with her husband, who was from the Baltic region. She was sleeping with other men, became pregnant, her husband could not have children, he left her, and she went through a bad time after she lost her son.

> Man interrupts monologue for the only time: Were you, in fact, seeing another man?
>   Sue: I screwin' a couple of guys for drinks. No big deal. This one guy, he was kinda cute.
>
> (chapter 22)

> Sue in monologue: I'm trying to tell you so as you'll understand how it went. The thing is I don't know what was before or what was after. I don't know what happened first. And it's kinda laid a mind fuck on me. My husband, he's fucking hiding something. He was acting all fucking weird one night before he left. He was talking this foreign talk and telling loud fucking stories. [The scene cuts to Smithy's living room where Sue, dressed in a slinky pink dress with her purse on her shoulder, and her husband are fighting. He punches her in the face. She falls to the floor. The husband strangles her and says, "I'm not who you think I am. You listen to me. I know for a fact I can't father children."] …
>   I guess after my son died I went into a bad time. When I was watching everything go around me while I was standing in the middle.
>
> (chapter 34)

This monologue cut scene repeats that of the two fighting Polish couples, where the Lost Girl is beaten for trying to leave and Ormand speaks the lines that Sue's husband speaks in the monologue. The repetition of the dialogue – and this is not the only instance – always repeats a little differently, always leaves a remainder that we cannot quite locate.

We can make a variety of connections between Sue Blue and the Lost Girl, but I will forward only one for the sake of brevity. The Lost Girl is the metaphoric "occulted signifier" (Lacan *Écrits* 422) of herself inside the fantasy structure. She is the signifier that holds the circular fantasy together as an extension of Nikki Grace. Through Sue Blue, Nikki can redeem the Lost Girl from her trap: freed by Sue's film death, Nikki is able to kill the Phantom and sacrifice herself when she kisses the Lost Girl and vanishes. Each of the women in the dynamic serves a metonymic function along the journey to liberation. Because the Lost Girl is a remote player both temporally and spatially, she functions as the metaphoric structure that holds the narrative together: in a particularly striking dream sequence when Sue's gaze pans into the catsup stain on her husband's shirt, we see the Lost Girl posed as if praying next to a candle. She says, "Cast out this wicked dream that has seized my heart." She is The Thing of meaning separated from the chain of fantasy signifiers, the ground control of fantasy, if you will.

The killing of the Phantom is also a significant moment that offers the other part of the film's frame, that is, the counterposed moment to his looking for an opening. The Phantom haunts all the characters and functions as the Law in most cases. He is the threat that the women must eliminate in order to be able to *situate* themselves in discursive subject positions that reflect their own desires and knowledge. As long as the Phantom hovers "out there" they are barred from access to that other jouissance. Sandwiched between our introduction to the Lost Girl and Nikki Grace, he functions as the gap that keeps them apart. Nikki, leaving the set of *On High*, wanders off set into a theater that is apparently showing the film we just saw, and she further wanders down a long corridor behind the screen (an alley behind the marketplace?). She comes face to face with the Phantom, shoots him, and her screaming face, which we have seen in the transition scene in Smithy's house as well as in a dark, dream like scene, is superimposed on the Phantom's (brutal fucking murder). He fades as if into her, and she continues wandering until she finds room 47 (the original screen-play title). Upon entering the room, Sue finds the Lost Girl, kisses her, and fades away. This aphanisis is an analog to the "end" of analysis: the subject, in producing a new S_1 and thus a new way to ground its relation to its own desire, replaces or eliminates the previous symptomatic blockage. Sue was a symptom, but so was the Lost Girl. The next time we see Nikki, she is in the very room that she walks out of upon our first seeing her. She is surrounded by characters from her monologue – many of whom we do not know unless we watch the footnotes – as well as by characters from the other films in the trilogy (specifically Camilla Rhodes, who exchanges blowing a kiss with Nikki). The Lost Girl escapes the hotel room after seeing via her screen the other girls escaping their rooms. She too walks down a long corridor to find herself in Smithy's house. She enters the living room, and Piotrek and a young boy enter through the front door to a joyous reunion.

The psychic dysphoria, the hysterical symptoms of self- and other-interrogation in the face of the violence of Woman as metaphor and the way in which the characters find one another through differential consciousness – as we see in the love Sue gives to the Lost Girl by the kiss that brings a simultaneous fading and separation, a "productive aphanisis" – are, I think, a beginning to the creation of non-masculinist narratives. The masculine logic is made to be so absurd in the sameness of these women's experiences, viz., their metonymical connections that bring the masculine logic into an overdetermined, hideous metaphor. Similar to the way in which the women of *Ni Una Más!* effect change through the metonymic reorganization of both their bodies and their culture's masculinist symbols, the women of *Inland Empire* take control of their psychic dealings. Walking off the set in a washed-out daze, Nikki walks away from the insistent trope of Woman proliferated in our cultural productions. The fading of each of these women to and from themselves, one another, and the men who oppress their ability to situate themselves allows for a fading of the masculinist narratives because these women ultimately create new ones. The lynch pin, for me, in this fading is that the Phantom, the haunting presence of the masculinist Law, desperately wants an opening into that excess as well. The killing of the Phantom and his fading into the character who seems to hold the key to the aphanisis of the masculinist subject promises the chaos of new modes of logic, new narratives, and new subjects, which we see in the eccentricity of the final crowd who celebrate an end to the Woman in Trouble.

Notes

1 Cf. Piotrek Świątkowski, *Deleuze and Desire: Analysis of the Logic of Sense*. Leuven University Press, 2015, p. 147; Nolan Boyd, "'Nature Is Satan's Church': Depression and the Politics of Gender in Lars von Trier's *Antichrist*." *Offscreen*, vol. 20, iss. 8, August 2016; Dorothy Geller, "Lars von Trier's *Antichrist*: Executioner at the Alter of the Other, Part 1." *Offscreen*, vol. 14, iss. 11, November 2010.

2 I co-wrote a seminar paper in the summer of 2008 with John Lowther, which was presented at the National Popular Culture Association Conference in April 2009. Much of the introductory material to this reading of *Inland Empire* is influenced by the paper. Later in 2009 an article was published that shared (uncannily) the premises on which we grounded our work: Anna Katharina Schaffner, "Fantasmatic Splittings and Destructive Desires: Lynch's "*Lost Highway, Mulholland Drive*, and *Inland Empire*." *Forum Modern Language Studies*, vol. 45, no. 2, June 6, 2009, pp. 270–91.

3 Out of the scope of this reading is another dimension to *Inland Empire* that is significant. It is a film about film-making and provides a critique of the process and disrupts the viewer's expectations of film viewing in the way in which it carries out the *mise-en-scène* via a *mise-en-abyme* of the filmic process.

4 In *Queen Kelly*, the problems of affairs and prostitution are the main elements of the plot, and the clip from *Queen Kelly* that Lynch replicates in *Inland Empire* is shown in *Sunset Boulevard*. Of course, we locate an immediate connection between *Sunset Boulevard* and *Inland Empire* in Nikki Grace's desire for a career comeback, which Norma Desmond (based on the notorious career of Norma Talmadge that dwindled ungracefully) also desires. Interestingly, *Sunset Boulevard* also aired as a radio play, which correlates slightly with the record player and content that opens and occasionally pops up in *Inland Empire*. Not only is Lynch alluding to the connections between his film and *Sunset Boulevard*, which we cannot help but notice toward the end when we are made aware of the film's filming during the Susan Blue death scene, but also a legacy in Hollywood film depictions of women, because this particular cut with the Lost Girl is a direct replica of a scene from *Queen Kelly*, a silent film that later was dubbed for an overseas audience. Erich von Stroheim, director. *Queen Kelly*, Gloria Swanson Pictures, 1929; Billy Wilder, director. *Sunset Boulevard*, Paramount Pictures, 1950.

5 This paragraph is a paraphrase of that Summer 2008 seminar paper co-written with John Lowther.

8   The dethroning of the father

Discourse is constantly touching on [jouissance], by virtue of the fact that this is where it originates. And discourse arouses it again whenever it attempts to return to this origin. It is in this respect that it challenges all appeasement.

Lacan, SXVII, 70

What's a myth? […] It's a manifest content.

Lacan, SXVII, 113

I have continued to work on the removal of the phallus as *the* quilting point from our understanding of sexuation and the way in which our subjectivities take form along the path of their directionality. In this chapter, I conclude this project by discussing first Lacan's moving beyond the Oedipus complex, then revisiting the hysteric's discourse in order to point out the labor of desire, replacing the ϕ with S_1 in the sexuation graph, and finally musing a beyond to masculine logic. The phallus is *a* quilting point for Lacan's reading of an historically patriarchal social structure but has been often misunderstood as *the* guiding concept of Lacan's teachings. To be fair, indeed, in the sexuation graph, the phallus serves as the primary signifier that ties the psychoanalytic narrative of sexuation together. However, and to be clear, shifting the primary signifier from the phallus to another signifier does not make the graph come unstitched.

As we see in the above figure and in the earlier explication of the mathematical logic, the graph does, in fact, tell a story, one that is at least partially rooted in Freud's narrative, based on his rendering of the Oedipal myth, of the way in which little boys and little girls grow up to be men and women with normatively organized libidinal drives. In the middle lectures of Seminar XVII (entitled post-seminar "Beyond the Oedipus Complex"), though, Lacan shifts his teaching from an adherence to Freud's work to a breakthrough in the way in which he understands the discursive manifestations of psychic structures based on jouissance. This breakthrough hinges on Lacan's deflation of the primacy of the Oedipus complex understood in psychoanalytic practice as that which shapes subjects' sexuated structure.

$$\begin{array}{c|c}
\exists x\ \overline{\Phi x} & \overline{\exists x}\ \Phi x \\
\forall x\ \Phi x & \overline{\forall x}\ \Phi x \\
\$ & S(\cancel{A}) \\
 & a \\
\Phi & \text{Woman}
\end{array}$$

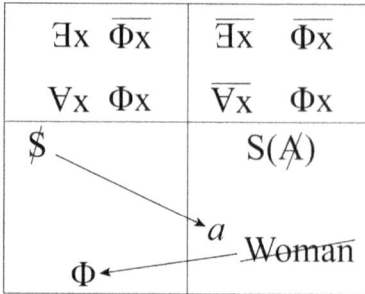

Figure 8.1 The sexuation graph

Freud's Oedipus complex is based on his own primal horde myth, which Lacan calls a "cock-and-bull story" (SXVII 114) for two reasons. Firstly, Lacan finds absurd the idea that the primal father of this myth would want all of the women, and, secondly, the myth tells us less about jouissance than about the truth of brotherhood founded on "segregation" (114), a segregation between and amongst men. Similar to the way in which I read "Woman as metaphor" as an Imaginary construction of patriarchy, Lacan reads Freud's Oedipus complex as nothing more than the *paternal metaphor* (112). Freud's primal horde myth and his "clinging to it" (112–13) is his attempt both to situate psychoanalysis within a larger scientific discourse, as well as to create psychoanalysis as a new scientific discourse. Freud wants to know and, as the first epigraph to this chapter describes, this double discursive move of alignment and creation touches his own access to jouissance. Situating his desire to know within the university's and master's discourses provides Freud with a subject position of having the phallus. Lacan understands the Oedipus complex that took such primacy in psychoanalytic practice as less dominant because of its manifest content, i.e., myth according to this chapter's second epigraph, as discursive. He explains this important critique of the field's placing the Oedipus complex in a dominant position by pointing up the hysteric's discourse, who speaks from the place of $, as the subject who "knows everything that he does not know even as he knows it" (113). In other words, it is the analysand who knows, not the analyst, and the analyst, based on the patent content of S_1, as master, only *interprets* what the analysand knows: "for [the analyst] the latent content is the interpretation that he is going to give, insofar as it is, not this knowledge that we discover in the subject, but what is *added on to it to give it a sense*" (113, emphasis added). (Recall here that sex and sense know nothing of each other.) The idea of the Father is a myth born out of the desire of the analyst (read: Freud) as master-supposed-to-know and, therefore, is an ego metaphor of masculinist fantasy. However, it is the analysand who actually fantasizes the analyst as such, and thereby manifests this Father, who s/he must overcome to reach an end point in analysis. The paternal metaphor, as Lacan reads the Oedipus complex, is the function by which all signification depends simply in the way in which one thing must be substituted for another in order for language to mean at all. And Lacan, in this rare moment of rebellion against Freud, is trying to explain that psychoanalysts are also "clinging to it" and, therefore, elevating its status via a retroversive causality that is not necessary.

Lacan shores up his talk on Oedipus and the primal father by claiming that "it is clear that it is truly incorrect to put everything in the same basket as Oedipus," and that we should "analyze the Oedipus complex as being Freud's dream" (117). We must understand this claim in the psychoanalytic (read: Freud's) sense of the dream; that is, as a way in which we can understand the unconscious's safeguarding us against "that other" jouissance and the way in which Freud's own desire plays out in his analytic methods. In creating the primal horde myth, Freud was presenting *an* interpretation, "*a sense*," of unconscious knowledge, not *the* interpretation. In *New Studies of Old Villains*, Paul Verhaeghe briefly catalogs the discrepancies in Freud's father theory with the "weak" fathers that Freud encounters in his practice, and the ways in which Freud fails to account for this collision (15–17).[1] Rather than restructuring his initial claim when the practice did not support the theory, Freud sticks to his theory "by introducing a new concept (primal phantasy) that he will ground in a self-constructed myth" (19). The myth, which Lacan points out as the paradoxical representation of brotherhood building by way of segregation, is, as Verhaeghe notices, absent of the mother and is guilt-inducing (19–21). To refer to guilt-enjoyment, I see this paradoxical moment of brotherhood/segregation and the instance of guilt-enjoyment as that which explains, to some degree, masculinist affect. The appearance of guilt is the mythic explanation of the opening for the Symbolic-Imaginary content of patriarchy. We band together under the Law filled with this hierarchical, boundary-laden content as guilty subjects. This system of transsubjectivity is one of exclusion and exception in that a hierarchy exists between men where some are exceptions that have access to certain signifying powers and where all *others* are excluded to varying degrees depending on their proximity or lack thereof to the exceptions. We know full well the ethical problems of this system, yet we labor to maintain recognition within it.[2]

Jouissance is at the core of psychoanalytic inquiry, and phallic jouissance is accessible to what Freud terms "the normal neurotic."[3] However, of interest to this project is the hysteric's interrogation of the master and the master's discourse, an interrogation ultimately of phallic jouissance. Lacan differentiates the Imaginary father (SXVII 128), which is a father of frustration (124) that marks a desire of the Other in the law, and the Real father (128), which is a father of privation (124), a father who does not exist, except as the signifier of castration. The Imaginary father is a source of frustration for the hysteric and the master: the hysteric is frustrated by the law that makes the master a master, and the master is frustrated by the father as that which denies him his ownership of his desire. As Žižek shows, the Real father, just as ~~Woman~~, marks the place where the Imaginary cannot hold, where we must face the sham of our desires for identity (*Enjoy!* 143–47). The hysteric, in asking "what/who am I?," interrogates the fantasy of the master's discourse in an attempt to access that which castration does not account for. The hysteric needs the master, indeed "wants a master," (SXVII 129) so as to expose the guilt-enjoyment that is a hegemonic feature in the very structure upon which the master rests. In this way, the hysteric refuses to absorb the affect of shame demanded of her by the master. Instead of embracing fully the shame-enjoyment, she splits herself between her access to it – which allows her to disconnect from and, therefore, interpret retroversively and differently the seemingly stable identifications in masculinist discourse – and the master's masculinist discourse from a resistant standpoint.

Psychoanalysts made Freud the master in their own hysteric desire: "Freud produced a number of master signifiers, which he covered with the name of Freud. […] [Psychoanalysts] are unable to untangle themselves from Freud's master signifiers, that's all. It's not so much to Freud that they adhere as to a number of signifiers" (130). I have been working toward a replacement, various replacements, of the phallus as the master signifier, which offers a theoretical account of the mobility in and between our subjectivities and the quilting point (read: empty signifier) that we use as a general stabilizer. If we can theorize the phallus as one of many possible quilting points and the Oedipus complex as myth, a structured manifest content, then new quilting points and new myths arise through emptying out the Symbolic of that Imaginary narrative. The hysteric's discourse, Lacan teaches, is a method by which we can access this new knowledge that can produce new content.

The revolution of the sexuation graph, of which I have only begun to illustrate in this project, provides a new way to view the structure of language and the way in which it uses us. Through our understanding of the lower portions of the graph to describe the structural implications of metaphor and metonymy on our subject formations and discourse positionalities, we see one way in which our inter- and transsubjective relations are figurally mapped. Also, the replacing of the ϕ with the general S_1 allows for the figural to reopen and acquire new content after a long legacy of patriarchal oppression that, if we can take Lacan at his symbolic logic word, bears down on those subjects who demand to possess the master signifier perhaps more than others who have an excess. In having the excess, the subject's body experiences variously. For example, the dermis responds in ways from which the phallically minded are barred in that having the excess and using it redefines the accesses of the body. Having the excess entails that the subject perceives the world as more than just a thing that provides answers to its desires and recognizes itself as an object among many varieties of objects. As an object that has the excess, it sees many possible narratives, many discursive positions for itself, because it recognizes other objects as immanent agents. The hysteric remains caught up in having, but what she has is significantly other than what the master is caught up in having. The hysteric demands knowledge of the excess, but s/he demands that knowledge from the subject foreclosed from it – the master. The hysteric causes the master to realize s/he knows nothing, whether or not s/he ignores that fact on the surface. The hysteric's interrogation of the master's logic of identity deconstructs the façade upon which it is built. The master, in turn, must work harder to maintain the structure that always fails because his desire lies to him.

An ethics of the hysteric's discourse and the labor of desire

> At the level of the hysteric's discourse it is clear that we see this dominant appear in the form of a symptom. It is around the symptom that the hysteric's discourse is situated and ordered.
>
> Lacan, SXVII, 43

In *Encore*'s opening lecture, "On Jouissance," Lacan rhetorically situates the dynamic between himself and his attendees within the analyst's and hysteric's discourses.[4] He says that his impetus for the lecture series stems from the claim "I don't want to know anything about it [re: the ethics of psychoanalysis]" (SXX 1). Rather than being compelled to continue the lecture series because he "could say a little more about it," he declares, "while it is true that with respect to you I can only be here in the position of an analysand due to my 'I don't want to know anything about it,' it'll be quite some time before you reach the same point" (1). Even though it is not entirely clear at this moment from where he sits as analysand – that is, whether he positions himself as analysand in the hysteric's or the analyst's discourse – I want to argue here that, particularly in these early lectures, he is in the position of the analysand, the $, of the hysteric's discourse. The hysteric asks the master, S_1, the subject-supposed-to-know, "am I a man or a woman?," but the hysteric does not want a definitive answer to this question. Rather, the hysteric asks the question to interrogate the master's discourse, to disrupt the hegemonic demand, to refuse that demand. Arguably, the hysteric, especially in the midst of analysis, does not want so much to know anything about it, but rather wants the master to admit that there is no definitive answer to the question (and to realize, perhaps, in the later stages of analysis, that s/he, the hysteric, does not have to know). In positioning himself as the $ of the hysteric's discourse, Lacan situates himself in what he refers to as the "feminine" position to an audience grounded mostly within either/both the university's and/or master's discourses.

In his "feminine" position as the hysteric analysand, Lacan occupies the position of *objet a* for the audience member as desiring subject in the university's or master's discourse. Let us first look at how he situates himself with his audience from their perspective in the university's discourse. On the receiving end of the trajectory of desire, Lacan, in "not wanting to know anything about it," occupies the position of *objet a* with the desired production of the barred subject, $. Knowledge, S_2, is that which speaks toward *objet a*, directly toward the cause of desire. Lacan acts amazed by this reversal of his position and the apparent demand of those to whom he speaks in his *encore*: the attendees of the lectures, who continue to come year after year and the numbers continue to rise, desire

$$\underset{\text{Master}}{\frac{S_1 \longrightarrow S_2}{\cancel{S} \quad a}} \qquad \underset{\quad}{\frac{S_2 \longrightarrow a}{S_1 \quad \cancel{S}}}$$

$$\underset{\text{Hysteric}}{\frac{\cancel{S} \longrightarrow S_1}{a \quad S_2}} \qquad \underset{\text{Analyst}}{\frac{a \longrightarrow \cancel{S}}{S_2 \quad S_1}}$$

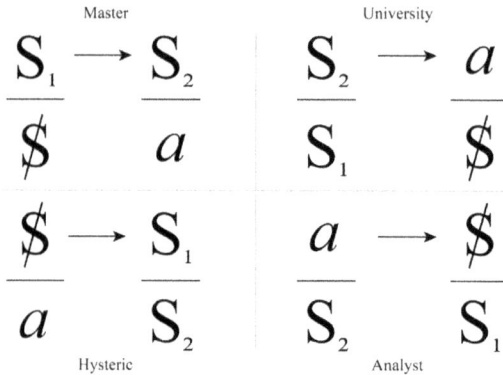

Figure 8.2 The four discourse formulae (again)

something he produces (if not actually him) (SXX 1). From the master's discourse perspective, Lacan occupies the place of S_2, knowledge, on the receiving end of the trajectory of desire, of speech. The audience, the desiring subjects, desire his knowledge and expect the production of *objet a*, the object cause of *their* desire. Arguably, the object cause of their desire is to know more about *it*, to know how to become better analysts, to know more about themselves.

As the hysteric, Lacan speaks latently from *objet a* and patently as $ to the master, S_1, arguably here our Enlightenment inheritance. He seeks to oppose anything having to do with the *cogito*, which has been the foundation of the university's and master's discourse content for hundreds of years. Lacan must speak as the hysteric in order to free his own thinking from this educative legacy. The more he speaks from this place, the more patent *objet a* becomes in the trajectory of his speech; that is, the trajectory of his desire. Hence, *objet a* becomes the speaking position "above the bar" in the analyst's discourse, and *objet a* arguably speaks to $ in her/his desiring to produce a new (or different) master signifier.

The hysteric's tension with the master, I think, is one way in which we can understand the subject's capacity to remove itself from the content of a dominant structure. The hysteric does not necessarily succeed at such a difficult endeavor, but s/he serves as the place from which Symbolic-Imaginary revision can occur. To think of a subject, specifically always split/barred, as capable of only one jouissance, namely phallic jouissance, is to ignore that the subject is at root/core a hysteric. If all subjects are inherently hysterical, then all subjects at least potentially have access to that *other* jouissance that Lacan says we do not know anything about and cannot say anything about. In replacing the φ, a manifest content, in the sexuation graph with S_1, the symbol of primary signification, then we can visualize, and therefore conceive of, the possibility not only of other manifest content, but also the entire sexuation graph as representative of the split/barred subject's experiences with jouissance. Verhaeghe succinctly explains that "jouissance arises from one's own body," and "Anxiety concerning jouissance then is basically anxiety about being overwhelmed by one's own drive and enjoyment" (58). The differences in jouissance as we see illustrated in the sexuation graph are differences in safeguarding against the limit, similar to the way Freud theorized the rising and subsiding of tensions in the pleasure principle. A subject, then, can always experience a level of phallic jouissance, but, to access the other jouissance, she must be willing to refuse the safeguard presented by the Other as prohibitive Law within the Symbolic and find an opening in the Other as her own body.[5] Guilt-enjoyment is an effect of phallic jouissance, a jouissance accessible through various invocations of *objet a*, in that we are trained by the mythic father to prohibit ourselves from the dangers of any enjoyment beyond this boundary. The subject experiences shame, however, when the prohibition fails to keep us from enjoying the Other as our own body differently than that which has been scripted for us.

What do I mean by an "ethics" of discourse and an "ethics" of sexuation? For me, a "good" or "better" ethics simply means not so abject-inducing. To clarify, the ethical does not involve a resistance to abjection so much as a refusal to punitively abject the other; after all, punitive abjection of the other is what masculine subjects are trained to do with their self-abjection. An ethics based on punishment of the other is a masculine logic. Earlier, I suggested that the normative, hegemonic subject, in assuming an identity, is occupying a subject position that extends oppressive power dynamics. As well, it demands a hierarchical desire – "to rise above." One sexed category assumes privilege and dominance over another, even in its failure and misidentification. To demand a little boy to grow up to be a masculine subject – and *only* and *always* a masculine subject – is to foreclose all the little boy's various capacities for enjoyment for himself and for others except in a way in which he will fail and hurt others in the process of his failing. One of the main reasons why this little boy will fail within this foreclosure is that all enjoyment will be phallic. Regardless, he will always place a value of and for meaning on his jouissance. To only enjoy as having the phallus, as a masculine subject, is to have a very limited trajectory of desire. To refuse this demand and foreclosure is important because the little boy will (hopefully) develop varying identifications full of understanding and empathy for whatever other occupies a place in the multiplicity of discourses he will encounter. To limit desire is to limit possibility. Hegemonically, we do not allow ourselves to enjoy outside of this limitation of desire. Of course, I am not suggesting here that desire must not have limits: desire must have limits to enjoy. I do not intend to suggest we need more and more trajectories of desire or accesses to jouissance; rather, I suggest we explore possible ways of desiring that do not have clearly oppressive consequences, that do not hurt others in the process of our failing.

Phallic jouissance is meaningful enjoyment, the enjoyment of meaning, and all subjects experience (something of) this jouissance – or, as subjects, should want to. *To always make and/or have one's enjoyment mean is labor.* As Lacan describes the difference between masculine and feminine subjects (as if a subject must be one or the other), the masculine subject laboriously constructs the fantasy of Woman out of the feminine subject position (SXVII 154–60). The construction of the Woman fantasy is so prolific in myth and narrative that hard and insistent labor persists in upholding the fantasy:[6]

> The space in which the creations of science are deployed can only be qualified henceforth as the *n-substance*, as the *a-thing*, *l'achose* with an apostrophe – a fact that entirely changes the meaning of materialism.
>   It is the oldest figure of the master's infatuation – write "master" as you will – for man to imagine that he shapes woman. I think you all have experienced enough to have encountered this comical story at one stage of your life or another. Form, substance, content, call it what you will – this is the myth scientific thought must detach itself from.
>
> (159)

Lacan's use of the courtly love phenomenon exemplifies this labor well.[7] Namely, within the phallic economy, phallic jouissance has the use value of establishing and sustaining meaning within Symbolic relations and between Imaginary relations. Women have an exchange value in the phallic economy, and Woman stands in as the signifier that sustains the phallic subject's Imaginary stability as One. Tracy McNulty, in "The Other Jouissance, A Gay *Sçavoir*," succinctly summarizes the exchange value of women:

> [capitalism] paradoxically establishes an illusory "oneness": one market, one currency, one standard of value – so many avatars of the phallus, the unary signifier. From the vantage point of capital, "supply and demand" becomes the two complementary halves of one holistic economy, in which excess is already reinscribed within the whole. (It is worth recalling that the French word "jouissance" derives from the language of economics, denoting the "surplus value" – usufruct – of what is "enjoyed" without being owned.) In such an economy, woman can never be anything more than a commodity, an object of exchange, reduced to embodying those imaginary *objets a* that promise plentitude or enjoyment to the subject who can append them to himself.
>
> (137)

Phallic jouissance, in the familiar capitalist economy, has value, often even a price tag. This price tag is one of the reasons that some scholars resist Lacan's use of the phallus as the master signifier and why their equating it with the penis is a misreading of Lacan's logic. The reading lacks the nuance between the masculine subject's "having" the phallus and the feminine subject's "being" the phallus. The masculine subject only ever has the phallus if he can pay the price of thinking he owns or enjoys the feminine subject or some other *objet a* who "is" the phallus; hence, the capitalistic economy's relevance to what is at stake.[8]

One of capitalism's founding tenets is property rights, and the institutionalization of women as property – as things to be had – is a tenet of phallic jouissance. The masculine subject's resistance to or incompetence at "being" the phallic subject weighs so heavily on his ability to access a desired sociodiscursive position that he, along with his pals, creates and sustains an entire market of human trafficking for possessing the phallus either for a lifetime or for momentary enjoyment. Simply put, the phallus is not the penis under Lacan's logic. The phallus is not the penis simply because those subjects who have a penis must always have something else to create and validate their position of power. Simply having a penis does not bring this creation and validation; a lot of labor goes into the masculine masquerade and the obtaining and enjoying of a phallic object. The phallic object is that which is precisely not the penis, but the object can be manipulated to provide enjoyment (read: orgasm) for the penis.[9] While occupying the masculine subject position, as McNulty points out at the end of the above passage, the subject engages with the social in order to obtain various *objet a* for a phallic jouissance.[10]

The seeking and obtaining of these *objets a* is the masculine trajectory of desire. To have to seek out, obtain, and then transform the object into *objet a*, then repress the object as the transformation into *objet a*, and then to find a way to enjoy it and economize that enjoyment is a whole lot of work. Phallic jouissance as a manifestation of desire is quite a bit of labor, and a labor, moreover, that separates subject from the thing and his enjoyment further. Lacan explains:

> Assuredly, what appears on bodies in the enigmatic form of sexual characteristics – which are merely secondary – makes sexed beings *(êtres sexués)*. No doubt. But being is the jouissance of the body as such, that is, as asexual *(asexué)*, because what is known as sexual jouissance is marked and dominated by the impossibility of establishing as such, anywhere in the enunciable, the sole One that interests us, the One of the relation "sexual relationship" *(rapport sexuel)*.
>
> (SXX 6–7)

This rumination immediately leads him to phallic jouissance.

> That is what analytic discourse demonstrates in that, to one of these beings qua sexed, to man insofar as he is endowed with the organ said to be phallic – I said, "said to be" – the corporal sex *(sexe corporel)* or sexual organ *(sexe)* of woman – I said, "of woman," whereas in fact *woman* does not exist, woman is *not whole (pas toute)* – woman's sexual organ is of no interest *(ne lui dit rien)* except via the body's jouissance.
>
> (7, emphasis in original)

He rephrases this explanation: "Analytic discourse demonstrates – allow me to put it this way – that the phallus is the conscientious objection made by one of the two sexed beings to the service to be rendered to the other" (7). The phallus is what stands between Man and Woman, the terrain and logic of negotiation between sexuation in discourse. In fact, it is phallic jouissance that "is the obstacle owing to which man does not come *(n'arrive pas)*, I would say, to enjoy woman's body, precisely because what he enjoys is the jouissance of the organ" (7). As Fink's footnote explains, *arriver* is the slang term for "to come" just as it means "to be unable" with the negative *n'arrive*. But I cannot help gesture back toward "to arrive" in the sense, as I discussed earlier, that the letter "always arrives." The letter, *a*, always arrives because, as Lacan explains in SXVII, the "bar is equal to *a*" (157).

We can locate the structure of the symptom within the advent of language upon the moment of castration – the castration that plunges the subject in the direction of *objet a* – and language, which is the elemental, manifest symptom of desire. The repetition of the symptom, though, "already costs and institutes, at the level of the *a*, the debt of language. *Something has to be paid* to the one who introduces its sign" (157, emphasis added). The debt paid is the adherence to phallic jouissance while simultaneously not foreclosing absolutely its excess. However, phallic jouissance is that thing that prevents arrival. Said differently, the trajectory that phallic jouissance takes – that is, toward *objet a* – is an unconscious blockage toward any arrival at being.

S₁ replaces φ in the sexuation graph

The narrative in Lacan's sexuation graph tells a story of the way in which subjects come into meaning as one of two discursive positions within the structural history of patriarchy. The master signifier is Lacan's semiotic concept for that which takes shape out of the Symbolic's emptiness. My proposal, then, is to remove the phallus from the sexuation graph and simply fill or replace it with the master signifier, S₁.

Lacan connects his claim that there is no sexual relation to the ancient father of law Moses, who declares that all relations with women are prostitution: "One thing is certain, all relations with women are [...] 'prostitution,'" and "What the master's discourse uncovers is that there is no sexual relation" (SXVII

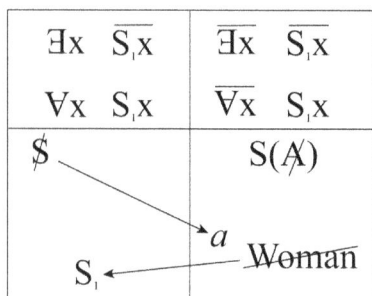

Figure 8.3 The sexuation graph with φ replaced by S₁

116). In order to cover over the non-existence of the sexual relation, we use the economy of sexual difference to define an Imaginary relation to make sense of ourselves.[11] Therefore, by minimizing the social demand of sexual difference through the discursive positioning of the subject not based on sexual difference, we can begin to equalize the playing field of hom(m)osocial relations. In other words, by replacing the phallus with the empty signifier, we open up at any given moment the possibility of engaging in inter- and transsubjective relations that must take form as they occur rather than as they have been predetermined by mythic, manifest content. The logic of immanence on the upper-right side begins to make more sense in that it is not so much that the subject's structure is understood as not-all within the phallic context, but that there is a jouissance that is not discernible in the Symbolic-Imaginary.

In the topography of this graph, we locate the "vel" on the side of imma-nence where the latent Real has a manifest presence. The vel – the lower portion of the lozenge as shown earlier in the matheme of desire, ◊ – is the locus of alienation, which is "the first essential operation" (SXI 210) in the subject's formation: "this *vel*, which [...] condemns the subject to appearing only in that division which, it seems to me, [...] if it appears on one side as meaning, produced by the signifier, it appears on the other as *aphanisis*" (210, emphasis in original). Aphanisis is the term Lacan uses to describe the disappearance, or fading, of the subject in the "lethal," paradoxical side of the Hegelian/Marxian being/meaning dyad *your money or your life*.[12] The hinge here is the *or*. Within psychoanalysis, though, this dyadic alienation-separation struggle between being and meaning is one wholly grounded within the field of desire, and is "supported only on the logical form of joining" (211):

> If we choose being, the subject disappears, it eludes us, it falls into non-meaning. If we choose meaning, the meaning survives only deprived of that part of non-meaning that is, strictly speaking, that which constitutes in the realization of the subject, the unconscious. In other words, it is of the nature of this meaning, as it emerges in the field of the Other, to be in a large part of its field, eclipsed by the disappearance of being induced by the very function of the signifier.
>
> (211)

The vel, as that which carries the subject into meaning only to put it back on the course to aphanisis, is closely tied to S(Ⱥ). The vel serves most productively in the hysteric's discourse as the locus from which the speaking $ can make evident that the "subject is not univocal," to refer to the "Either I am thinking or I am not" problematic of the *cogito* (SXVII 103), so that "to be in effect quite certain that the subject is confronted by this 'vel'" (103). Said differently, the vel is a useful place from which the subject encounters the unconscious and recognizes that s/he is not in control of her/his consciousness.

In turning the lower portions of the graph again, but this time with S_1 replacing ɸ, we perhaps can begin to recognize the interaction with the vel,

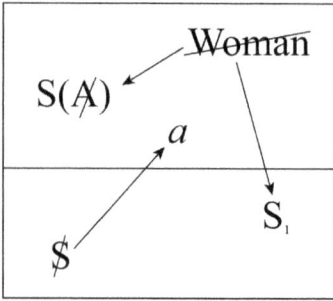

Figure 8.4 The lower portions of the graph turned with ϕ replaced by S_1

as the trajectory from ~~Woman~~ drops below the bar to reach the empty, master signifier waiting to be filled with productive signification. I find great potential in possibilities of inter- and transsubjective relations through the reconfiguration of Lacan's algorithm for Demand (S◊D) as ~~Woman~~ ◊ S_1, then, because the function of the lozenge "is designed to allow for a hundred and one different readings, a multiplicity that is acceptable as long as what is said about it remains grounded in the algebra" (*Écrits* 691). If Woman does not exist, yet there is a subject substance behind that Imaginary veil, who demands a trajectory of jouissance toward the empty yet full of potential S_1, then that subject can take myriad forms as a signifier to other signifiers linked by a quilting point possibly devoid (at least for a time) of the demand for structural oppression or violence. As well, the algorithm ~~Woman~~ ◊ S(Å) signifies a knowledge of desire that puts the Other into an ethical relation with the subject. Rather than the Other occupying a place in the subject's consciousness as a point of anxiety, the ~~Other~~ bears the weight of constraint and limitation, thereby allowing itself to be known, at least in terms of the subject's extimacy, by taking on a form that is not so abjection-inducing.

Beyond masculinist logic

I have set up a tension between the master's discourse as we know it in its patriarchal manifest content and the potential for replacements to that content. I locate the potential for replacements in the knowledge and identifications produced in the hysteric's discourse and a reworking of the narratives that inform the initial discourse of sexuation.

I mean a couple of things when I refer to masculinist logic. Firstly, as I have already discussed implicitly and briefly concerning the *cogito*, this mode of logic is most evident in our inherited Western Enlightenment tradition of positivism, as well as in the linearity of knowledge and the paradigmatic myths and tropes by which knowledge is rendered, validated, and proliferated. In the opening paragraph of the "Prelude" to *Masculine Domination*, Pierre Bourdieu finds the logic of domination (and violence) inextricable from the masculine:

> And I have also seen masculine domination, the way it is imposed and suffered, as the prime example of this paradoxical submission, an effect of what I call symbolic violence, a gentle violence, imperceptible and invisible even to its victims, exerted for the most part through the purely symbolic channels of communication and cognition (more precisely, misrecognition), recognition, or even feeling. This extraordinary social relation thus offers a privileged opportunity to grasp the logic of domination exerted in the name of a symbolic principle known and recognized both by the dominant and by the dominated.
>
> (1–2)

Bourdieu articulates that which feminists for decades have forwarded, which is that masculinist logic is violent and takes both active and passive forms of violence, but is inseparable from it. Iris Marion Young's article on the U.S. post 9/11 security regime recaps these active and passive forms: "Much feminist theory and gender theory has focused on forms of masculinity characterized by selfishness, coarse domination, and desires to exclude," but there is "another, more benign, image of masculinity, more associated with ideas of chivalry. The gallantly masculine man faces the world's difficulties and dangers in order to shield women from harm" (224). It is within these definitions of masculinist logic that I situate my own understanding of the concept. Of course, I do want to acknowledge that most subjects function under a masculinist mode of logic most of the time, whether we are men or women, masculine or feminine subjects, as these concepts and terms are all born out of this logic.

The writing subject is an affective production of Kristeva's semiotic and symbolic functions. The unconscious surely has some kind of uncontrollable, yet reined in, presence in the creative production of a series of vignettes of hideous men, or the contradictory sex-object but autonomous Tarantinian women, or the way in which von Trier's She always finds a way to refuse He's Imaginary pathological desire of her. My goal here is to propose a psychoanalytic way of engagement that not only disrupts masculinist logic, but also recognizes the grammar of the subject as different from the discourses of the subject. The beloved Virginia Woolf in her 1938 *Three Guineas* highlights (it is not the first and obviously will not be the last to do so) the irony and multivalent fascism embodied in men's continual demand to their sole right to education, income, and career pursuits at the expense of women having rights as subject all the while fighting against the Nazis (98–99). Whether through the writing subject or through conscientious differential logic, the disruption of masculinist logic is the refusal of the normalized rupture expected from language in a common discourse. The disruption of the expected, normalized ruptures in language results in a metonymy of new content within the Symbolic-Imaginary axis that reorients sexuated signifiers.

In "Against Neoliberal Blackmail," Christopher William Wolter and Alice Barrena argue that the focused turn to affect that accompanies identity politics is the privatization of individuals, which fits square within the neoliberal ideological framework (read: discourse): "the valorization of affect functions hand in hand with certain formations of contemporary identity politics to allow for a fetishistic disavowal of universality and to continue the reification of society as a society of privatized individuals – privatized in all senses of the word" (35). I tried to demonstrate earlier the way in which affect, viz. guilt and shame, is a structured part of ideological discourse, rather than as "particularities removed from politics and history, that is, to elide the structural dimension of trauma" (35). Referring to von Trier's *Nymphomaniac*, Barrena-Phipps[13] locks in on the moment of the rape attempt, the exchange of words between Joe and Seligman: when Joe says "No" to Seligman's rape attempt he replies, "But you, you've fucked thousands of men." In her reading the film, "Joe's sole recourse within the boundaries of both the circumstance she finds herself in and the discursive structure available to her" (26) is one only of negation that the feminine subject has at her disposal when confronted with a violent act upon her, itself a negation of her subjectivity and autonomy. This sole recourse is not only personal, but also structural and discursive and intimately, unequivocally connected to sexual difference and the masculine dominated structure of sexuation. Not only to work on the disruption of these dominate, oppressive discourses, but also to conjure and build new discourses is an ethical act.

Notes

1 Here, Verhaeghe also distinguishes between different camps of psychoanalysis in the ways in which they interpret and develop theories and practice around this tension. Some people think that "analysis praxis ought to analyze this necessity for the master figure, instead of endorsing it," while others, including Lacan in his later work, "will stress the role of the mother" and "denounce the Freudian fallacy" (18). The myth, Verhaeghe says, allows Freud to "safeguard his theory" (21) in a "typically neurotic solution" (22).
2 Recently, the term "gate-keepers" has become the mainstream way of recognizing this ethically problematic behavior.
3 Indeed, the subject is (in part) in question, but it is the subject's jouissance that is really in question, that produces interpretations of his/her repetition, directionalities of desire, and anxiety over lack.
4 Because Lacan inserts himself and his position intentionally into his lectures, particularly in the opening segments, I do not think I am guilty of intentional fallacy in what follows. I think that he often inserts himself and his position into his lectures in order to set up an analogy, to put into context the lecture content that will follow (and even perhaps have these supposedly intimate or vulnerable moments function as an allegory).
5 For a clear differentiation of the Other as these two different things, Symbolic Law and the body, see Verhaeghe's account in *New Studies* 47–59.

6 One could argue the obverse and say that the construction of the Woman fantasy is so prolific and normalized that there is no labor involved in upholding it; however, the expectation of that fantasy will always be met with disappointment, and the masculine subject has to work to maintain it, or live in utter denial, which produces alienation whether inter- or transsubjectively. In accepting wholly the fantasy as one of the givens of his position of dominance in patriarchal culture, I think, the masculine subject's own fantasy of identity meets obstacles consistently. The threatening of one's fantasy of identity can produce, for example, violent outbreaks of resistance, such as the epidemic of domestic violence, specifically "wife beating." As the theory goes, when a man's dominance is threatened or removed from one realm – e.g., losing a job or being subordinate at work – then he will often try to regain that dominance in another realm – e.g., abusing his wife and children. Similarly, if his wife consistently does not fit into the Woman fantasy, then he will try to make her fit.

7 See *Television* and *Encore* for Lacan's treatments of courtly love.

8 For more detail on this point see Jacques Lacan, "The Direction of Treatment and the Principles of Its Power," *Écrits*, 523–26; Tim Dean, *Beyond Sexuality*, 49–50.

9 Irigaray emphasizes the point in *Speculum of the Other Woman* in her juxtaposition of the male and female reproductive organs, as the male organ must be stimulated from the outside and the female organ touches and stimulates itself.

10 I recall the popular T-shirt back in the Reagan-era 1980s that American middle-aged men wore: "The one with the most toys wins." This seems to be an overly simplified statement of phallic jouissance.

11 In this declaration, I understand that Lacan's intended audience is only, or mostly, men, and heterosexual ones at that, which mimics my gripe with the condescension that Freud shows to women. My desire is for this not to be the case, but, nevertheless, I am having difficulty imagining that all women's relationships with other women is one of prostitution. I suppose that a mother marrying off her daughter is prostitution, just as her role as wife, if she is one, is also a representation of prostitution to her children, but these examples hardly cover the spectrum of women's relationships.

12 This concept is covered often and thoroughly, so I do not want to belabor it here. Briefly, it shows the paradox of man's social existence in Hegel's master-slave dialectic and Marx's appropriation of it: "If I choose the money, I lose both. If I choose life, I have life without money, namely, a life deprived of something" (SXI 212). For Lacan, it is a matter of language or existence, "This *or* exists" (212). But we cannot have one without joining it with the other; there is always an overlap, a grey area.

13 Barrena(-Phipps) name is documented differently in two points in the article, so I'm choosing to document as such in those two points.

Works cited

Adams, Parveen. *The Emptiness of the Image: Psychoanalysis and Sexual Difference.* Routledge, 1996.

Aristotle. *Poetics. The Complete Works of Aristotle: The Revised Oxford Translation*, edited by Jonathan Barnes, vol. 2, Princeton UP, 1984, pp. 2316–340.

Barthes, Roland. "Myth Today." *Mythologies.* Translated by Annette Lavers, Hill and Wang, 1972, pp. 109–59.

Benveniste, Émile. *Problems in General Linguistics.* Translated by Mary Elizabeth Meek, U of Miami P, 1971.

Bersani, Leo. *Homos.* Harvard UP, 2009.

Bourdieu, Pierre. *Masculine Domination.* Translated by Richard Nice, Stanford UP, 2002.

Bracher, Mark. "On the Psychological and Social Functions of Language: Lacan's Theory of Four Discourses." Lacanian Theory of Discourses: Subject, Structure, and Society, edited by Mark Bracher, Marshall W. Alcorn, Jr., Ronald J. Corthell, and Françoise Massardier-Kenney, New York UP, 1994, pp. 107–28.

Bryant, Levi R. *The Democracy of Objects.* Open Humanities Press, 2011.

Butler, Judith. *Bodies that Matter: On the Discursive Limits of 'Sex.'* Routledge, 1993.

———. "Restaging the Universal." *Contingency, Hegemony, Universality: Contemporary Dialogues on the Left*, edited by Judith Butler, Ernesto Laclau, Slavoj Žižek, Verso, 2006, pp. 90–114.

Copjec, Joan. *Read My Desire: Lacan against the Historicists.* The MIT Press, 1994.

———. "May '68, The Emotional Month." *Lacan: The Silent Partners*, edited by Slavoj Žižek, Verso, 2006, pp. 90–114.

Cornell, Drucilla. *Beyond Accommodation: Ethical Feminism, Deconstruction, and the Law.* Rowman & Littlefield, 1999.

Cuarón, Alfonso, director. *Children of Men.* Universal Pictures, 2007.

Curtis, Margaret Miller. "Times Have Changed." *Atlanta Journal Constitution*, Friday, December 5, 1980, Margaret Miller Curtis Collection, Special Collections and Archives, Georgia State University.

Davidson, Arnold I. "Foucault, Psychoanalysis, and Pleasure." *Homosexuality & Psychoanalysis*, edited by Tim Dean and Christopher Lane, University of Chicago Press, 2001, pp. 43–50.

Dean, Tim. *Beyond Sexuality.* University of Chicago Press, 2000.

———. "Lacan and Queer Theory." *The Cambridge Companion to Lacan*, edited by Jean-Michel Rabaté, Cambridge University Press, 2003.

———. *Unlimited Intimacy: Reflections on the Subculture of Barebacking.* University of Chicago Press, 2009.

Evans, Dylan. *An Introductory Dictionary of Lacanian Psychoanalysis.* Routledge, 1996.

Fink, Bruce. *The Lacanian Subject: Between Language and Jouissance.* Princeton University Press, 1995.

Fisher, Mark and Amber Jacobs. "Debating Black Swan: Gender and Horror." *Film Quarterly*, vol. 65, no. 1, fall 2011, pp. 58–62.

Foucault, Michel. *The Archaeology of Knowledge and the Discourse on Language.* ranslated by Sheridan Smith, Pantheon Books, 1972.

———. "Preface." *Anti-Oedipus: Capitalism and Schizophrenia.* Gilles Deleuze and Felix Guattari, Continuum International Publishing Group, 2004.

Franks, M.A. "The Insistence of Lacan on Woman as the Letter." *The Symptom,* vol. 2, spring 2002, no pagination. www.lacan.com/franks.htm

Freud, Sigmund. Excerpt from *The Interpretation of Dreams.* rpt. *The Freud Reader*, edited by Peter Gay, W.W. Norton & Company, pp. 129–42.

———. "A Comparative Study of Traumatic and Hysterical Paralyses." *The Standard Edition of the Complete Psychological Works of Sigmund Freud*, vol. I (1893c), edited and translated by James Strachey, The Hogarth Press, 1961, pp. 160–72.

———. *Civilization and Its Discontents* (1930[1929]). *The Standard Edition of the Complete Psychological Works of Sigmund Freud*, vol. XXI (1927–31), edited and translated by James Strachey, The Hogarth Press, 1961, pp. 64–145.

Fuss, Diana. *Essentially Speaking: Feminism, Nature, & Difference.* Routledge, 1989.

Geller, Dorothy. "Lars Von Trier's *Antichrist*: Executioner at the Alter of the Other, Part 1." *OffScreen*, vol. 14, iss. 11, November 2010, no pagination.

Grigg, Russell. Lacan, Language, and Philosophy. SUNY Press, 2009.

Irigaray, Luce. *Speculum of the Other Woman.* Translated by Gillian C. Gill, Cornell University Press, 1985.

———. *This Sex which Is Not One.* Translated by Catherine Porter and Carolyn Burke, Cornell University Press, 1985.

Jakobson, Roman. Excerpt from "Linguistics and Poetics." *The Critical Tradition: Classic Texts and Contemporary Trends*, 3rd ed, edited by David H. Richter, Bedford St. Martin's, 2007, pp. 852–59.

Jameson, Fredric. "Lacan and the Dialectic: A Fragment." *Lacan: The Silent Partners*, edited by Slavoj Žižek, Verso, 2006, pp. 365–97.

Johnson, Barbara. "The Frame of Reference: Pose, Lacan, Derrida." *The Purloined Poe: Lacan, Derrida, and Psychoanalytic Reading*, edited by John P. Muller and William J. Richardson, The Johns Hopkins University Press, 1988, pp. 213–51.

Johnson, Sonia. Interview by Janet Paulk. April 19, 2010, Activist Women Oral History Project, Special Collections and Archives, Georgia State University.

Keisner, Jody. "*Do You Want to Watch?* A Study of the Visual Rhetoric of the Postmodern Horror Film." *Women's Studies*, vol. 27, 2008, pp. 411–27.

Kristeva, Julia. *Revolution in Poetic Language.* Translated by Margaret Waller, Columbia UP, 1984.

Lacan, Jacques. *Écrits.* Translated by Bruce Fink, W.W. Norton & Company, 2006.

———. *My Teaching.* Translated by David Macey, Verso, 2008.

———. The Seminar of Jacques Lacan, Book III: The Psychoses 1955–1956. Translated by Russell Grigg, edited by Jacques-Alain Miller, W.W. Norton & Company, 1993.

———. The Seminar of Jacques Lacan, Book VII: *The Ethics of Psychoanalysis 1959–1960.* Translated by Dennis Porter, edited by Jacques-Alain Miller, W.W. Norton & Company, 1992.

————. The Seminar of Jacques Lacan, Book XI: *The Four Fundamental Concepts of Psychoanalysis*. Translated by Alan Sheridan, edited by Jacques-Alain Miller, W.W. Norton & Company, 1998.

————. The Seminar of Jacques Lacan, Book XVII: *The Other Side of Psychoanalysis*. Translated by Russell Grigg, W.W. Norton & Company, 2007.

————. The Seminar of Jacques Lacan, Book XX: *Encore: On Feminine Sexuality, the Limits of Love and Knowledge*. Translated by Bruce Fink, edited by Jacques-Alain Miller, W.W. Norton & Company, 1999.

Libbrecht, Katrien. "The Body." *A Compendium of Lacanian Terms*, edited by Huguette Glowinski, Zita Marks, and Sara Murphy, Free Association Books, 2001, pp. 33–37.

————. "The Real." *A Compendium of Lacanian Terms*, edited by Huguette Glowinski, Zita Marks, and Sara Murphy, Free Association Books, 2001, pp. 154–59.

"Loud & Proud." *L Word*, season 2, episode 11, written by Elizabeth Hunter, directed by Ilene Chaiken, Showtime, 2005.

Love, Heather. *Feeling Backward: Loss and the Politics of Queer History*. Harvard UP, 2007.

Lynch, David, director. *Inland Empire*. Studio Canal, 2006.

————. *Lost Highway*. October Films, 1997.

————. *Mulholland Drive*. Asymmetrical Films, 2001.

Mabbott, Thomas Ollive. "Text of 'The Purloined Letter'." *The Purloined Poe, Lacan, Derrida, and Psychoanalytic Reading*, edited by John P. Muller and William J. Richardson, The John Hopkins University Press, 1988, pp. 6–23.

McGowan, Todd. "Introduction: The Bizarre Nature of Normality." *The Impossible David Lynch, Columbia UP*, 2007, pp. 1–25.

McNulty, Tracy. "The Other Jouissance, A Gay Sçavoir." *Qui Parle: Literature, Philosophy, Visual Arts, History: A Special Issue on Lacan*, University of California Press, vol. 9, no. 2, spring/summer 1996, pp. 126–59.

Miller, Jacques-Alain. "Extimité." *Lacanian Theory of Discourse: Subject, Structure, and Society*, edited by Mark Bracher, Marshall W. Alcorn, Jr., Ronald J. Corthell, and Françoise Massardier-Kenney, New York University Press, 1994, pp. 74–87.

Morel, Geneviève. *Sexual Ambiguities*. Karnac, 2011.

Mulvey, Laura. "Visual Pleasure and Narrative Cinema." *The Sexual Subject*, Routledge, 1992, pp. 22–34.

Nietzsche, Friedrich. "On Truth and Lies in an Extra-Moral Sense." Rpt. *The Nietzsche Reader*, edited by Keith Ansell Pearson and Duncan Large, Blackwell Publishing, 2006, pp. 114–23.

————. *Twilight of the Idols*. in *The Anti-Christ, Ecce Homo, Twilight of the Idols and Other Writings*, edited by Aaron Ridley and Judith Norman, translated by Judith Norman, Cambridge University Press, 2005, pp. 153–229.

Padawer, Ruth. "What's So Bad about a Boy Who Wants to Wear a Dress?" *New York Times Magazine*, August 8, 2012, www.nytimes.com/2012/08/12/magazine/whats-so-bad-about-a-boy-who-wants-to-wear-a-dress.html?smid=fb-share

Pluth, Ed. "On Sexual Difference and Sexuality 'as such': Lacan and the Case of Little Hans." *Angelaki*, vol. 12, no. 2, August 2007, pp. 69–79.

Poisson, Jayme. "Footloose and Gender-Free: Parents Keep Child's Gender a Secret." *Star* iss. 21, May 2011, www.parentcentral.ca/parent/babiespregnancy/babies/article/995112

Rothenberg, Molly Anne. *The Excessive Subject: A New Theory of Social Change*. Polity, 2010.

Salamon, Gayle. Assuming a Body: Transgender and Rhetorics of Materiality. Colombia UP, 2010.

Salecl, Renata, Ed. *Sexuation*, Sic 3. Duke University Press, 2000.

Samuels, Robert. "The Fear of Women in *Spellbound*: Kaja Silverman and the Question of Castration." *Hitchcock's Bi-Textuality: Lacan, Feminisms, and Queer Theory*, State University of New York Press, 1998, pp. 27–43.

Sandoval, Chela. *Methodology of the Oppressed*. University of Minnesota Press, 2000.

de Saussure, Ferdinand. *Course in General Linguistics*. Open Course Classics, 1972.

Schaffner, Anna Katharina. "Fantasmatic Splittings and Destructive Desires: Lynch's *Lost Highway*, *Mullholland Drive* and *Inland Empire*." *Forum for Modern Language Studies*, vol. 45, no. 3, 2009, pp. 270–91.

Schlafly, Phyllis. "Feminists Double Standard about Child Care." *Eagle Forum*, January 11, 2006, www.eagleforum.org/column/2006/jan06/06-01-11.html

Shepherdson, Charles. *Vital Signs: Nature, Culture, Psychoanalysis*. Routledge, 2000.

Shklovsky, Victor. "Art as Technique." Translated by Lee T. Lemon and Marion Reis, in *The Critical Tradition: Classic Texts and Contemporary Trends*, 3rd edition, edited by David H. Richter, Bedford St. Martin's, 2007, pp. 775–84.

Silverman, Kaja. *The Subject of Semiotics*. Oxford University Press, 1983.

———. *Male Subjectivity at the Margins*. Routledge, 1992.

Spivak, Gayatri Chakravorty. "Scattered Speculations on the Subaltern and the Popular." *Postcolonial Studies*, vol. 8, no. 4, 2005, pp. 473–86.

Stavrakakis, Yannis. *Lacan and the Political*. Routledge, 1999.

Tarantino, Quentin, director. *Death Proof*. Dimension Films, 2007.

Thomas, Calvin. "'It's No Longer Your Film': Abjection and (the) Mulholland (Death) Drive." *Angelaki*, vol. 2, no. 2, August 2006, pp. 81–98.

———. *Ten Lessons in Theory: An Introduction to Theoretical Writing*. Bloomsbury, 2013.

United States of Tara. Dreamworks Television, 2009–2011.

Verhaeghe, Paul. *New Studies of Old Villains: A Radical Reconsideration of the Oedipus Complex*. Other Press, 2009.

Vilensky, Daniel. "*Antichrist*: Chronicles of a Psychosis Foretold." *Senses of Cinema*, vol. 53, December 30, 2009, no pagination.

von Trier, Lars, director. *Antichrist*. Zentropa Entertainments, 2009.

———. *Melancholia*. Zentropa Entertainments, 2011.

———. *Nymphomaniac*. Zentropa Entertainments, 2013.

Wacjman, Gérard. "The Hysteric's Discourse." *The Symptom*, vol. 4, spring 2003, no pagination.

Wallace, David Foster. *Brief Interviews with Hideous Men*. Little, Brown and Company, 1999.

Winterbottom, Michael, director. *Code 46*. British Broadcasting Company, 2003.

Wolfreys, Julian. *Critical Keywords in Literary and Cultural Theory*. Palgrave MacMillan, 2004.

Wolter, Christopher William and Alicia Barrena. "Against Neoliberal Blackmail." *International Journal of Zizek Studies*, vol. 13, no. 2, 2019, pp. 1–37.

Woolf, Virginia. *Three Guineas*. Penguin, 1977.

Wright, Elizabeth. *Lacan and Postfeminism*. Icon Books, 2000.

Young, Iris Marion. "Feminist Reactions to the Contemporary Security Regime." *Hypatia, Feminist Philosophy and the Problem of Evil*, vol. 18, no. 1, winter 2003, pp. 223–231.

Žižek, Slavoj. *Enjoy Your Symptom!: Jacques Lacan in Hollywood and Out*, 2nd edition. Routledge, 2001.

———. *Looking Awry: An Introduction to Jacques Lacan and Popular Culture*. The MIT Press, 1992.

———. *The Sublime Object of Ideology*. Verso, 1989.

Index

For Product Safety Concerns and Information please contact our EU
representative GPSR@taylorandfrancis.com
Taylor & Francis Verlag GmbH, Kaufingerstraße 24, 80331 München, Germany

www.ingramcontent.com/pod-product-compliance
Lightning Source LLC
Chambersburg PA
CBHW070338270326
41926CB00017B/3907